UNDERSTANDING AND USING READING ASSESSMENT, K–12

Also by Peter Afflerbach

Teaching Readers (Not Reading):
Moving Beyond Skills and Strategies to Reader-Focused Instruction

UNDERSTANDING AND USING READING ASSESSMENT, K–12

fourth edition

Peter Afflerbach

THE GUILFORD PRESS
New York   London

Copyright © 2025 The Guilford Press
A Division of Guilford Publications, Inc.
www.guilford.com

All rights reserved

Except as indicated, no part of this book may be reproduced, translated, stored in a retrieval system, or transmitted, in any form or by any means, electronic, mechanical, photocopying, microfilming, recording, or otherwise, without written permission from the publisher.

Printed in the United States of America

This book is printed on acid-free paper.

Last digit is print number: 9   8   7   6   5   4   3   2   1

LIMITED DUPLICATION LICENSE

These materials are intended for use only by qualified professionals.

The publisher grants to individual purchasers of this book nonassignable permission to reproduce all materials for which permission is specifically granted in a footnote. This license is limited to you, the individual purchaser, for personal use or use with students. This license does not grant the right to reproduce these materials for resale, redistribution, electronic display, or any other purposes (including but not limited to books, pamphlets, articles, video or audio recordings, blogs, file-sharing sites, internet or intranet sites, and handouts or slides for lectures, workshops, or webinars, whether or not a fee is charged). Permission to reproduce these materials for these and any other purposes must be obtained in writing from the Permissions Department of Guilford Publications.

Library of Congress Cataloging-in-Publication Data

Names: Afflerbach, Peter, author.
Title: Understanding and using reading assessment, K–12 / Peter Afflerbach.
Description: Fourth edition. | New York : The Guilford Press, [2025] |
   Includes bibliographical references and index.
Identifiers: LCCN 2024042386 | ISBN 9781462556137 (hardcover) |
   ISBN 9781462556120 (paperback)
Subjects: LCSH: Reading (Elementary)—Ability testing—United States. |
   Reading (Secondary)—Ability testing—United States.
Classification: LCC LB1050.46 .A36 2025 | DDC 372.48—dc23/eng/20240914
LC record available at *https://lccn.loc.gov/2024042386*

*To the teachers—past, present, and future—
who help students reach their reading potentials*

About the Author

Peter Afflerbach, PhD, is Professor Emeritus of Education at the University of Maryland, College Park. His research interests are individual differences in reading, factors influencing reading achievement, reading comprehension strategies, and reading assessment. Dr. Afflerbach has served on National Academy of Education and National Academy of Sciences committees related to literacy and literacy assessment. He is a member of the 2025 Reading Framework Development Committee of the National Assessment of Educational Progress (NAEP) and has served on other NAEP committees and on the board of directors of the Literacy Research Association. Dr. Afflerbach is an elected member of the Reading Hall of Fame and a Fellow of the American Educational Research Association. A founding editor of the journal *Metacognition and Learning,* he has published his work in numerous theoretical and practical journals and several books. Prior to his university career, Dr. Afflerbach served as a Chapter 1 remedial reading teacher, a middle school reading and writing teacher, and a high school English teacher. He is a proud graduate of New York City public schools.

Contents

	Introduction	1
CHAPTER 1	Important Issues and Concepts in Reading Assessment	14
CHAPTER 2	Assessing Early Reading	36
CHAPTER 3	Assessing Strategies and Skills: Tests and Reading Inventories	50
CHAPTER 4	Teacher Questioning as Assessment	76
CHAPTER 5	Performance Assessment	99
CHAPTER 6	High-Stakes Reading Tests	117
CHAPTER 7	Assessment and Accommodating English Learners and Special-Needs Students	140
CHAPTER 8	Assessing "the Other": Important Noncognitive Aspects of Reading	158
CHAPTER 9	Formative and Summative Assessment	178
CHAPTER 10	Promoting Self-Assessment to Help Students Build Reading Independence	188
CHAPTER 11	Assessing Digital and Critical Reading	201
	Appendix	225

References 243

Index 259

> Purchasers of this book can download and print select materials at *www.guilford.com/afflerbach2-forms* for personal use or use with students (see copyright page for details).

Introduction

Assessment is central to students becoming successful readers. Assessment informs our understanding of students' development so that we can provide effective instruction. It helps us demonstrate accountability. Assessment is a key for creating equity, as it describes students' strengths and needs and helps us shape our teaching. Assessment assists us in communicating with homes and communities to optimize student learning.

Assessment is created and used in relation to educational, political, and social contexts. Schools' reputations, teachers' salaries and tenure, and reading program selection are regularly linked to assessment results. Test scores are used to promote legislation that determines what should be taught. For example, many states mandate instruction based on a "science of reading." A result is assessment that focuses on basics of reading, including discrete skills and strategies. These skills and strategies include phonemic awareness, phonics, fluency, vocabulary, and comprehension, and there is no shortage of tests to help us determine student achievement in relation to each.

While these skills and strategies are essential, it is important to ask, "What else is basic in students' reading development?" Is student ability to distinguish fact from opinion, to confront propaganda, and to challenge an author and text also basic? Can students navigate the internet and understand multimodal texts? Is student ability to apply what is learned from reading to solve real-world problems also essential? Should we consider motivation and metacognition as basic for student reader success? Assessment that addresses these questions provides valuable information on the full range of students' reading development and reading achievement.

Assessment highlights equity and inequity in students' opportunity to learn. High-stakes test results describe persistent achievement gaps between groups of students. Based on these results, funding for programs to address inequities may be proposed. Furthermore, effective classroom-based formative assessment assists in the creation of instruction that can diminish those gaps. Assessment developed without acknowledgment of students' cultural differences contributes to bias and skews assessment results, furthering inequity. In contrast, assessment that is informed by an understanding of cultures and communities can place our students in the best position to demonstrate their reading growth and accomplishments. Throughout this book, I argue that effective assessment helps us better understand students' individual differences and thus provide optimal instruction.

Assessment is a key aspect of the accomplished teacher's repertoire. Expertise in assessment contributes to expertise in teaching. However, the reading assessments we can conduct in classrooms rarely receive the attention they deserve. Throughout this book, there is an emphasis on what teachers can do in classrooms to optimize reading assessment and related reading instruction. Thus, the book's title: *Understanding and Using Reading Assessment, K–12*.

READING ASSESSMENT ACROSS THE SCHOOL DISTRICT: A TOUR

Imagine for a moment that you spend the day visiting different classrooms in a school district noted for exemplary practices in reading assessment. Students are reading and achieving throughout the community. Reading assessment informs focused and timely reading instruction and plays a vital role in fostering student growth. Teachers are supported in their efforts to best understand and use reading assessment.

The first stop on our tour is kindergarten. Four language-rich kindergarten classrooms occupy a wing of the school. Students regularly experience and explore the uses of language: to learn, to inform, to enjoy, and to reflect. The students are involved in classroom discussions and read-alouds. They create meaning with dictated stories, focus on vocabulary with word walls, build listening comprehension, and maintain their enthusiasm for language through play with words. In one classroom, we see and hear students mouthing /b/ as they connect speech sounds with the print form of the letter *B*. The teacher circulates around the room, listening to determine whether students understand. She assesses their ongoing progress in matching print with speech and finds some students struggling to make this connection. Her ability to assess, which she considers central to successful teaching, allows her to provide immediate and focused instruction that meets students at their current level of understanding.

Using the assessment information gathered through screening tests, careful listening and ongoing oral exercises, and her knowledge of early reading curriculum, she creates a teachable moment. Based on her knowledge of individual students' development of phonics, she provides instruction that focuses on familiar things in and around the classroom to help students cement the connection of the letter *B* to its corresponding speech sound. We hear, "Bugs. Book bags. Best. Butter. BFF." Smiles spread around the group, and the students and their teacher acknowledge their accomplishments and are ready to move on. Many children in this classroom choose to spend time with books during their independent work time. This inclination to try to read is valued by the school and the teacher. She makes note of students' widespread willingness to try. This is important information, to be included in the students' narrative report cards. Throughout the school day and school year, assessment helps the teacher know her students, their individual strengths and needs, and how reading fits in their lives.

Next, we visit a fourth-grade classroom. The teacher works with a small group of students while other children read their self-selected books and articles. Students choose books wisely for independent reading: A rich classroom library provides choice for the students, and many know their capabilities as readers. Students ably navigate the internet to locate texts to gain information for their problem-based learning tasks and to further their interests. Their self-assessment ability allows them to select books and texts that present an engaging reading experience, including the comfortable challenge of stretching themselves as readers. These students continue to develop the ability to self-assess their reading in relation to the goals of reading and their abilities.

While many students work independently, several work on strengthening the skills and strategies that help them read the texts encountered in fourth grade. A quick paper-and-pencil assessment, in which students are asked to write what they know about key vocabulary words, reveals that several students do not understand *ecosystem, symbiosis, prey,* and *predator*—words that are key to constructing meaning in the new science unit. The teacher decides that the small group will engage in three tasks that provide both learning opportunities and assessment opportunities related to vocabulary. An enrichment lesson focuses on the common features of ecosystems, and the teacher encourages a small-group discussion of the important vocabulary words. She asks the students to write definitions of the words and answer questions to demonstrate their understanding. Each of these activities provides valuable assessment information—converging evidence of student knowledge and progress. The teacher is sensitive to the fact that several of her students are reluctant to participate, given their negative self-concepts as readers. Reading assessment that gives students useful feedback while shoring up their self-esteem is important to the students and the teacher. Her feedback to students is direct and supportive. Three sources of assessment information describe the status of her students' growth and knowledge: classroom discussions, the students' writing, and student responses to teacher questions. Combined, these assessments afford her high confidence in her determination that all students in the group now understand the key words and concepts of the unit.

Just as important, the teacher of this diverse group of students recognizes the different levels of self-efficacy and motivation that each student shows in relation to reading. Students in the small group work to understand the key vocabulary words. The teacher, an advocate of assessing students' attitude toward reading, attends to both the cognitive and affective aspects of learning. She assesses her students' knowledge of words as she assesses their motivation and perseverance. The teacher's careful work here is evident: The students who sometimes struggle at reading meet the reading challenges with positive motivation and complete the lesson with their self-esteem intact. The teacher considers this a critical outcome of her instruction.

Across town, students in a middle school classroom are progressing through an extended language arts period. The students in this class use digital portfolios, which help them organize their work. Most important, the portfolios provide a context for reading assessment. One virtual pocket holds reading logs and the students' ongoing accounts of their understanding of the stories and their reactions to the stories. Another pocket contains the weekly quizzes that focus on students' knowledge of the literary devices used by authors and the content of the texts that are read. Yet another pocket contains the vocabulary words that the students have independently chosen and determined to be important. Within this pocket, the students regularly sort vocabulary words into and among the categories "I don't know," "Getting to know," and "I definitely know." This self-sorting process demonstrates the ability of students to assess their own learning. The opportunities for students to conduct reading assessment are enhanced by the school district's commitment to portfolios and digital technology. The teacher consults each student's portfolio to regularly gauge student growth. The portfolio is shared with parents at open school night. In addition to demonstrating their children's achievements, the portfolio provides parents with a model of valuable and (for them) nontraditional reading assessment. Finally, the portfolio provides motivation for students. Viewed via laptop or tablet, the portfolio helps them see the connection of their consistent hard work to their accomplishments.

The next stop on our tour of reading assessment is a high school. Students read primary and secondary source documents, including diaries, newspapers, and textbook chapters related to the American Revolutionary War. The students' reading tasks include establishing a literal understanding of the historical content of the text. Students are expected to investigate when the texts were written, where they first appeared, and who wrote them. Students consider the trustworthiness of the texts they read and the reliability of the historical accounts provided by the authors. Students' success revolves around the prior knowledge and strategies needed for reading in the content area of history. These sophisticated reading strategies build on students' existing reading achievements and their ability to construct literal and inferential meaning from content-area texts.

The students' work is guided by a series of assessments, and throughout the year the teacher refers students to the publicly displayed and often-discussed rubrics for performance assessments in history. The rubrics serve as road maps for students, guiding their performances. The rubrics remind students to search for clues in the text that help determine sources and that may reveal an author's biases. The rubrics also provide details that assist the teacher in assigning scores to students' final projects. As such, the rubrics and performance assessment are an example of transparent assessment: They are developed not only to measure but also to educate. They inform students about what is expected to earn a particular grade, and they help students learn how to conduct self-assessment in complex reading tasks.

At our final stop, we observe students analyzing and interrogating advertisements. Students in 12th grade download advertisements from the internet—a readily available resource—for critical evaluation with classmates. The curriculum regularly references digital resources and uses them as objects for students' critical reading. Students are well versed in asking questions that include "Why does this text exist?," "Who wrote it?," "What is the purpose of this text?," "What are the claims?," "Is there evidence to support the claims?," and "What in this text is fact, opinion, or outright fabrication?" The questions are a culmination of the district-wide focus, from kindergarten through high school, on critical reading, understanding complex texts and then analyzing them. The questions serve as focused assessment of students' ability to access and critique digital resources.

Upon completion of our tour of the district, we understand that there are stories of success and challenge related to reading assessment across the school district community. Reading assessment is central to knowing students' reading progress and achievement. Reading assessment helps teachers construct understanding of how their students are developing as readers. In doing so, reading assessment provides critical information for making important instructional decisions. The relationship between reading assessment, teaching, and student progress in reading could not be more important.

What undergirds the natural, seemingly seamless approach to reading assessment developed by this district? The assessments derive from detailed and consensus-based understandings of both reading and reading assessment. Assessment is aligned with district and state standards for reading achievement and content-area curricular goals. Assessment is also aligned with the well-researched theories of the development of students' reading skills and strategies. In addition, assessments measure students' metacognition, self-efficacy, and motivation and engagement related to reading. The assessments are developed in relation to psychometric standards and issues related to fairness and the consequences of assessment. Reading assessment in this district is planned and systematic. The teachers know reading assessment and understand the strengths, weaknesses, and appropriate uses of different reading assessments. Throughout the district, assessment is used in accordance with the goal of helping each student become an accomplished reader.

READING ASSESSMENT PRINCIPLES AND PRIORITIES

Operating behind the scenes in the school district are principles and priorities that guide the development and use of reading assessment. They are presented in the following section.

1. All reading assessment is high-stakes assessment.

It is common to label standardized tests as "high stakes." In contrast, *all* assessment conducted in district schools is considered consequential and high stakes. The reasoning behind this idea is that if teacher time and effort—and school resources—are given to an act of assessment, the expected result is useful assessment information. Consider the teacher who is gathering detailed data on a second grader's oral reading fluency *in situ*, using a reading inventory. Or the teacher who follows silent reading with questions, noting that a student does well with literal comprehension, but not with inferences and critical comprehension. The information provided by such daily assessment is immediately useful in helping to shape subsequent reading instruction. And it is this shaping of reading instruction to the individual student's needs that is at the heart of "high stakes." Teachers know that accountability is demonstrated by year-end tests, but that accountability is created by instruction and learning informed by careful, daily classroom-based assessments. Nothing could be more high stakes.

2. Assessment should be conducted with the goal of bettering students' reading and students' lives.

Assessments range from daily teacher-conducted questions and observations to year-end summative tests. Assessment provides fine-grained detail of students' progress with the strategies and skills of reading and informs end-of-year reports on students' attainment of grade-level standards. Throughout the school year and through careful planning, each assessment is scrutinized for how it can foster student reading and how it helps all students reach their potential. All relevant audiences—teachers, students, parents, administrators, legislators, and the general public—are considered as the potential consumers of assessment results. Priority is given to assessments that give teachers actionable information to shape lessons to student needs. Be it measures of phonics development, fluency rate, digital literacy, literal and inferential comprehension, or critical reading, assessment provides details that inform instruction. In addition, assessment helps teachers understand the conative and affective aspects of becoming a successful reader. Motivation and engagement, self-efficacy, and metacognition are all accounted for in the assessment regimen. One result of this broad-based assessment perspective is the understanding of each student's reading progress and challenges. A second result is understanding how students are developing as individuals. Assessment serves to support student attainment and positive attitudes toward school. Across the district, teachers and administrators consistently ask, "How can this assessment help our students become better readers?"

3. Assessment should focus on reading processes and reading products.

A focus on reading processes allows for assessing students' strategies and skills as they read. Reading processes include matching sounds and symbols, deriving word meanings, fluently reading, constructing meaning, evaluating and critiquing texts, navigating the internet to locate appropriate texts, and managing the act of reading. Process-oriented assessment allows teachers to make inferences about student strengths and needs as students read. For example, insight into a student's decoding process results from listening to the sounding out of the *fl-* consonant blend. And, observation of students slowing or stopping to clarify meaning as they read allows for assessing a metacognitive process. These process assessments describe the nature and success of strategies and skills, as students are actually reading and engaged with constructing meaning.

In contrast, product-oriented assessments provide an after-the-act record of student reading. Assessments focused on reading products include quizzes, tests, and questions related to text comprehension. Product assessments measure student development and achievement. Scores on quizzes and tests allow for inferences about student learning in relation to lesson and unit goals and district and state standards. Product assessments provide test scores, report card grades, and other critically important assessment information. However, product assessment allows only backward inferences about student development. Asking if reading instruction was successful requires a similar set of backward inferences. A worthwhile analogy is trying to determine how a sports team won or lost a game by examining the final score. Of course, the final score is important, yet the score is silent as to how it was achieved. An informed blend of process and product information helps optimize the reading assessment system.

4. Assessment should describe how students use what they understand from reading.

Readers read to do things: Learn more about a school topic, hobby, or passion; be entertained; solve a complex problem; or share ideas with friends and family about a text just read. Reading lessons may end with students answering comprehension questions. Using assessment to check that students have comprehended text is important. Yet, assessment should not send the implicit message to students that we read to answer teachers' questions. While answering comprehension questions as *the* follow-up to reading is common school practice, it is uncommon for reading done outside of school. Reading assessment should increasingly focus on how students use the meaning they construct from text in reading-related tasks. When students read advertisements prior to analyzing and critiquing them, or when they follow detailed guidelines prior to conducting a lab experiment, reading involves at least two goals: comprehending text and using what is comprehended in a related task. This type of reading is the norm outside of the classroom, and it should be practiced in classrooms and increasingly reflected in our assessments.

5. Assessment should describe students' higher-order thinking, as well as the mechanics of reading.

Many reading assessments include multiple-choice and short-response items. These items help determine if students learn details, identify themes, derive vocabulary meaning, and comprehend main ideas. However, such assessments often fail to investigate students' complex thinking, which includes synthesizing and analyzing texts, evaluating and critiquing texts and authors found on the internet, and applying what is learned from reading. Such higher-order thinking is required by increasingly complex state and nationwide standards.

Students' basic skills and strategies in reading are necessary for higher-order reading skills and strategies: The latter are dependent on the former. It is important to conduct reading assessments that gauge all order of students' reading skills and strategies. However, there should be movement away from a preponderance of assessments that require students to fill a short answer, choose one answer from several choices, or dwell only on the mechanics of reading development, as is developmentally appropriate. Using assessments that connect students' reading with related performances helps with this progress.

6. Assessment should describe students' single-text reading as well as reading from multiple sources, including the internet.

A predominant goal of reading instruction is to help readers construct meaning from text. Many reading comprehension assessments focus on understanding single texts. Typically, and after reading a single text, students are asked to determine details and main ideas, answer literal and inferential questions, and demonstrate vocabulary knowledge. While this assessment approach focuses on comprehension of single short passages, students' success at reading in the 21st century involves more.

The environment of reading changes with hypertext and the internet. In this dynamic environment, students must construct meaning from multiple sources of information, decide which information sources are reliable, and integrate information taken from various sources. Related reading assessments must be capable of describing how students make sense of verbal and nonverbal information such as texts populated with graphs, photos, drawings, and maps. These assessments must describe how students distinguish and identify the relationships between multiple sources. Assessment should help us understand student readers' progress at reading multiple texts and identifying the relative strengths and weaknesses of claims and evidence presented in different texts. Finally, assessment should describe students' developing ability to determine the credibility and usefulness of the different texts they locate on the internet.

7. Assessment should focus more broadly on the different factors that influence reading development and reading achievement.

Diagnostic reading assessments and high-stakes assessments focus on the skills and strategies that contribute to reading comprehension, as do most classroom-based assessments. Unfortunately, there may be little or no attention paid to other factors that support students' reading development. Consider that across the United States, systematic reading assessment in elementary school involves universal screening and then diagnostic assessment and progress monitoring—all focused exclusively on reading skills and strategies. These strategies and skills are essential, but they do not guarantee students' reading success. Many factors influence reading development and reading achievement, including motivation and engagement, self-efficacy, and metacognition. Successful readers are engaged readers. These readers are motivated to read, they identify themselves as readers, they persevere in the face of reading challenges, and they consider reading to be an important part of their daily lives.

Across this district, teachers know that teaching success is measured not only by high test scores but also by helping students change from reluctant readers to enthusiastic readers, and helping students evolve from being easily discouraged to having the motivation to persevere when facing challenges. Accomplished teachers know the great impact of affect and conation on reading achievement and reading development. Related assessments inform teachers and students how these powerful factors are operating in each student. These assessments also help deliver the message that instruction that acknowledges the power of these "other" factors helps student readers develop and achieve.

8. Assessment should be coordinated across grades and across content areas, including formative and summative assessments.

There are several advantages to coordinating assessment. First, students and teachers become familiar with the ways and means of assessment. Students who are introduced to simple scoring rubrics in early elementary school can continue to develop their ability to use increasingly complex rubrics across their school careers. Second, coordination can streamline and make more efficient all assessment efforts. Students who work with similar types of assessment in reading, science, social studies, and mathematics develop a working familiarity with the expectations and procedures of the particular assessment program. Third, coordination facilitates cross-talk between summative assessments and formative assessments. Information gained from formative assessments helps teachers consider best paths for students to attain unit and year-end goals.

Schools, school districts, classrooms, states, teachers, and students are evaluated and ranked in relation to annual series of tests: summative reading assessments. These assessments summarize reading achievement as a grade-level equivalent, a raw score, and a percentile rank. Summative assessment is important as it helps us understand if students reach grade-level benchmarks, unit and lesson goals, and standards in classrooms, districts, and states. However, summative assessment is, by nature, after the fact of teaching and learning. Summative assessment is less able to inform instruction and to address individual needs as students are developing.

In contrast, the degree of detail that is provided by formative assessment may help a classroom teacher determine a teachable moment, identify the need for reteaching an important concept or skill related to ecosystems, or move forward to new instruction with confidence that students possess the requisite knowledge to succeed. Formative assessment describes students' ongoing reading growth as it occurs, and summative assessment provides summary statements about students' literacy achievement. Successful teachers use formative assessments in their classrooms because they know the importance of understanding students' reading development.

9. Assessment should be used to help students learn to assess their own reading.

Is reading assessment done *for* students? Or is it done *with* students and *by* students? Consider the first question as students read and respond to a multiple-choice test. The students submit answers that are then evaluated and graded. The scored test is returned to the student, but the student is kept at arm's length as to how assessment works. One consequence of this approach to assessment is that students do not learn to do reading assessment for themselves. Students' questions of "How do I do assessment?" remain unanswered.

When teachers ask assessment questions, they can explain to students why they are asking them and how they evaluate student responses. Through these explanations, students gain an understanding of evaluation and assessment. Likewise, using rubrics to help students understand the detail of how they will be assessed adds transparency to the assessment enterprise. Assessment that is consistent in providing insights into assessment across school years provides opportunities for students to learn to "do" reading assessment on their own and move toward independence.

Independent student readers must assume responsibility for assessing their reading, just as metacognitive, accomplished readers do. Students are not born with this ability: It is learned through teachers modeling and explaining assessment. Teachers provide opportunities in which students learn the value of self-assessment and the means to do accurate and useful assessment for themselves. Eventually, students can internalize assessment routines. A good start is modeling simple assessment procedures and helping students learn to initiate and successfully complete the routines independently. Throughout the district, teachers know that if students do not learn how to do self-assessment, they will not become independent readers.

10. Teacher and school accountability should be supported by helping teachers develop expertise with assessment.

Classroom-based reading assessment requires that teachers develop expertise. Specifically, teachers must be supported in developing effective formative assessments, interpreting assessment results, and then using the results to inform instruction. Teachers as assessment experts know what aspects of reading to assess, choose the texts and tasks to best capture student performance, make inferences about the students' reading from the assessment information, and use the understanding of students' reading to create effective instruction.

Teachers develop expertise with classroom assessment when they are supported by their administrators and school districts. The array of student factors to be assessed is large, ranging from reading strategies and skills to motivation, self-efficacy, and metacognition. There are zones of proximal development for each. Teachers who are assessment experts use assessment data to define these zones of proximal development and provide effective instruction. The teachers and administrators in this district know that effective reading instruction is informed by the insights made with classroom assessment, and effective classroom assessment is enabled by teachers' professional development.

In summary, effective reading assessment results from attention to the nature of students' reading development and reading achievement, paired with understanding of the different types and uses of assessment, and with knowledge of how assessment and instruction work together to foster change. This, combined with careful planning and consideration of the different assessment audiences, positions assessment to benefit teachers and students as they work through reading challenges and realize reading success.

WHAT'S NEW AND DIFFERENT IN THE FOURTH EDITION

New Chapters

The fourth edition of *Understanding and Using Reading Assessment* includes two new chapters: Chapter 2, "Assessing Early Reading," and Chapter 11, "Assessing Digital and Critical Reading." Chapter 2 focuses on how we assess young students' concepts of print and concepts of reading: assessments that help us understand children's language experiences that contribute to learning to read. In addition, the chapter examines the role of assessment in multi-tiered systems of support (MTSS), including a detailed example of how assessment works with phonemic awareness within MTSS. Chapter 11 describes assessments that mirror students' developmental path in learning keyboarding skills, navigating the internet, identifying and evaluating sources, and constructing meaning from multimodal texts. The chapter also examines assessment at the interface of critical reading and digital reading, focusing on students' ability to identify facts and opinions, claims and evidence, and to critically evaluate propaganda and advertisements.

Equity and Assessment

This fourth edition emphasizes the relationship of reading assessment with equity in education. Equity is addressed in two ways. First, the book describes how assessment can (and must) be fair for all students. Each chapter includes a focus on how assessment is administered and how assessment results are interpreted to achieve equity in acts of assessment. Second, each chapter describes how we can use assessment results to guide our efforts to achieve equity. Assessment is positioned as central to our determination of what students need to meet their full potential—and what teachers can do to help each do so.

Sciences of Reading

Reading assessment is always influenced by contextual factors that include the dynamics of research and practice, as well as politics and economics. The popularity—and necessity—of the science of reading offers the opportunity to examine our conceptualizations of students' reading development, the factors that influence this development, and reading achievement. It also demands that we examine our assessments in relation to our understanding of reading development. Does the array of assessments used in schools and classrooms fully reflect what research tells us is essential for reading development? Are particular aspects of students' reading development overassessed? Are some underassessed (or not assessed at all)? This fourth edition was written, in part, to present a broad view of how the science of reading can inform assessment. I propose that the science of reading—research on aspects of reading development that include phonemic awareness, phonics, fluency, vocabulary, and reading comprehension—should be expanded to the *sciences* of reading. This allows for assessment that maintains a focus on essential cognitive strategies and skills, while complementing our view of reading development with motivation, self-efficacy, attributions, and metacognition.

Updated Research

Finally, the fourth edition benefits from the copious research and theory that marks the vibrant sciences of reading. Throughout the book, I strive to include new information on what we have learned—about reading and about assessment—since the last edition of this book.

CHAPTER 1

Important Issues and Concepts in Reading Assessment

Reading is a key to students' success in school and in life, and reading assessment done well guides our efforts to foster this success. As we strive to understand and use reading assessment, it is important to consider three questions: First, why do we assess reading? All reading assessment should be conducted with the purpose of helping students achieve in reading. Second, what do we assess when we assess reading? Asking this question allows us to focus on reading program goals and outcomes and what we hope for our students as we teach and support their reading development. Third, how, where, and when do we assess reading? This query anticipates the array of reading assessment materials and procedures that are examined throughout this book in individual chapters.

THREE KEY QUESTIONS

Why Do We Assess Reading?

Reading assessment helps us understand the strengths and needs of each of our students: their reading development and reading achievement. Although all reading assessments should share this purpose, the manner in which individual assessments provide information and the manner in which we use the particular assessment information are varied. Consider the different formative and summative purposes for assessment that are demonstrated in the following scenario.

Hannah, a third-grade teacher, uses a reading inventory to gather detailed information about a student's oral reading strategies and skills. The reading inventory provides information for ongoing analysis of student reading. She determines that the student reads with high confidence but also reads through sentence boundaries. The student does not reread after obvious meaning-changing miscues. The teacher uses this new assessment information to update her understanding and determines that the student needs to concentrate on developing self-awareness in general, and comprehension-monitoring strategies in particular. Hannah uses the assessment information in the next day's instruction, the goal of which is to encourage the student to regularly monitor the meaning-making process that is reading. Using think-alouds, Hannah models the types of questions that good readers ask themselves as they read, including "Why am I reading?" and "Does that make sense?" In this case, the answer to the question of why we assess reading is that it provides detailed and timely information that is used by a talented teacher to shape instruction to the student's needs.

Late in the school year, Hannah administers a statewide high-stakes reading assessment. The test provides information on students' reading strategies and skills. Results of this test may be used for several purposes. The mean student scores, derived from multiple-choice and short fill-in items, will be used to determine if the school meets federally mandated levels of adequate yearly progress at reading achievement. The test is considered by some to be a judge of accountability, helping to determine if the teacher, school, and school district are working successfully to help students develop as readers and meet state standards in reading. The results of this test are also reported at the individual student level, and parents receive their child's raw scores and percentile rankings in vocabulary knowledge and literal and inferential comprehension. Thus, test results inform parents of their children's general reading achievement levels.

In each of the preceding scenarios, reading assessment is conducted for specific purposes and specific audiences. One assessment is more direct: The classroom teacher is accomplished at using the reading inventory to understand the nature of a student's reading, how it relates to a model of highly efficient reading, and how it anticipates the instruction and learning that the teacher plans for the student. The process orientation of the reading inventory provides a window into the reading strategies and skills that the student uses, or needs. The reading assessment information is immediate and fleeting, and the teacher knows how to focus on and interpret the information that the reading inventory produces. The teacher's knowledge of the nature of students' self-monitoring of reading is matched with the teacher's ability to use the reading inventory to provide information related to this important instructional goal.

In contrast, the end-of-year test is composed of items that describe the students' vocabulary knowledge and text comprehension. The test focuses on reading comprehension products. The results signal that a certain percentage of students meet state and federal reading benchmarks and communicate to particular audiences that the teaching of reading in the district is going well and that taxpayers' money has been well spent.

Throughout this book, the question of why we assess reading frames our consideration of the diverse purposes for assessing reading. These purposes include determining students' reading development, informing instruction, demonstrating teacher and school accountability, describing a reading program's strengths and weaknesses, motivating and encouraging students, and teaching students how to self-assess. Representative purposes for reading assessment and the audiences that use assessment information are presented in Table 1.1. If you are interested in an accounting of the different assessment audiences and purposes in your school or district, you can use the Reading Assessment Inventory: Audiences and Purposes reproducible form in the Appendix.

The question of why we assess reading is answered in different ways because reading instruction and reading assessment are influenced by the larger society in which students, teachers, administrators, and schools work. Consider that diverse theories and bodies of research inform the successful teaching and learning of reading (Tierney & Pearson, 2024). These theories emanate from domains of knowledge that include cognitive psychology, developmental psychology, linguistics, pedagogy, sociology, anthropology, critical race theory, and critical theory. Each theory may suggest different priorities for reading instruction and reading

TABLE 1.1. **Representative Audiences and Purposes for Reading Assessment**

Audience for assessment	Purpose for assessment
Students	• To report on learning and communicate progress • To motivate and encourage • To learn about assessment and how to self-assess • To build independence in reading
Teachers	• To determine the nature of student learning • To inform instruction • To evaluate students and construct grades • To diagnose students' strengths and weaknesses in reading
School administrators	• To determine reading program effectiveness • To prove school and teacher accountability • To determine resource allocation • To support teachers' professional development
Parents	• To be informed about children's achievements • To help connect home efforts with school efforts to support children's reading development
Politicians	• To establish accountability of schools • To inform the public of school progress
Taxpayers	• To demonstrate that tax dollars are well spent

assessment, which will signal different purposes for doing reading assessment. For example, research on reading strategies describes their importance for constructing meaning, whereas research in motivation provides evidence of the need to engage students as they develop into independent, committed readers (Afflerbach et al., 2008; Guthrie & Klauda, 2016). A successful reading program has varied, important outcomes that should include students' growth in the ability to use reading strategies and skills as well as students' increased motivation to read. Reading assessment must have strong connections to these outcomes and describe them well.

The assessment of reading takes place in a context that is influenced by social and political forces. There are assessment practices that may be favored politically, practiced locally, widely supported, or widely questioned. Legislators, taxpayers, parents, school administrators, teachers, and students may all claim legitimately that part of the question of why we assess reading is answered: to provide useful information. However, "useful information" varies, from the parent seeking assessment information that will help coordinate classroom and home reading efforts, to the legislator seeking districtwide reading assessment information in anticipation of an upcoming vote for school funding, to the administrator interested in documenting reading program effectiveness. In these contexts, each purpose for reading assessment must have the potential result of the betterment of student reading. Ideally, one group's need for particular reading assessment information should not displace another group's need. The goal of improving the teaching and learning of reading should help us determine our reading assessment priorities in all cases.

What Do We Assess When We Assess Reading?: The Focus of Assessment

Asking what we assess helps us focus on the goals of the reading instruction program and the relationship of reading instruction to reading assessment. The answer may demonstrate that our conceptualization of reading achievement, as reflected in the reading assessments used, is broad or narrow. The answer may help us determine whether the diverse goals of reading instruction are adequately reflected in the assessments that are intended to measure progress toward those goals. Or, the answer may indicate that whereas school district standards and the curriculum conceptualize reading development broadly, reading assessment measures it narrowly. We should plan to assess what we plan to teach.

Effective instruction contributes to the development of students' reading strategies and skills, motivation, and commitment to reading. Effective instruction broadens students' conceptualization of reading as contributing to success in life. Given the characteristics of successful readers, the array of reasons for reading, and the diverse outcomes of successful reading instruction, should we expect reading assessment to be similarly broad? Does our assessment describe the many beneficial outcomes of becoming a better reader? How are the outcomes of reading instruction weighted in relation to the assessment that is conducted in states, districts, schools, and classrooms? An examination of popular reading assessments reveals that there are clear gaps between the rhetoric of why reading is important and what is assessed.

Most reading assessments focus narrowly on one set of important reading outcomes: the cognitive strategies and skills of reading. We are familiar with these outcomes because of our experiences with them in school as teachers and former students. Phonemic awareness, phonics, sight word recognition, and fluency (National Institute of Child Health and Human Development, 2000), as well as vocabulary knowledge (Stahl & Bravo, 2010) and literal and inferential comprehension (Snow, 2002), contribute to reading success. Although these are essential elements of successful student reading, they do not fully represent the growth and development that students experience in exemplary reading programs (Afflerbach, 2022). Related, few reading assessments measure student motivation to read or the range of students' social uses of reading. Many reading assessments sample a small portion of student accomplishment and growth—and by implication, teacher and school success. Bracey (2001) notes that standardized tests regularly miss the following outcomes of effective teaching and student learning: "creativity, critical thinking, resilience, motivation, persistence, humor, reliability, enthusiasm, civic-mindedness, self-awareness, self-discipline, empathy, leadership, and compassion" (p. 158). If we want reading assessment to mirror students' accomplishments, we must avoid reading assessment practice that provides, at best, only a partial reflection of those accomplishments.

The question of what we assess when we assess reading must be asked because it can help us become better at assessment. This question helps us prioritize our reading instruction goals and focus on the most appropriate assessment materials and procedures. Schools use an array of assessments conducted across the school year, from reading inventories at the beginning of the year to standardized, norm-referenced tests at the end of the year. An accounting is necessary to optimize this variety of assessments that are intended to serve different audiences and purposes. Our reading assessments include those mandated by the district, the state, and the federal government and those selected by teachers and administrators in schools. An assessment inventory can help us better understand the relationship between the things that a school community values in relation to students' reading development and what is actually assessed. A sample reading assessment inventory, which may be used to investigate the variety, breadth, and focus of assessment, is presented in Figure 1.1. A reading assessment inventory allows us to rank assessment in terms of the match between our teaching and learning priorities and time demands. An assessment inventory helps us compare what is with what could be. This information may be used to create an action plan with the goal of achieving

	Assessment is a measure of students' . . .					
Assessment type	Cognitive reading strategies and skills	Motivation for reading	Social uses of reading	Independence in reading	Using reading in collaborative learning environments	Choosing reading over attractive alternatives
Tests and quizzes	X					
Portfolios	X	X	X	X	X	X
Performance assessments	X		X	X		
Teacher questions	X	X	X		X	X
Reading inventories	X					
Teacher observations	X	X	X	X	X	X

FIGURE 1.1. A sample reading assessment inventory. X = demonstrated ability of a particular type of reading assessment to serve the indicated purpose.

better alignment among valued and agreed-upon outcomes of reading instruction, what is taught, and what is assessed. If you are interested in an accounting of the different assessments you use and the focus of these assessments in your school or district, you can use the Reading Assessment Inventory: What Is Assessed? reproducible form in the Appendix.

How, Where, and When Do We Assess Reading?

The determination of why we assess and what we assess must be followed by informed decisions of how best to examine and evaluate students' reading development. Indeed, the majority of this book addresses the different means for assessing students' reading. Part and parcel of a description of how to assess reading is the determination of where and when such assessment should occur. This is where the logical relationship between why we assess, what we assess, and how we assess should be evident. If we assess students' reading comprehension strategies and skills to determine the general success of a districtwide reading program, standardized and norm-referenced tests may be the first choice of school administrators and other educational decision makers. In contrast, if we assess students' progress to gauge the effectiveness of daily reading lessons, our assessment must be sensitive to the detailed goals of the lessons, and the information provided by the assessment must be immediately useful. Here, we could focus on questions about the contents of the chapter being read, with students' responses providing formative assessment information.

Just as reading assessment should be matched to particular purposes and audiences, how we assess students' reading achievement must be informed by the nature of the reading we expect of them. Much is known about the complexities of reading and the manner in which student readers develop (Kim et al., 2021; Tierney & Pearson, 2024; van den Broek et al., 2016; VanSledright, 2010). Reading is described in detail, and research reminds us that reading is a stunning human accomplishment. Although we are far from any claim that we know all we need to know about reading, what we know should be reflected in our assessments. For example, the necessity of learning phonics and comprehension strategies is well documented, and we have many useful approaches to assessing phonics and comprehension.

In some districts, these assessments are regularly called on to tell the story of students' reading achievement. In other districts, the aggregate results of reading assessments may underrepresent how students have developed as readers. Doing our best work with reading assessments demands that we understand the available assessment materials and procedures and that we use them expertly.

DEFINING READING IS CENTRAL TO USEFUL READING ASSESSMENT

Reading assessment must be clearly linked to a definition of what reading is. The accuracy and detail of this definition will figure largely in the process of determining the validity and usefulness of all reading assessments. This definition of reading should consistently serve as a touchstone as we consider different reading assessment materials and procedures. As we proceed through this book, the assessments we examine must map clearly onto a definition of reading. If not, then the definition or the choice of assessment is faulty. The definition of reading should inform the goals of reading instruction and the reading assessment program that is developed for a particular classroom, grade, school, school district, or state. I note that developing a definition and description of reading can be challenging for one individual. Developing a consensus definition—for a district, school, or grade—is more challenging when many stakeholders are involved, as indicated by the ongoing and contentious process of defining "science of reading." We are not wanting for definitions and descriptions of reading, but it is exceedingly difficult to create a consensus definition with which all teachers, administrators, parents, students, legislators, and the general public agree. This creates a complex situation in which there is universal agreement about the importance of reading, but not universal agreement on what reading is, how children learn to read, and how reading is best taught.

Our professional knowledge of reading should inform our conceptualization of reading and students' reading development. Thus, I believe that it is imperative that teachers compare their understandings of what reading is with others' definitions. Reading assessment can be narrowly focused, missing aspects of students' development that are keys to lifelong, accomplished reading. Following is an overview of how I construct an understanding of reading, based on research and professional knowledge. I consider reading as defined in the frameworks of two major national and international reading assessments. First, I focus on the definition of reading comprehension that is provided by the framework of the National Assessment of Educational Progress (NAEP):

> Reading comprehension is making meaning with text, a complex process shaped by many factors, including readers' abilities to
>
> - engage with texts in print and multimodal forms;
> - employ personal resources that include foundational reading skills, language, knowledge, and motivation; and
> - extract, construct, integrate, critique, and apply meaning in activities across a range of social and cultural contexts. (National Assessment Governing Board, 2023, p. 10)

The NAEP reading framework portrays reading as a dynamic and goal-oriented process that involves strategies, skills, and prior knowledge, as well as motivation. I note that the inclusion of motivation in the definition of reading comprehension is a watershed moment; it serves as acknowledgment of the essential nature of motivation. I also appreciate that the definition reminds us that students read across different media. Furthermore, the definition includes what readers may do with what they comprehend (i.e., "integrate, critique, and apply meaning") and notes that reading is situated in social and cultural contexts.

A dynamic, strategic, and goal-oriented conceptualization of reading also serves as a foundation for the Progress in International Reading Literacy Study (PIRLS; Mullis & Martin, 2021), which assesses reading achievement across the globe. The PIRLS definition of reading provides further details on the nature of reading and anticipates the types of reading assessment that are necessary to gauge student growth in reading across the school year: *"Reading literacy is the ability to understand and use those written language forms required by society and/or valued by the individual. Readers can construct meaning from texts in a variety of forms. They read to learn, to participate in communities of readers in school and everyday life, and for enjoyment*" (italics in original; Mullis & Martin, 2021). The further explanation of reading in relation to the PIRLS definition is critical, in my opinion, for built into this definition of reading are reader motives and the subtexts for why we read and what we read.

We can appreciate the reading that the NAEP and PIRLS reading frameworks describe. However, there is one major wrinkle. The NAEP (conducted in the 4th, 8th, and 12th grades) and the PIRLS (conducted with 9- and 10-year-old students) are based on the premise that the majority of students who take the tests are capable of reading. These students can decode language, recognize words, read fluently, understand the concepts represented in text, and comprehend. The challenge, then, is to create a definition of reading that reflects the development that students undergo as they learn to read. We are fortunate to have considerable research information related to the development of reading ability in young children (Clay, 1979; Heath, 1983; Metsala & David, 2016; Rasinski et al., 2021; Sleeman et al., 2022). We also have recent research syntheses that describe the importance of language knowledge in helping students learn to read and continue their development as readers (National Institute of Child Health and Human Development, 2000). This research demonstrates that success in reading is attributable, in part, to the development of strategies and skills related to phonemic awareness, phonics, fluency, vocabulary, and comprehension. Within each of these areas are developmental benchmarks and trajectories that are helpful to me as I construct an account of successful student reading and consider reading assessment suitable for different students.

At this point, my understanding of reading includes the ideas that we read to construct meaning and that we use strategies and skills to do so. These strategies and skills are developmental in nature. While cognitive strategies and skills are essential to success in reading, they do not guarantee success. When I compare my evolving definition with known and valued outcomes of teaching readers, I find that there are several missing pieces. These include students' motivation to choose to read, whether it is in the face of what might be attractive alternatives that may (or may not) involve reading (e.g., TikTok, Instagram, sleeping, soccer), and students' motivation to persevere with reading when the going gets tough. Self-efficacy is a powerful influence on student performance (Bandura, 1998), but it is rarely considered in models of reading development. Another missing piece is how reading experience and reading accomplishment make ongoing contributions to a student's personality development and sense of self. Fortunately, there is research that describes these essential elements of reading development. Reading consists of identifiable cognitive components (e.g., word recognition, comprehension) that interact to make reading successful (Alexander, 2005). Reading development and success are influenced by students' metacognition (Xie et al., 2023), motivation (Barber & Klauda, 2020), self-efficacy (Schunk & Bursuck, 2016), and prior reading experiences (Anderson & Pearson, 1984). These powerful factors are operating not only in individual acts of reading but also on students' reading development. Students who are not motivated, who struggle to be metacognitive, and who lack self-efficacy find that it is difficult to become a better reader (Afflerbach, 2022).

As I contemplate the nature of reading and what is currently assessed, I am reminded of the need to develop assessments that measure the complexity of student achievement. Too often, reading assessment is a thin account of a robust phenomenon (Davis, 1998). For example, we might ask students to determine the main idea of a text that describes the economic concept of opportunity cost. Determining the theme or main idea of a text is an important reading ability, but it can be complemented with assessment that asks students to apply the main idea related to opportunity cost to an economic decision that the student makes (e.g., How should Reg spend his allowance? Should Maryann buy running shoes or a bicycle helmet with the money she received from her parents for her birthday?) to explain the relation of the main idea to other important economic concepts, or to critique the author's stance toward the main idea.

As to my definition of reading, I am confident that it includes a breadth of conceptualization that informs my reading instruction goals and the nature of the reading assessments I will use:

> Reading is the act of constructing meaning from text. We use cognitive and metacognitive skills, strategies, and prior knowledge, all of which are developmental in nature, to understand what we read. The act of reading is supported by reader motivation and positive self-efficacy, which are also developmental. We read to help us achieve our goals, within and outside of school.

In summary, the definition of reading that we construct must reflect an accurate understanding of what reading is, for this definition becomes a benchmark for determining the reading assessments in our classrooms. We must assess our assessments to determine that they get into the nooks and crannies of students' strengths and needs, and that they describe students' immediate and long-lasting achievements in reading. We must build, maintain, and revise our understandings of what reading is to make informed decisions about the quality of our reading assessments. Our detailed definition and characterization of reading will help us vet reading assessments.

A MODEL OF READING ASSESSMENT

Just as we need a clear definition of reading to help us determine what we must assess, we also need a clear understanding of how assessment works to develop effective assessments. Pellegrino et al. (2001) describe three components of useful assessment: cognition, observation, and interpretation. We engage these aspects whenever we assess, although we may not have considered them in such formal terms.

To the degree that we understand what developing students do when they read, we can use this information to specify the things we would like to assess. The cognition component of reading assessment focuses on the strategies and skills that students use to decode, understand words, and construct meaning. Related research contributes to the building of detailed theoretical constructs that reflect successful reading, which in turn informs our instruction. For example, we know that the ability to summarize a text is an important comprehension strategy (Snow, 2002) that is frequently applied by student readers in school reading tasks. Research provides considerable detail on the nature of summarization strategies (Pressley & Afflerbach, 1995), the usefulness of the strategies, and how they are used with traditional and electronic texts (Cho, 2014; Pečjaka & Pircb, 2018). We know that students must be able to ignore unimportant text information and recognize and synthesize important text information, using processes that determine connections, similarities, and repetitions within the text. Students must be able to clearly synthesize and state the content and the purpose of the text read. This detailed understanding of the phenomenon to be assessed—summarization, in this case—is the first component in Pellegrino et al.'s (2001) model of assessment. Our model of reading tells us that summarization is important and worthy of teaching and assessing.

Our ability to describe the detailed nature of summarization informs the second component of the reading assessment model: observation. Another way to view observation is that it is what we get from the assessment itself, and a related challenge is to design an assessment task that will provide us the opportunity to observe students as they summarize text. The observation component of reading assessment must accurately represent our knowledge related to the domains of reading *and* assessment. As research contributes to our evolving understanding of how reading works, a concurrent evolution is taking place in educational measurement. That is, theories of how to evaluate student progress are informed by research. This research, in turn, informs our conceptualization of how we can assess those things that we deem critical for reading success. We can propose reading assessments that reflect classroom reading practice and require students to use summarization strategies:

- Do we ask students to write and construct a summary as opposed to choosing the correct summary in a multiple-choice format?
- Do our assessments allow for different interpretation and summary of the text, or is there a single, "correct" meaning?

- Do we ask for retellings of text that can be checked against a detailed list of the text's contents?
- Do we ask for summary accounts of several related texts?
- Are summarization assessment tasks related to the types of summarization regularly done in the classroom?

The observation component of the assessment model (Pellegrino et al., 2001) reminds us that an effective assessment reflects our understanding of how students read in relation to a particular task, text, and setting. How can we evoke, record, and evaluate student summaries? What are our options? We may consider constructed-response questions, think-alouds, short fill-in responses, and answers to questions as the means to gather and then observe students' work with summarization. Or we may require students to perform tasks in which success is contingent, in part, on their ability to summarize text. An assessment task worthy of our intent to observe students' summarization strategies and skills is to create a summary statement of the author's argument for addressing global warming.

Interpretation is the third component of Pellegrino et al.'s (2001) assessment model. So far, we have designed an assessment that focuses on students' summarization ability, combining our understandings of reading and assessment. We expect that careful development of the assessment will yield valuable assessment results. Our faith in our understanding of the nature of summarization and in the assessment materials and procedures that we have developed to assess summarization figure largely in the confidence we have in the inferences that we then make about student achievement and ability.

All reading assessment involves interpretation, and assessment is always related to acts of inference (Johnston, 1987). Reading assessment done well allows us to make inferences about students' needs and strengths. This basic process of reading assessment, generalizing to students' reading performances from a sample of their reading, demands that our inferences be accurate and born of high confidence. The importance of accurate inferences from assessment information cannot be understated, given that we assess to help students become better readers. However, we can make inferences only about those things that we sample. An incomplete assessment agenda, including one that ignores how students develop in terms of motivation and self-efficacy in relation to reading, or their ability to construct meaning from multiple texts on the internet, will limit the inferences that we can make about students' reading development, our teaching effectiveness, and the value of the reading curriculum. To make valid inferences from our summarization assessment, we use a rubric that indicates the degree of student success at summarizing the author's argument for addressing global warming.

The assessment model proposed by Pellegrino et al. (2001) focuses on reading. However, we should also assess related aspects of reading performance and development. We should conceptualize assessment of reading in addition to—and other than—the cognitive. We know that students' motivations and self-efficacy matter in single acts of reading and across time as student readers develop. We must construct assessments with the rigor and attention to detail that are equivalent to those that measure students' cognitive strategy and skill growth. For example, an assessment of students' motivations for reading must demonstrate our understanding of the construct of motivation. This understanding allows us to specify what aspects of motivation are to be assessed, inform the development of the observation instrument, and guide our interpretation of results.

Pellegrino et al.'s (2001) assessment model includes the three elements of cognition, observation, and interpretation. In the previous extended example, we considered each of these components separately, and then in relation to one another. We contemplated what happens when students summarize text, and we considered the nature of an assessment that would capture and describe this important reading ability. Also, we considered the inferences that we can make about students' reading and summarization, based on our understanding of the reading assessment we have planned. We examined the factors involved in successful student performance, beyond cognitive strategies and skills.

DETERMINING THE SUITABILITY OF READING ASSESSMENT: THE CURRV MODEL

Our final consideration for this chapter is the suitability of reading assessments:

- What is the optimal mix of reading assessments that we use across a school year?
- How do we choose one assessment over another, given what are often limited resources?
- On what basis can decisions about the suitability of a reading assessment be made?

The CURRV model (Leipzig & Afflerbach, 2000) encourages us to examine a reading assessment using five criteria: consequences, usefulness, roles/responsibilities, reliability, and validity. This model supports us in determining if a reading assessment is appropriate for measuring and describing our students' learning. The knowledge gained from applying the CURRV model brings us closer to an informed use of reading assessment.

The CURRV model was developed, in part, as a reaction to the historical practice of using only the criteria of reliability and validity to argue for the quality of reading assessments. Reliability and validity are traditional and critical aspects

Important Issues and Concepts 27

of assessment. Yet, they are psychometric principles that cannot help us ultimately determine whether an assessment is suitable for particular teachers, students, and reading situations and assessment tasks. The CURRV model retains the criteria of reliability and validity and adds three necessary considerations:

1. What are the consequences of the reading assessment?
2. What is the usefulness of the reading assessment?
3. What are the roles and responsibilities related to effectively using the reading assessment?

The five different components of the model allow us to analyze different reading assessments and make choices and suggestions based on our understandings of the nature, strengths, and weaknesses of these assessments. The model allows us to judge the situational appropriateness of an assessment. A sampling of the questions that the CURRV model allows us to ask of a reading assessment is presented in Figure 1.2. If you are interested in using the CURRV criteria to evaluate the reading assessments in your school or district, you can use the Using the CURRV Model to Evaluate Reading Assessment reproducible form in the Appendix.

Consequences of Assessment

All reading assessments have consequences. If we return to the question of why we assess, we are reminded that a reading assessment must have the primary consequence of helping students continue their development as readers. Yet, not all reading assessments may effect this change. It is essential to consider all the possible consequences of a reading assessment, positive or negative. Students may

---

- What are the positive consequences of the use of this assessment?
- What are the negative consequences of the use of this assessment?
- What is the usefulness of this assessment to teachers, students, administrators, and others?
- What are the specific roles and responsibilities for the teachers, students, and administrators associated with this assessment?
- What are the reliability issues related to this assessment?
- What are the validity issues related to this assessment?

FIGURE 1.2. The CURRV model's framework (Leipzig & Afflerbach, 2000): Questions to help determine the suitability of a reading assessment. CURRV = consequences, usefulness, roles and responsibilities, reliability, and validity.

experience consistent support in their reading development as a consequence of careful classroom-based assessment. High-quality reading assessment will help them become better readers. Students may feel increased self-esteem when their high-stakes test scores demonstrate learning. Students could become motivated to read as a result of encouraging teacher assessment feedback. In contrast, students may lose class reading time as school resources are allocated to test preparation. Inappropriate assessment will not provide the type of information that best shapes classroom instruction to students' immediate and long-term needs. A teacher's insensitivity to a student's response to a question stifles student engagement. Additionally, a history of low test scores may teach students to avoid reading. Ultimately, their motivation to read suffers.

The positive or negative consequences of different types of reading assessments influence teachers. Reading inventories and careful teacher questioning provide important information with which accomplished teachers practice the art of teaching. These assessments allow teachers to adjust instruction and influence student learning in a dynamic manner. Performance assessments allow a teacher to better understand the depth and breadth of student achievement related to content-area reading and learning. High test scores garner a salary increase for some teachers and may help build parental and community support for teachers and schools. In contrast, inappropriate assessments take valuable class time from the teaching of reading without yielding valuable information. Decisions made in relation to high-stakes test scores may constrict the curriculum: The content of what is taught in reading blocks and the time to teach it both shrink. Assessing our assessments from the perspective of their intended and unintended consequences will help us determine their suitability.

Usefulness of Assessment

A second aspect of the suitability of a reading assessment, closely related to consequences, is the usefulness of the assessment. If the criterion of usefulness were applied to the mix of reading assessments selected and mandated in schools, the assessment landscape might look different. The array of assessments found in classrooms represents a legacy of tradition and habit, insight and oversight. Reading assessments accompany districtwide initiatives and are mandated under federal and state laws. Some are developed by teachers, some are bought off the shelf, and others are inherited from earlier times. There may be no strategy for coordinating reading assessment efforts. Thus, it is important to take stock of available assessments to consider their usefulness.

A useful assessment is one that allows teachers to gather accurate and actionable information about students' reading. As teachers, we need reading assessments that help us address the different audiences for the information garnered.

We need assessments that provide both formative and summative information. We need assessments that focus on the processes and products of student reading. We also need assessments that are sensitive to the breadth and depth of students' accomplishments in reading at different levels of reading achievement.

Criteria for usefulness include how well the assessment describes student achievement, how easily the assessment information is communicated, and how well the assessment works with curricular goals. Using such criteria, we can create a ranking system that informs and allows us to make sometimes difficult decisions about which assessments are first-order and keepers, which are optional, and which we might do well without. Please note that in some of the chapters that follow, I combine our consideration of the consequences and uses for particular assessments as guided by the CURRV framework because they are tightly interwoven.

Roles and Responsibilities Related to Assessment

The third component of the CURRV framework (Leipzig & Afflerbach, 2000) reminds us that reading assessments come with roles and responsibilities. For example, performance assessments offer distinct advantages over many machine-scored, multiple-choice tests because the performance assessments can describe detailed student learning and achievement. Not all parents are aware of this fact, and administrators and teachers may be charged with informing parents about the potential advantages of performance assessments. In addition to the need to communicate these potential advantages to parents, we must become familiar with the important components of different reading assessments. If we adopt a series of performance assessments to measure students' reading and learning in the content areas, then we must be able to use rubrics to score students' complex performances. In addition, we should be able to use rubrics to help students anticipate the nature of the performance expected of them and to provide models for student learning. We should also be prepared to use performance assessments and rubrics to help students develop their self-assessment abilities (Afflerbach, 2002a).

Reliability of Assessment

The reliability of a reading assessment relates to the consistency and precision of the assessment instrument and process (Kerlinger, 1986). When we assess students, we want to make inferences about the students' learning and performances. Reliability theory posits that the information we gather through assessment is composed of two components: (1) the true component, which reflects the student's real reading achievement, and (2) the error component, which signals "noise" and is the component of an assessment result that does not reflect the student's reading achievement. We must be vigilant in recognizing and controlling the error component. If we recall the model of assessment presented by Pellegrino et al. (2001), we can immediately appreciate the need for high reliability. If our assessments are unreliable, then the inferences we make about our students' learning and achievements may be erroneous, or worthless. We may miss a student's need for developing critical reading strategies, mistakenly teach decoding skills to a student who already has them, or fail to recognize an increase in a student's motivation to read.

We must strive to determine that assessment practices are consistent and focused on important aspects of student learning. The goals of evenhandedness in dealing with different students and of clear and fair communication with our reading assessments are imperative. When we assess student reading, we must have confidence in the reliability of our assessment. Otherwise, assessment is not worth administering and the results are not worth considering.

Validity of Assessment

The fifth component of the CURRV model (Leipzig & Afflerbach, 2000) is validity (Messick, 1989). We want our assessment efforts to matter, and we must ask questions related to validity before we invest valuable time in any assessment. There are several types of validity. For our purposes here, it is important to consider the construct validity and ecological validity of a reading assessment. (Within the chapters, I only discuss the particular forms of validity that pertain to the chapter topics.)

How do we conceptualize reading? The construct of reading represents our best theory of what reading is. If we view reading as a series of strategies and skills, then we likely believe that phonemic awareness and reading comprehension are critical to students' development as readers. We should make every effort to assess students' growth and achievement related to their comprehension and phonemic awareness. If we believe that reading achievement can be influenced by student motivation, then we should use a reading curriculum that addresses student readers' motivation, as well as assessments that help us understand growth in student motivation.

If we believe a student's self-efficacy influences reading development, we should signal that importance with appropriate assessments. When we invest time in ascertaining the links between our assessment, curriculum, standards, and constructs, we may arrive at the determination of construct validity for an assessment without surprise.

An additional consideration is ecological validity, or the degree to which assessment items and tasks reflect what students do when they read in the classroom. Schmuckler (2001) describes ecological validity as a test of "whether or not one can generalize from observed behavior in the laboratory to natural behavior in the world" (p. 419). This description leads us to two questions:

1. Does student work on an assessment generalize to what is normally done in the classroom?
2. Does student work in the classroom generalize to important tasks and accomplishments in the world outside the classroom?

Contrasting a reading inventory conducted while a student reads orally from a self-chosen text and a series of comprehension questions that follow a two-paragraph reading selection on a standardized, norm-referenced reading test helps us consider ecological validity. A talented teacher conducting a reading inventory can, in this instance, gather information from a student reading texts that are part of the school curriculum and that are read in a normal manner, reflecting the classroom routine. The assessment focuses on students' real-time use of strategies and skills. Compare this with the ecological validity of a multiple-choice, machine-scored reading test. There may be a very limited relationship between daily classroom reading instruction routines and students' reading behaviors, except for those classrooms where test preparation is a focus, with test-like reading materials and assessments used regularly. When the reading and reading-related tasks demanded on an assessment vary greatly from the reading and reading-related tasks done regularly in the classroom, we may see considerable challenges to ecological validity.

THE PLAN FOR THIS BOOK

The CURRV framework (Leipzig & Afflerbach, 2000) described in this chapter is used as an organizing principle for many of the chapters in the book. After an examination of assessments for early reading in Chapter 2, Chapters 3 through 6 focus on particular types of reading assessment, including reading inventories, teacher questioning, portfolios, performance assessments, and high-stakes tests. These chapters begin with a brief introduction and historical overview of the particular assessment, followed by a detailed accounting of the characteristics of the assessment. We then examine the consequences, usefulness, roles and responsibilities, reliability, and validity of each type of assessment as it is situated in a particular teacher's classroom. The consideration of these different types of reading assessment is done in relation to the reading development that most students experience across their school careers. Thus, we determine the suitability of an assessment in relation to students' development as readers. Chapters 7 and 8 focus on important issues that are not given the attention they deserve: the accommodation of English learners (ELs) and students with learning disabilities in reading assessment, and how reading development other than cognitive strategy and skill growth may be assessed. Chapter 10 focuses on using reading assessment to help students learn to self-assess and become truly independent readers, and Chapter 11 examines assessment related to digital reading and critical reading.

The array of reading assessments now available to teachers and students is broad. To this end, I acknowledge that successful reading assessment programs sample and choose from this wide assortment and tailor these assessments to the programs' particular needs. It is not uncommon to encounter individualistic approaches to portfolios and performance assessment, or hybrid assessments that combine positive features of checklists and performance assessment, and issues that surround high-stakes testing. Thus, my chapter-by-chapter approach to understanding and using reading assessments may appear artificial in some respects. Guiding my plan here is the goal of presenting each assessment separately and providing details related to the assessment, while noting the ways in which it might be complemented by other, valuable reading assessments.

Throughout this book, issues are framed in relation to the educational, social, and political factors that exert varied degrees of influence on reading assessment. There are sharp divides in how different stakeholders, from teachers to legislators, conceptualize reading, the teaching of reading, and reading achievement. It follows that there are disparate ideas related to the nature and role of reading assessment. I attempt to represent reading assessment in relation to the frames of reference and agendas that different people bring to the assessment arena, for consideration of any reading assessment divorced from the school and societal contexts in which it is used does not pass the reality test. Furthermore, I attempt to represent the thinking and rationale behind particular reading assessment initiatives and programs. My purpose here is to anchor reading assessment to the classrooms, the schools, and the society in which our students read and are assessed. Each chapter ends with a section called "Enhancing Your Understanding," in which I provide questions and tasks that invite the readers of this book to apply the knowledge they gain from each chapter to their own assessment practices.

Each chapter is followed by a section called "Reading Assessment Snapshot." Each snapshot addresses an important reading assessment issue that pertains to some or all of the assessments covered in this book. For example, the reading assessment snapshots include examination of the confounds in reading assessment, technology and assessment, and task analyses of our assessments as a check on their suitability.

Throughout this book, I stress the need to examine reading assessment in relation to our current understanding of the reading process, students' development, and the culture of schooling. I reflect on Huey's (1908) observation, made over 100 years ago: "To completely analyze what we do when we read would almost be the acme of a psychologist's achievements, for it would be to describe very many of the most intricate workings of the human mind" (p. 6). When we are successful in our attempts to assess the range of students' development in reading and use this information to help our student readers thrive, we will have accomplished a similarly remarkable, and necessary, feat.

THE PURPOSE AND INTENDED AUDIENCES FOR THIS BOOK

My purpose is to help us understand and use reading assessments. Through reading this book, readers will become familiar with different types of reading assessments, and together we examine important issues in reading assessment. Never has there been a more promising time for the implementation and productive use of assessments to help us understand students' growth in reading. It is my hope that this book will help readers become familiar with the characteristics of different types of reading assessments and become accomplished in the assessment of reading. Herein, we consider the suitability of different reading assessments for particular purposes and audiences. In doing so, we examine the means for developing, conducting, and using reading assessments to help foster students' reading achievements.

This book is intended for those who are interested in developing a more detailed understanding of different reading assessments, their characteristics, their usefulness and possible consequences, and their requirements. As such, this book can be used in undergraduate and graduate teacher-preparation courses that focus on reading assessment. This book may also be useful in graduate courses that include a comprehensive overview of reading assessment materials and procedures. Finally, this book is inspired by and intended for K–12 teachers and the administrators that support them.

SUMMARY

Using assessments well demands our knowledge and vigilance. The informed use of reading assessments may be accomplished when we attend to the issues discussed in this chapter. First, we must regularly ask the following questions:

- Why do we assess reading?
- What do we assess?
- How do we assess reading?

Second, all of our work in reading assessment must be guided by a detailed understanding and definition of what reading is and a clear conceptualization of reading assessment. We are fortunate that our evolving understanding of reading parallels an evolving understanding of how to best assess reading. A model of reading assessment provides useful guidelines for us to assess assessments. Finally, we must examine the suitability of a reading assessment. The psychometric standards of reliability and validity are central to any successful reading assessment. Yet, these aspects of assessment must share the stage with our consideration of the consequences, usefulness, and associated roles and responsibilities of particular reading assessments. Equipped with these important understandings of assessment, we are now ready to begin our consideration of the different types of reading assessments.

Enhancing Your Understanding

1. An important use of reading assessment is the inferences we make about students' reading from assessment information. Chart an inference that you make from a reading assessment about a student's reading development. Where does the information that you use to make the inference come from? What degree of confidence do you have in the inference? How could you gather complementary information about the student and the inference? How does the inference help you plan and deliver instruction?

2. Assess your assessments. Are there assessments that provide information about student reading that is not otherwise obtainable? Are there assessments that you cannot live without? Are there assessments that are not worth the time and effort put into them in relation to the quality or type of information they provide?

3. Talk with your students about a particular assessment. Do they understand what it is? Do they understand how it works and why it is valuable?

4. Working with administrators and teachers, develop an assessment inventory. Identify the different types of reading assessments that are used in your classroom, grade, and school. Describe their frequency of use and their usefulness.

5. Use the CURRV model to analyze an assessment that you use or are considering using.

Reading Assessment Snapshot
ASSESSMENT AND EQUITY

Assessment and equity are in a dynamic relationship. We conduct assessment to learn about students' needs and strengths and to then provide suitable instruction. We want all assessment to be fair and reliable—to treat students equitably. We want to use the results of assessment to establish equity of opportunity and to promote achievement in all schools, for all students.

Assessment plays several roles related to educational equity. First, assessment results can be used to identify inequities. For example, reading scores on the NAEP indicate a consistent achievement gap between students from higher and lower socio-economic conditions. The NAEP assessment results can be used to address inequity, as they provide evidence for the claim that economically disadvantaged students should be better supported in schools and communities. We attain educational equity for all students when we provide instruction and support that helps them reach their potential. In doing so, assessment is in service of achieving equity.

In addition to using test scores to evaluate the equity of students' opportunity, assessment itself may be equitable or inequitable. For example, a reading comprehension test that privileges prior knowledge of particular groups of students will result in assessment results that are biased and that give less-than-accurate portrayals of students (or groups of students). Teacher bias may be unconsciously triggered by a student's spoken dialect. Students recently arrived from another country may speak little English, hindering our ability to fully understand their language competencies. These examples remind us that we should examine our assessment materials and procedures to determine if bias is present, and then work to eliminate that bias. This examination helps us determine if an assessment positions students to do their best and if the assessment provides accurate information in relation to reading development. Promoting equity in all assessments, be it tests, teachers' questions, or worksheets and quizzes, results in information that best serves the goal of helping every student. When assessment is fair and reliable, bias against (or for) particular students is lessened or removed, and equity is encouraged.

CHAPTER 2

Assessing Early Reading

Most young children arrive at school with substantial language experience (Clay, 1989; Scarborough, 2001), and an essential role of assessment is to determine the nature of this experience. In doing so, assessment describes students' language as they begin school and helps us determine what instruction will best support students' beginning reading and continued literacy development.

In a single classroom there may be students who have years of formal prekindergarten education, who have parents who regularly read aloud to them, who have home environments where talk and language play are encouraged, and whose home language is a good fit with the language of the classroom. In contrast, there may be students who do not have the privilege of formal prekindergarten education, whose parents' circumstances hinder home literacy practices like reading aloud, whose home environments are devoid of language play and discussion, and whose daily language does not mesh well with the language of school (Lee & Burkam, 2002; Weisleder & Fernald, 2013). Research demonstrates that such social and socioeconomic differences in the daily lives of children have significant influence on language development and readiness for reading (Hoff, 2006; Lonigan et al., 2000; Nag et al., 2019). Thus, it should be expected that there is wide variation in young children's language experience. Assessment helps us come to know the nature of each student's language, their strengths, and their needs. Assessment helps us shape early reading instruction to students' individual differences.

In this chapter, we examine assessments that focus on foundations for reading: students' emergent literacy and early reading knowledge. We also consider the assessments that are used in multi-tiered systems of support to address struggling readers' strategy and skill needs. Next, we meet Max and Raoul—teacher and student—and examine how different assessments are used to find, diagnose, and address reading challenges in early elementary classrooms.

EMERGENT LITERACY AND EARLY READING ASSESSMENT

Young children develop awareness of spoken and written language in relation to their environments and experiences. This knowledge serves as a foundation on which to further build students' reading development. A key goal for assessment is to help us determine the nature of this foundational knowledge so that our teaching efforts meet students at their current understandings and abilities. I note that the following assessment types are often incorporated into commercially produced tests that focus on reading readiness and language development, and I encourage the reader to check on the availability of such assessments.

Recognizing Letters and Sounds

An early developmental benchmark in understanding print is knowing letters and sounds (Adams, 1990; Schatschneider et al., 2004). Knowing letters and sounds is required for developing phonemic awareness and phonics, which themselves are essential for students becoming successful readers. In fact, letter-sound knowledge is a strong predictor of students' future reading achievement (Clayton et al., 2020). This knowledge figures centrally as students learn that speech streams (i.e., how spoken language "sounds" to young children) are composed of sentences, words, letters, and sounds. Assessment of students' knowledge of letters and sounds is straightforward. While many tests of early reading measure this knowledge, in classrooms we can determine students' understanding of letters and sounds based on the two following questions:

"What is the letter?"
"What sound does it make?"

The above two questions can be asked on an as-needed basis, when we are working with students and the opportunity for assessment presents itself. A more systematic approach to assessing students' knowledge of all letters, in both upper and lower case, is included in Form 2.1.

Closely related, we can modify the form in Form 2.1 and use it to assess students' knowledge of letter sounds, as in Form 2.2. This assessment affords the opportunity to record any student mismatches of letters and their sounds, which then provides an instructional focus for follow-up lessons on letter-sound matching.

Concepts about Print and Reading

Concepts about print and reading include knowing differences between letters and words, where to start reading a text, different punctuation marks, and that stories

FORM 2.1 Checklist: Naming Upper- and Lowercase Letters

Knowing lowercase letter names: Teacher asks students to point to each letter and then name the letter.

Student name: _____

a____ p____ b____ f____ g____ n____ x____ w____ m____ i____

d____ k____ l____ c____ s____ q____ j____ o____ h____ e____

r____ u____ v____ z____ y____ t____

Number correct: _____/26

Knowing uppercase letter names: Teacher asks students to point to each letter and then name the letter.

X____ R____ M____ A____ G____ F____ D____ U____ C____

V____ E____ Z____ J____ Q____ H____ I____ N____ K____

O____ S____ W____ B____ Y____ T____ P____ L____

Number correct: _____/26

From *Understanding and Using Reading Assessment, K–12, Fourth Edition*, by Peter Afflerbach. Copyright © 2025 The Guilford Press. Permission to photocopy this material, or to download and print enlarged versions (*www.guilford.com/afflerbach2-forms*), is granted to purchasers of this book for personal use or use with students; see copyright page for details.

FORM 2.2 **Checklist: Knowledge of Letter Sounds**

Teacher asks students to speak the sound of each letter. Letter sound spoken is recorded in space.

Student name: _____

a____	i____	h____
p____	d____	e____
b____	k____	r____
f____	l____	u____
g____	c____	v____
n____	s____	z____
x____	q____	y____
w____	j____	t____
m____	o____	

Number correct: ____/26

From *Understanding and Using Reading Assessment, K–12, Fourth Edition*, by Peter Afflerbach. Copyright © 2025 The Guilford Press. Permission to photocopy this material, or to download and print enlarged versions (*www.guilford.com/afflerbach2-forms*), is granted to purchasers of this book for personal use or use with students; see copyright page for details.

have beginnings and endings. Concepts about print and reading also include a child's orientation to read, knowing that we read a text from top to bottom and left to right. While this knowledge has great value for beginning reading, not all students develop it prior to formal schooling. In addition, students' knowledge about reading varies as they enter school. Thus, assessment of students' emerging knowledge of concepts of reading is essential.

The assessment of students' concepts of print and reading can be done through observing students as they work with books and texts. We can also detail our understanding of concepts of print and writing with questions and with checklists. A sample checklist on concepts about print and reading for use in the classroom is presented in Form 2.3. The items on this checklist represent a wide range of knowledge and understanding that are necessary for students to progress. Assessment of this essential knowledge helps us plan instruction to further foster reading development.

Comprehensive assessment of students' emerging understanding of reading should be a goal, as the more we know about student development, the more options we have for providing meaningful instruction. One example of comprehensive early reading assessment is the *Observation Survey of Early Literacy Achievement* (Clay, 2016), which contains six tasks that provide broad perspective on young children's developing reading behavior. The assessment tasks include letter identification, word tests, concepts about print, writing vocabulary, hearing and recording sounds in words, and text reading. Letter identification focuses on children's knowledge of letters and how letters are identified, word tests focus on children's vocabulary building, and concepts about print examines what children know about how spoken language is represented in print. Writing vocabulary focuses on children's expressive vocabularies (i.e., those words that children use in their writing), and hearing and recording sounds in words examines phonemic awareness and how children represent sounds in written and graphic form. Finally, text reading is used to record children's behaviors as they read continuous text, using running records. Text reading also helps teachers determine students' instructionally appropriate reading levels if the student is already reading connected text. Finally, text reading allows us to observe children as they coordinate different strategies and skills to comprehend text.

The wealth of information that can be gathered using the *Observation Survey of Early Literacy Achievement* (Clay, 2016) requires teacher expertise in analyzing and then using this information to develop suitable instruction. Here, teachers' ability to consistently gather and interpret assessment data contributes to the validity and reliability of the assessment. I mention this requirement because the overall program of assessment chosen by a school or district involves costs and benefits. Resources given to purchasing a wide range of tests of discrete strategies and skills cannot be used to provide professional development for teachers becoming experts

FORM 2.3 Checklist: Concepts about Print and Reading

Student name: _____

_____ Describes why we read (purpose)

Knowledge of print:
_____ Identifies letters
_____ Identifies words
_____ Identifies sentences
_____ Identifies spaces between words
_____ Identifies beginning of sentence
_____ Identifies end of sentence
_____ Identifies and distinguishes single letters and single words
_____ Identifies and distinguishes words and sentences

Knowledge of punctuation:
_____ Identifies different punctuation marks
_____ Describes purpose of each punctuation mark

Book and text orientation:
_____ Holds book appropriately
_____ Identifies front of book
_____ Identifies back of book
_____ Locates title of book
_____ Locates author of book
_____ Knows to read top to bottom
_____ Knows to read left to right

Knowledge of story parts:
_____ Identifies beginning of story
_____ Identifies middle of story
_____ Identifies end of story

From *Understanding and Using Reading Assessment, K–12, Fourth Edition,* by Peter Afflerbach. Copyright © 2025 The Guilford Press. Permission to photocopy this material, or to download and print enlarged versions (*www.guilford.com/afflerbach2-forms*), is granted to purchasers of this book for personal use or use with students; see copyright page for details.

at classroom assessment—and vice versa. A carefully planned reading program will proactively develop a list of assessment priorities and then match these with an assessment plan that maps onto these priorities.

Multi-Tiered Systems of Support

Multi-tiered systems of support (MTSS) are widely regarded as a fruitful approach to helping students develop as readers. The state of California describes MTSS as follows: "Multi-Tiered System of Support provides a basis for understanding how . . . educators can work together to ensure equitable access and opportunity for all students to achieve" (California Department of Education, n.d.). The American Institutes for Research describes MTSS thus: "A multi-tiered system of support is a proactive and preventative framework that integrates data and instruction to maximize student achievement and support students' social, emotional, and behavior needs from a strengths-based perspective" (American Institutes for Research, 2024). And the State of Massachusetts Department of Elementary and Secondary Education describes MTSS and reading in this way: "High-quality, evidence-based literacy instruction for all students is a central tenet of an effective MTSS framework." (Massachusetts State Department of Education, 2024).

Using an array of well-integrated assessments to identify and address students' specific reading skill and strategy needs is a signature of MTSS. Within MTSS for student readers, assessments of reading skill and strategy are used for different purposes, including *universal screening assessment, diagnostic assessment, progress monitoring assessment,* and *summative assessment*. The four types of assessment are typically used in the order presented in Table 2.1, which also provides brief descriptions of the purpose of assessments used in MTSS.

To the four types of assessment listed above, I add *ongoing classroom-based assessments*, although these assessments are not included in formal MTSS plans. Classroom-based assessment, conducted on a regular basis, can play a vital role in providing timely and "fresh" data related to students' ongoing development. Progress monitoring assessments serve the primary purpose of letting us know how well our instruction is working in relation to students' documented reading needs. However, progress monitoring—even when conducted frequently—may not be of sufficient detail or recent enough to inform our instruction as it takes place. Ongoing classroom-based assessments serve this special function.

ASSESSING EARLY READING IN QUESTIONING IN MAX'S KINDERGARTEN CLASSROOM

In the following scenario, I describe the five types of early reading assessments and how they work together in MTSS. I focus on Max's kindergarten class and one student—Raoul—who is receiving intensive instruction with phonemic awareness.

TABLE 2.1. **Assessments Used in Multi-Tiered Systems of Support**

Type of assessment	Purpose of assessment
Universal screening	Provide initial identification of students who are challenged and at risk of failure in reading Identify general areas of student need and strength
Diagnostic	Provide detailed information about specific areas of students' reading need
Progress monitoring	Provide regular check-in on student development in relation to indicated reading need
Summative	Indicate student progress toward reading goals for identified need(s)
Ongoing classroom-based assessment	Inform daily reading instruction

Universal Screening

Like his classmates, Raoul begins the school year with a universal screening assessment. This screening test yields a general overview of students' concepts of print and reading, as well as reading strategies and skills. Universal screening provides an initial indication that a student's reading achievement is at, above, or below grade-level expectancy. The universal screener also provides a first indication of students who are at risk for reading problems. A guiding idea here is that using assessment to identify reading challenges early in the year places teachers and schools in the best position to help students.

The universal screener is not intended to give a detailed account of a student's strengths or needs. Rather, it is a valuable first assessment of students' general reading ability. Many universal screening assessments have strong predictive validity, meaning that students who score below a certain cutoff score can be reliably classified as at risk for future reading failure. Thus, the results of the universal screening test can serve as an early warning system to identify and classify students as "at risk" or "minimally at risk," while also identifying those "not at risk." With a related high-priority designation, school resources can be given to help students meet reading challenges early on. I note that this is the same ethos that undergirds Reading Recovery (Clay, 1989), with the focus on identifying struggling students and meeting their specific needs early in their reading careers.

The results of a universal screening assessment describe areas of students' strengths and needs, and here indicate that Raoul needs to better develop phonemic awareness. Given these results, the next step is to further assess and identify the specific challenges related to Raoul and phonemic awareness and gather more information for appropriate instruction.

Diagnostic Assessment

Within MTSS, this second type of assessment is diagnostic assessment. These assessments "dig deeper" into the nature of students' reading strategies and skills. As Raoul's universal screening indicated the need for focused instruction in phonemic awareness, the diagnostic assessments provide the finer-grain detail that is necessary to identify specific (as opposed to general) needs. For example, the diagnostic assessment—focused on phonemic awareness—yields information that Raoul needs to learn and practice both phoneme blending and phoneme segmenting. Max develops phonemic awareness lessons in accordance with the detailed diagnostic results, and reading instruction is directly informed by this assessment.

Max supplements the MTSS assessment plan with regular classroom-based assessment. Working with the data from both the universal screener and diagnostic assessments, he identifies lessons in the early reading curriculum that should benefit Raoul. The complementary information from Max's classroom-based assessments is combined with data from the MTSS assessments to further specify Raoul's needs and to fine-tune instruction.

Progress Monitoring

The third type of assessment within MTSS is progress monitoring. These assessments are a logical partner, in that they focus on students' development in the area of need identified by the universal screener and then detailed by the diagnostic assessment. As such, progress monitoring assessment describes Raoul's ongoing development with blending and segmenting phonemes. The progress monitoring assessments provide "check-in" opportunities that describe both Raoul's progress and the effectiveness of Max's phonemic awareness instruction. Progress monitoring may be scheduled for once a week, every other week, monthly, or by marking period. In addition to this more formal progress monitoring, Max regularly conducts his classroom-based assessments.

Summative Assessment

The fourth type of assessment in MTSS is summative assessment. Summative assessments are typically given at the end of a unit, marking period, or school year. They provide a summary of student growth and achievement and an account of instructional effectiveness. For example, the summative assessment in Max's classroom describes Raoul's progress toward longer-term goals of developing and using phonemic awareness. The summative assessment shows that Raoul has mastered phoneme blending and segmenting and describes Raoul's attainment of benchmark outcomes in phonemic awareness. Combined, the group of assessments used

Assessing Early Reading

in MTSS represent the coordinated efforts to continually measure and support individual students' progress in areas of indicated need.

Ongoing Classroom Assessment

While not typically considered an essential component of MTSS, a fifth type of assessment—classroom assessment conducted on a regular basis by the teacher—is certainly worthy of our consideration. When Max listens to students attempting to read and sound out words, observes students working in small groups on phonemic awareness exercises, examines students' early writing and spelling, and asks language-related questions, he is in an excellent position to gather assessment information that is complementary to the MTSS data.

Max uses Elkonin boxes, or sound boxes, to gather up-to-the-moment assessment information on phonemic awareness. Elkonin boxes help students develop phonological awareness as they segment words into individual sounds, or phonemes, and place the individual sounds into separate boxes. Elkonin boxes require that students take intact words and segment them into their individual, constituent sounds. Max presents Raoul with an Elkonin box for each word under consideration. The number of boxes is matched to the number of phonemes (e.g., *cat* has three phonemes and the Elkonin box used to examine Raoul's phonemic awareness development has three spaces). Raoul must provide the individual sounds that make up the word in correct sequence. As Raoul works, Max uses his observations of Raoul to assess. Thus, Elkonin box exercises provide a concrete, visual account of word segments that is matched by students sounding out the segments—and they provide a stream of assessment data. Here, Max notes that Raoul has progressed to the point where he can segment phonically regular and irregular words, specifically *C-A-T* and *P-EE-P*.

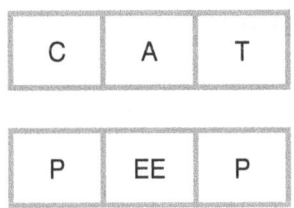

Max views ongoing classroom-based assessment as necessary for enhancing teaching and learning. These assessments are valuable because they have the potential to inform—to "fine-tune"—instruction as it takes place. For example, Max observes that while Raoul is making good progress with phoneme segmentation, he is regularly challenged when asked to blend individual sounds to make a word. This observation leads to focused instruction on blending sounds as the lesson takes place. Figure 2.1 provides details on the questions, items, and tasks that Max uses to best understand Raoul's ongoing challenges and accomplishments.

Assessment done regularly in the classroom helps fill gaps in understanding children's ongoing progress and challenges and then informs instruction. Classroom assessment provides information that may not be available from the MTSS assessments. Notice the specificity and detail regarding Raoul's phonemic

---

Sample items and tasks:

Matching
> What words start with the same sound? *ball, pin, boy, fall, bike*
> Answer: *ball, boy, bike*

Blending
> What word do these sounds make?
> Max (teacher) pronounces: /c/-/a/-/t/
> Answer: *cat*

Segmenting
> What sounds do you hear in *cat*?
> Max pronounces: *cat*
> Answer: /c/-/a/-/t/

Isolation of initial sound
> What is the first sound in *toy*?
> Max pronounces: *toy*
> Answer: /t/

Isolation of medial sound
> What is the middle sound in *cat*?
> Max pronounces: *cat*
> Answer: /a/

Isolation of final sound
> What is the last sound in *sun*?
> Max pronounces: *sun*
> Answer: /n/

Substitution
> Say "bog."
> Change the /b/ to /f/.
> What is the word?
> Answer: *fog*

Deletion of initial sound
> Say "bin" without the /b/ sound.
> Answer: *in*

Deletion of final sound
> Say "pin" without the /n/ sound.
> Answer: *pi*

FIGURE 2.1. Sample phonemic awareness assessment.

awareness that is provided "in the moment." Should Max forgo this regular classroom-based assessment practice, he would have to wait for progress monitoring assessment information to influence his instruction.

Combined, the information from the five types of assessment described above and used in MTSS helps us create detailed accounts of student readers, the challenges they face, and the growth they experience. Related, the combined assessments inform our choices for the most effective instruction. I note that in well-organized MTSS, assessments are chosen carefully and in relation to one another. Thus, the assessments provide complementary information and help the teacher "drill down" to identify and address the most salient student reading challenges. Within such a system, individual assessments are chosen so that they can be used in creating a comprehensive portrait of each student.

Our examination of Raoul's learning phonemic awareness illustrates the breadth of assessment choices available. However, a potential limitation of the assessment data gathered through MTSS is that many of the tests used focus on single components of successful reading, and not on intact acts of reading. Thus, we may gain detailed knowledge of how a student develops and uses phonemic awareness, applies phonics knowledge, increases fluency, grows vocabulary, and constructs meaning, but not have an indication of how the student orchestrates all necessary strategies and skills and knowledge to read successfully. A critical question counterpart to the detailed information provided by assessments of students' discrete reading skills and strategies is, "Can the student coordinate all the strategies and skills in real time to read successfully?" This question is addressed in Chapter 3, "Assessing Strategies and Skills: Tests and Reading Inventories."

SUMMARY

The assessment of early reading benefits students as it identifies areas of strength and need and informs effective instruction. A successful assessment program helps teachers determine what language experiences and language assets each student brings to school. Students' early reading is fostered by assessments that survey students' language experiences and emergent literacy, including letter and sound knowledge and concepts of print and reading. These assessments inform the development and selection of reading instruction best suited to meet students at their current levels of understanding. The assessment program also documents students' attainment of essential reading development benchmarks.

Effective MTSS includes a formalized approach to identifying students early in their reading careers who are at risk. Assessments used in MTSS describe students' specific strategy and skill needs and then chart and certify progress across marking periods and school years. Within MTSS, specific assessments include universal screeners, diagnostic tests, progress monitoring, and summative assessments, and each works in concert with the others to support teaching and learning. Throughout, teachers' classroom-based assessments can provide complementary and immediately useful information.

Whether our assessment takes place in MTSS or not, all successful assessment programs share specific features. These include initial assessment that provides valid and reliable information regarding the state of each student's strategies and skills. At the beginning of the school year, these assessments provide baseline information on which we can begin to plan instruction. As these initial assessments are necessarily broad, the required follow-up involves diagnostic assessments with a specific focus on student needs that are indicated by the initial assessment. We can consider the results of initial assessment and the more focused diagnostic assessment as arrows that point toward the classroom instruction that will address student needs.

As we implement our assessment-informed instruction, we want to evaluate the effectiveness of our teaching. Progress monitoring fills this need, giving valuable information on students' progress and related instruction. At the completion of units of study, marking periods, and school years, we are, of course, interested in the sum of our efforts and students' learning outcomes. Summative assessment provides this information, giving a summary statement of accomplishment. Summative assessment is necessarily tied to both curriculum and district or state learning standards. A final and essential type of assessment is that which is conducted on a regular basis in the classroom, during teaching and learning. The effectiveness of these classroom assessments is tied to teachers' professional development to conduct the assessment, analyze the results, and use them to inform instruction.

Finally, I note that this chapter focuses on the cognitive aspects of early reading development and reading achievement. Indeed, the commercially developed assessments and tests used in MTSS focus exclusively on cognitive strategy and skill development. It is important to remember that our young students are not only cognitive strategy and skill users. Our students' reading development is also influenced by the motivation and engagement that fuel effort and attention (Guthrie & Klauda, 2016), metacognition that guides students to independence (Veenman et al., 2006), and self-efficacy (Bandura, 2006) that reflects students' beliefs that they can succeed at reading. Young readers do not become better readers only because of our well-planned strategy and skill lessons. They thrive in environments that support motivation to read and engaging texts and tasks. They excel when our instruction focuses not only on cognition but on metacognition, which is the key to successful and independent reading. And, our young readers must build positive self-efficacy, just as they build their repertoires of strategy and skill. The students most in need of developing strategy and skill are also the students most in need of believing that they can succeed at reading. For detailed consideration of assessment and support for student readers in areas other than cognitive strategy and skill, see Chapter 8, "Assessing 'the Other': Important Noncognitive Aspects of Reading."

Enhancing Your Understanding

1. What are the four different types of assessment that are typically used in MTSS?

2. How do these four types of assessment work together to provide teachers with information to optimize their instruction?

3. Why are concepts of reading and concepts of print important to assess as children begin formal schooling?

4. What is the value of concentrated assessment of a particular reading skill, as demonstrated by the focus on phonemic awareness in this chapter?

Reading Assessment Snapshot
TASK ANALYSIS

How can we determine that student work within an assessment is clearly related to the specific reading skills, strategies, and attitudes that we teach and intend to measure? How can we determine that our assessment is clearly focused on the knowledge that students gain from reading? How can we be certain that what we ask students to do in a reading assessment is a legitimate request?

Conducting an assessment task analysis can provide confidence that we are getting what we ask for from our assessments. Effective assessment is aided by the process of piloting, or trying out, the assessment. Piloting an assessment allows us to determine if it actually elicits the assumed student thinking and student work. We can walk through the very assessment tasks that we demand of our students. What are we seeking? What will students actually do?

A common result of a detailed task analysis is a realization of the necessary commitment of time and resources to create and use truly worthwhile assessments. We may determine that our reading assessments involve student capabilities that are not necessarily specific to reading. If students write to demonstrate what they have understood in a textbook chapter or are called on to verbalize their understanding of a poem, we need to consider how writing and speaking figure in the assessment. In summary, task analysis is a critical part of assessment development and determining the congruence of an assessment with its purported purpose. It helps verify that we are getting what we ask for. If you are interested in task analyses related to the reading assessments that are used in your school or district, you can use the Conducting a Task Analysis to Enhance Reading Assessment reproducible form in the Appendix.

CHAPTER 3

Assessing Strategies and Skills
Tests and Reading Inventories

As students progress with their reading knowledge and development, assessment should provide regular and consistent information that helps us shape instruction and determine our students' attainment of learning outcomes. There are several approaches to such valuable assessment, and in this chapter we consider two: tests of discrete strategies and skills and reading inventories.

Research demonstrates that students must develop specific strategies and skills to be successful readers. These include phonemic awareness (Melesse & Enyew, 2020; Snowling & Hulme, 2012), phonics (Hoover & Tunmer, 2021; Sleeman et al., 2022), fluency (Datchuk & Hier, 2019; White et al., 2021), vocabulary (Cain & Oakhill, 2011; Paris, 2005), and comprehension (Kendeou et al., 2016; Kim et al., 2021). Related, there is a wide array of tests of these individual reading strategies and skills. Figure 3.1 lists tests that are commonly used to gather information related to these essential strategies and skills. Many of the assessments benefit from extensive development in relation to reading research and psychometric standards. Each comes with practical and technical manuals that explain the development and recommended uses of the specific test, as well as their psychometric properties. I also encourage you to investigate those assessments that are used in your school or district so that you may make the most of the instructionally useful information they provide. The information gained from these assessments places us in a good position to identify and address student needs and influence their reading development.

Table 3.1 focuses on the "five pillars" of reading associated with the report of the National Reading Panel (National Institute of Child Health and Human Development, 2000): phonemic awareness, phonics, fluency, vocabulary, and comprehension. The table lists representative assessments that are suitable for

- AIMSweb
- Comprehensive Test of Phonological Processing (CTOPP)
- Dynamic Indicators of Basic Early Literacy Skills (DIBELS)
- Easy CBM
- Gates–McGinitie Reading Tests
- Gray Oral Reading Test (GORT)
- Kauffman Assessment Battery for Children (KABC)
- Phonological Awareness Literacy Screening (PALS)
- Stanford Diagnostic Reading Test (SDRT)
- Test of Reading Comprehension (TORC)
- Test of Word Reading Efficiency (TOWRE)
- Woodcock–Johnson Test of Achievement

FIGURE 3.1. Commonly used tests of reading strategies and skills.

investigating student performance, along with brief descriptions of the nature and necessity of each of the five pillars. Each assessment can provide valuable information about students' accomplishments and needs in relation to the specific strategy and skill.

Figure 3.2 contains sample items and tasks related to phonemic awareness, phonics, fluency, vocabulary, and comprehension and that are representative of those found on large-scale, commercially published tests. The items and tasks may also prove useful in shaping classroom-based assessments.

The types of assessment described in the preceding section provide valuable information about student need and achievement. However, the majority of these assessments are focused on particular "parts" of reading, such as phonics or fluency. For example, fluency assessment typically measures how many words are read accurately in 1 minute and phonics assessment focuses on the student's ability to match sound and symbol. Such assessments inform our instruction and help us determine that our students have met specific learning goals. However, they do not give us a view as to how students use strategies and skills in concert, in acts of actual reading.

Our students vary in their ability to recognize words, unlock word meanings, read fluently, build and use vocabulary, comprehend texts, and monitor the construction of meaning. Moreover, students exhibit differences in how they coordinate reading strategies and skills to understand what they read. Assessment that helps us understand students' growth and the reading challenges that they face is a

TABLE 3.1. **Reading Strategies, Skills, and Related Assessments**

Reading strategy/skill	Nature and necessity of strategy/skill	Assessment options
Phonemic awareness	Phonemic awareness helps students segment spoken words into onset–rime or syllables; it helps students manipulate phonemes within a word to segment, blend, or substitute.	Assessments focus on student ability to isolate, blend, segment, add, delete, and substitute phonemes. Commercial assessments include the Comprehensive Test of Phonological Processing (CTOPP), Phonological Awareness Literacy Screening (PALS), and Test of Word Reading Efficiency (TOWRE). Classroom-based assessments focus on isolating, blending, segmenting, adding, deleting, and substituting phonemes.
Phonics/word recognition	Phonics helps students decode print to sound and match the printed form of a word with the spoken word. Word recognition helps students unlock meaning; automatic word recognition contributes to reading efficiency.	Assessment provides an opportunity to determine and analyze errors in relation to different classes of words, including decodable words, high-frequency words, single syllable words, and multisyllable words. Commercial assessments include Dynamic Indicators of Basic Early Literacy Skills (DIBELS), Easy CBM, and TOWRE Sight Word and Phonemic Decoding. Classroom-based assessments focus on demonstrating knowledge of sounds of letters and combinations of letters in isolation and within words, pronouncing nonsense words, and reading common spelling pattern words.
Fluency	Fluency reflects students' ability to coordinate different reading strategies and skills with appropriate rate, accuracy, and expression.	Assessment focuses on oral reading rate, accuracy, and expression. Commercial assessments include DIBELS. Classroom-based assessments of students' oral reading of passages yield information on rate, accuracy, and expression. Words correct per minute (WCPM) is a major focus.
Vocabulary	Vocabulary represents knowledge, and this knowledge is useful for students constructing meaning from texts. Student readers with large vocabularies are better comprehenders and perform better on reading tests.	Commercial assessments include the Peabody Picture Vocabulary Test (PPVT), Gates–McGinitie Reading Tests, Stanford Diagnostic Reading Test (SDRT), Test of Reading Comprehension (TORC), and Woodcock–Johnson Test of Achievement. Classroom-based assessments focus on student ability to define and use words, be they specific to a content area or general vocabulary, and on the means to determine vocabulary including morphological analysis, context clues, and dictionary aids.
Comprehension	Comprehension is the product of successful reading. Students coordinate reading strategies and skills and combine these with relevant prior knowledge to construct meaning. Comprehending what is read is a key for success in school and in life.	Commercial assessments include AIMSweb, the Gates–McGinitie Reading Tests, the SDRT, the TORC, and the Woodcock–Johnson Test of Achievement. Classroom-based assessments focus on student ability to construct understanding of text, including literal, inferential, and critical comprehension, as indicated by student retellings and responses to comprehension questions.

Phonemic awareness

Sample items and tasks:

Matching

> What words start with the same sound? *car, bat, fall, cat, cart*
> Answer: *car, cat, cart*

Blending

> What word do these sounds make?
> Max (teacher) pronounces: /b/-/e/-/t/
> Answer: *bet*

Segmenting

> What sounds do you hear in *bet*?
> Max pronounces: *bet*
> Answer: /b/-/e/-/t/

Phonics

Sample items and tasks:

Reading nonsense words

> Read the words on this list:
> Nonsense words (e.g., *gonk, bleck, falt, chun, zast, quimp, lat*)

Reading real words with common spelling patterns

> CVC words (e.g., *bat*)
> VCC words (e.g., *aft*)
> CVCC words (e.g., *felt*)
> CCVC words (e.g., *brig*)

Reading with prefixes

> *nonsense, disappear, redo, prevent, misplay*

Fluency

Sample items and tasks:
- Students read a connected, unpracticed text aloud for one minute.
- Students' reading is analyzed for words correct per minute (WCPM).
- An error is any word that is substituted, omitted, or mispronounced.
- Each time a student reads a word incorrectly, it is counted as an error.
- When a student self-corrects, it is not an error.
- If a word is mispronounced because of a student's dialect or speech difficulty, it is not an error.
- The total number of errors is subtracted from the total number of words read to determine WCPM.

Vocabulary

Sample items and tasks:
- Students define and use words in speaking and writing. Students demonstrate knowledge of words specific to a content area or general vocabulary.
- Students derive word meanings using morphological analysis, context clues, and dictionary aids.

(cont.)

FIGURE 3.2. Sample assessment items.

> **Comprehension**
>
> *Sample items and tasks:*
>
> Literal questions (students use information stated in the text)
> - What was the name of John's dog?
> - How did Amy get to school when the bus broke down?
>
> Inferential questions
> - Why do you think John took his dog to school?
> - Do you think Amy got to school on time?
>
> Critical/evaluative questions
> - Did the author do a good job of describing the broken-down bus?
>
> Retelling
> - Tell me about the story you just read.
>
> For more on comprehension questions, see Chapter 4; for more on retelling, see the earlier section in this chapter.

FIGURE 3.2 *(cont.)*

priority in each classroom. Reading inventories provide us with the means to assess diverse aspects of students' reading performance and growth.

A most important point regarding differences in reading inventories and tests of discrete reading strategies and skills can be made through the following extended analogy, focused on student readers and automobiles. Imagine your car sitting in the shop, getting a regular diagnostic checkup. The mechanic uses individual tests to diagnose the engine, exhaust system, braking system, steering, tires, interior and exterior lights, ventilation, and fluids. The list is long. Each of these tests is important as it can pinpoint a need or help determine that components are in operating order. Based on the results of the diagnostic, the mechanic addresses all indicated needs. The bill is settled (always too high!) and we head out from the garage.

But how does the car drive? How is the acceleration under different weather conditions? Is performance good on dry and wet roads? Can the car negotiate turns? What is the braking distance? How does the car handle when obstacles are encountered? Does it perform well in snow and ice? Does the car get us to the desired destination? Answers to these questions depend on the overall performance of the car. Likewise, there is great value in an assessment that allows us to observe our students as they coordinate and effectively use all the "parts" of reading—here the discrete skills and strategies—that are needed to read and understand text. The reading inventory is such an assessment. In addition, reading inventories allow us to ask, "How mindful is the driver?"

To illustrate the importance of determining how (and if) all the "parts" of reading (i.e., phonemic awareness, phonics, fluency, vocabulary, and comprehension) work together for our student readers to comprehend text, consider the *Reading First Impact Study Final Report* (Gamse et al., 2008). This research found "a positive and statistically significant impact on amount of instructional time spent on the five essential components of reading instruction promoted by the program (phonemic awareness, phonics, vocabulary, fluency, and comprehension) in grades one and two" (Gamse et al., 2008; p. xv). In addition, results indicated that the Reading First initiative "produced a positive and statistically significant impact on decoding among first grade students tested in one school year." However, the research also found that Reading First did not "produce a statistically significant impact on student reading comprehension test scores in grades one, two or three." (Institute for Educational Sciences, 2008).

This research reminds us that success in teaching a specific strategy—here decoding—does not guarantee that our students become better readers. It also reminds us that a wide range of assessments is necessary to investigate the detail of students' reading development, as well as their ability to comprehend text.

I characterize reading inventory assessment as a set of diagnostic materials and procedures, ranging from commercially published to teacher created. Reading inventories can vary in the depth and breadth of the information they provide, and each may share theoretical bases and practical applications. In this chapter, I focus on the commonalities of these related reading assessments and note their differences.

READING INVENTORIES

Reading inventories, in one form or another, have existed for as long as teachers have been interested in better understanding their students' reading development. Teachers who carefully analyze their students' oral reading, check their students' fluency, encourage their students to retell what they have read, and ask comprehension questions use assessment information to inventory student reading behaviors and achievement. The ongoing popularity of reading inventories is a testament to their usefulness (Paris & Carpenter, 2003; Pikulski & Shanahan, 1982; Walpole & McKenna, 2006). Contemporary reading inventories can provide information related to each of the five target areas identified by the No Child Left Behind Act (NCLB; i.e., students' phonemic awareness, phonics, fluency, vocabulary, and comprehension) as developmentally appropriate. In addition, some inventories provide information on students' prior knowledge for particular texts and students' metacognitive processes. Typical components of reading inventories include graded word lists, graded passages that can be read orally or silently by the student or read aloud to the student, retelling rubrics, and comprehension questions.

Commercially produced reading inventories include literal and inferential comprehension questions. The advent of standards that require higher-order thinking (e.g., Council of Chief State School Officers & National Governors Association [CCSSO & NGA], 2010) suggests that reading inventories should help to determine how well (or if) a student can answer questions that demand application, synthesis, and evaluation (Afflerbach et al., 2011). However, the relatively brief texts that are found in most reading inventories may not lend themselves to higher-level thinking questions, or to answering these questions in relation to state and Common Core State Standards (CCSS; CCSSO & NGA, 2010). Going forward, it is important to consider how higher-order thinking questions can be included for the particular reading inventory passages.

A key feature of most inventories is the means to identify a student's independent, instructional, and frustration reading levels. *Independent* signifies an approximate reading level on which students can read successfully on their own, *instructional* suggests a reading level on which students can read successfully with a teacher's support, and *frustration* represents reading situations in which students will not be successful, with or without teacher support. The conceptualization of these levels is often traced to the work of Betts (1946), as is the idea of gauging a student's reading level in relation to text difficulty.

Although the characterization of independent, instructional, and frustration levels has been consistent over the past 75 years, students' performances in reading inventories should be examined in relation to our continually evolving knowledge of reading. How we interpret students' oral reading and comprehension-question performance should be informed by our most recent research understanding. In the following example, a student's oral reading miscues include rereading of words and clauses, and substitutions:

> *Text:* The former president bowed in gratitude to the hosts.
> *Student reads aloud:* The farmer president. . . . The former president bowed in great. . . . The former president bowed in gratitude to the hosts.

We can develop different interpretations of this student's reading using different lenses, polished by research and teaching knowledge, to explain the student's reading behavior. The student may be considered needy, unable to give a fluent reading of the text. Words are repeated and sections reread, and there are substitution miscues, including *farmer* for *former* and *great* for *gratitude*. The reading is choppy. Alternatively, we can infer that the reader possesses important reading strategies. The student is aware of a difficulty (i.e., misreading particular words), and the rereading strategy addresses the difficulty. This rereading indicates that the student is metacognitive (Paris et al., 1983; Veenman, 2016). We infer that rereading is initiated by the student's realization that comprehension is not occurring to the degree that it must in relation to the reader's goal. We know the value of metacognition and self-corrections to students' reading, and our interpretation of reading inventory data derives from particular reading research and theory. Based on reading inventory data, we determine that the student must work toward increased accuracy and speed in reading, but underlying this performance is the student's clear focus on making meaning from the text and related metacognition.

Reading inventories build on our understanding that children are mindful processors and users of language and that the examination of their oral reading can shed light on how they use language to construct meaning (Betts, 1946). For example, miscue analysis (i.e., the examination of developing readers' oral reading, including their missteps and hesitations) emanates from a perspective that readers strive to make meaning from text. It is not expected that children will read text perfectly because few people, including expert readers, do so. Careful attention to the miscues and processes that are part of oral reading can illuminate those aspects of students' language processing that are working smoothly and those that need further development. The process-oriented nature of the reading inventory allows us to observe the interaction and coordination of different reading strategies and skills that might otherwise be assessed separately, in piecemeal fashion. For example, a rich reading inventory session can yield information about students' decoding, metacognition, and comprehension, all in relation to fluency. Remember the automobile/reading analogy? Individual tests can describe miles per gallon, acceleration, braking speed, and the like, but the true test is how the driver coordinates all of these in the real time of driving. Similarly, we can test individual aspects of reading, but reading inventories allow for observing how they are coordinated in the real time of reading.

Fundamental to this approach is a respect for what children try to accomplish in learning to read. Use of the term *oral reading miscue* precludes use of the term *oral reading mistakes*. This word choice results in an assessment perspective that is forward-looking: Examination of miscues, along with those aspects of reading done well, provides assessment information of considerable usefulness. It is anticipated that students are on a developmental path to become better readers. The talented teacher uses a student's miscues in oral reading to construct an account of what a developing reader can and cannot do. Informed by cognitive, psycholinguistic, and child development theories, assessment information from reading inventories can provide rich information about students' ongoing reading achievement.

CHARACTERISTICS OF READING INVENTORIES

Commercial reading inventories typically contain graded word lists, reading passages, and a series of comprehension questions and requests to retell that are used to gauge students' understanding of text. Reading inventories also provide us with opportunities to assess silent reading and listening comprehension. Each of these components provides useful diagnostic reading information for a particular student. A listing of typical components of reading inventories and the related information they provide is presented in Table 3.2.

In this section, we review the constituent sections and procedures of reading inventories in the order that teachers and students commonly use them. I note that the sequence is necessarily flexible to allow for accommodation of different students, their varied reading achievement levels, and our specific diagnostic assessment needs (Leslie & Caldwell, 2021).

The placement of students in the reading inventory is guided by our best estimate of their current reading ability, as each word list and reading passage is intended to represent an approximate grade-level difficulty. When in doubt, it is

TABLE 3.2. **Representative Components of Reading Inventories and the Diagnostic Information They Provide**

Reading inventory component	Provides information related to . . .
Word lists	• Sight word vocabulary • Mediated word recognition processes • Self-corrections at the word level
Reading passages • Oral reading	• Word recognition • Decoding 　Phonics • Sight word vocabulary • Fluency 　Rate of reading 　Accuracy 　Prosody • Comprehension 　Retelling 　Literal understanding 　Inferential understanding • Metacognition 　Monitoring 　Fix-up strategies
• Silent reading	• Comprehension 　Retelling 　Literal understanding 　Inferential understanding
• Listening	• Comprehension 　Retelling 　Literal understanding 　Inferential understanding

Assessing Strategies and Skills

---

1. The teacher estimates the student's reading achievement level.
2. The student is placed in the appropriate level of the graded word list(s).
3. The student reads the graded word list(s).
4. Based on the student's graded word list performance, the teacher determines the student's oral reading passage placement.
5. The student reads the passage(s) orally until his or her frustration level is reached for word recognition, fluency, comprehension, or a combination of these.
6. The teacher determines the student's silent reading passage placement.
7. The student reads the passage(s) silently until his or her frustration level is reached for comprehension.
8. The teacher determines the student's listening comprehension placement.
9. The student listens and answers questions until his or her frustration level is reached for listening comprehension.
10. The student is tested via specific subtests.*

---

*These subtests may include parts of speech, such as consonant blends and long and short vowel sounds, and may be included in the published reading inventory or added by the classroom teacher.

FIGURE 3.3. A typical sequence of administration of a commercially published reading inventory.

best practice to underestimate a student's achievement levels, therefore increasing the probability of the student experiencing initial success and a positive reading inventory experience overall. The placement of students in a zone of current ability means that the reading inventory is positioned to provide detailed information related to independent, instructional, and frustration levels of reading. An overview of the typical sequence of administration of a commercially published reading inventory is presented in Figure 3.3.

Word Lists and Reading Inventories

Students often begin a reading inventory with graded word lists. Each word list in commercially published reading inventories is composed of 10 to 30 single words that are designated at an approximate grade level and listed in order of increasing difficulty. The grade-level distinction for a particular word is based on the frequency of occurrence of the word in common instructional materials and the regularity of the word's sound–symbol correspondences. It is assumed that more frequently occurring words are easier to recognize. For example, the first five words in the primer-level word list of the Qualitative Reading Inventory–7

(Leslie & Caldwell, 2021) are *from, need, going, what,* and *special,* and the final five words of the second-grade word list are *breathe, insects, weather, noticed,* and *season.*

Word lists serve several purposes. Performance on word lists provides information about students' decoding ability, which is particularly helpful in our determination of those students who need continued attention to word recognition skills. Word list reading also provides us with information on a student's sight word vocabulary. Students read the word list until they encounter continued difficulty, suggesting that they have reached a ceiling in their performance.

McCracken (1966) proposes that approximate reading levels can be derived from students' performance on word list reading. Specifically, independent level is 90% and above for words read correctly, instructional level is 70% to 85%, and frustration level is less than 70%, or more than 3 words missed for every 10 encountered. Although the specific criteria for continuing or discontinuing students' reading of words varies across reading inventories, these percentages are useful, approximate guidelines for determining when a student encounters difficulty and should stop word list reading.

We then calculate the number of words correctly pronounced and determine the level of this baseline performance. Based on the student's performance on word list reading, we choose the appropriate difficulty level in an initial oral reading passage. Note that all subsequent decisions for placement in reading passages are made in relation to this initial word list reading performance, as each student task in a reading inventory is sequential and interdependent.

Reading Passages with Reading Inventories

Having completed the word list reading, the student begins the oral reading passages. As we listen, we attend to the student's oral reading miscues and oral reading fluency. Miscues are determined by examining the student's oral reading in relation to the printed text, with miscues representing the student's verbalizations that do not match the text. Fluency is determined by the number of words read correctly per minute. Analysis of the student's oral reading miscues may provide details about his or her specific reading strategies and skills. Miscue analysis requires that we learn to identify specific reader behaviors and then record these behaviors accurately. The typical miscue analysis rubric focuses on important reader behaviors that include omissions, repetitions, substitutions, and insertions. Figure 3.4 contains examples of these miscues and illustrates the symbol system used to signify particular miscues in a student's oral reading.

Experienced teachers create a record of a student's oral reading behavior, noting the miscues and categorizing each miscue. Many teachers find it helpful to record reading inventory sessions, as the opportunity to listen again to students'

Printed sentence read by student: The cowgirl rode into the sunset on her horse.	
Omission	• *Student reads:* The cowgirl rode into sunset on her horse. • *Miscue notation:* The cowgirl rode into ⟨the⟩ sunset on her horse.
Repetition	• *Student reads:* The cowgirl rode rode into the sunset on her horse. • *Miscue notation:* The cowgirl <u>rode</u> into the sunset on her horse.
Insertion	• *Student reads:* The cowgirl rode into the sunset on her spotted horse. • *Miscue notation:* The cowgirl rode into the sunset on her ^spotted^ horse.
Substitution	• *Student reads:* The cowgirl rode into the sunset on her house. • *Miscue notation:* The cowgirl rode into the sunset on her ^house^ horse.
Self-correction	• *Student reads:* The cowgirl rode into the sunset on his on her horse. • *Miscue notation:* The cowgirl rode into the sunset ^on his^ on her horse.
Notes	• *High meaning-change miscue:* Substitution of *house* for *horse*. • *Low meaning-change miscue:* Omission of *the*.

FIGURE 3.4. Examples of oral reading miscues and their notation.

reading allows for checking codings of miscues and gaining further insights into the student's reading ability.

Oral reading continues for as long as the student meets acceptable criteria for reading accuracy, comprehension-question responses, and reading rate. As the student scores within the parameters of instructional- or independent-level reading (95% and 98% accuracy and correctness, respectively), oral reading can continue until a ceiling is hit (i.e., the student is unable to read accurately and fluently and/or cannot answer a minimum number of comprehension questions correctly). This is the point beyond a student's zone of proximal development (Vygotsky, 1978), and the text and task demands are too difficult.

Through examination of the student reader's performance, we can use miscue analysis to create a detailed portrait of the reader. For example, we may detect students' patterns of guessing words, reading without regard to punctuation, challenges to decoding final consonant blends, and other important behaviors. Analysis of oral reading may indicate that a student is using context to self-correct and varying the rate of reading in relation to the difficulty of the text. Each observed and coded behavior provides the opportunity for us to add to our understanding of student readers.

Oral reading allows teachers to examine the processes of decoding, word identification, meaning construction, and metacognition *in situ*. The skill and strategy use that we witness and record is embedded in an act of reading. We are not examining consonant blends as they appear on a consonant blend worksheet; we observe how students blend consonants as they read text and as this important process relates to other reading strategies and skills. We are not examining answers to comprehension questions to determine only the state of passage comprehension; we also are privy to the word identification and meaning-construction processes that contribute to comprehension. Comprehension processes may be glimpsed through miscue analysis, and comprehension products are tapped by the series of literal and inferential questions and student retellings.

Reading inventories are also used to assess reading rate and fluency. Across several oral readings, fluency is observed and calculated. This information, combined with the approximate grade levels of each oral reading passage, can be used to represent students' reading fluency by grade level, or Lexile level. Thus, students' oral reading on reading inventories is a veritable storehouse of important information about reading strengths and needs. (For more on this important process and product distinction, see the Reading Assessment Snapshot, "Process and Product Assessment," that follows Chapter 4.)

Like the word lists, the reading passages in reading inventories vary in difficulty. Passages are assigned specific grade-level equivalents, such as 1.0, 3.5, or 5.0, or Lexiles. These numbers and levels represent an approximation of the passages' difficulty, based on readability formulas. Students' reading performance can be described in relation to these graded reading passages. For example, reading inventory results may document that a fourth-grade student is reading at a 4.5 independent grade level orally and a 5.0 independent grade level silently and that the student's listening comprehension is at a 6.5 independent grade level. Most reading inventories contain several passages at each grade level so that students can demonstrate their reading proficiency on oral, silent, and listening comprehension tasks without having to repeat reading a particular text.

The texts included in reading inventories, like those encountered in daily instruction, are influenced by students' prior knowledge, which may lead to an inaccurate portrayal of students' reading achievement level. Thus, reading passages represent a judgment of the reading inventory's developer that the familiarity of text content is acceptable—not too familiar to privilege particular groups of student readers and not so unfamiliar that it prevents readers from using some prior knowledge in constructing meaning. As teachers administering the reading inventory, we must check this assumption.

Retelling and Comprehension Questions

The reading process information that we collect during oral reading is thus complemented by product information: students' understanding of the reading passages, as indicated by students' comprehension-question responses and retellings. Retellings allow students to use their own words to give an account of the passage they have just read. By using retelling checklists, we can determine students' comprehension by combining relevant parts of their retellings with their comprehension-question responses. As the student retells, the teacher focuses on the content of the retelling and its relation to the existing comprehension questions. This involves knowing the gist of each of the comprehension questions and determining that the student's retelling answers particular questions.

The passages in reading inventories are followed by sets of related comprehension questions, typically between 5 and 10 in number. Questions may be designated as focusing on details or main ideas and on literal or inferential comprehension. Question-type designation as literal or inferential is intended to provide details about students' comprehension beyond whether or not they got the correct answer. For example, a student answering the minimum acceptable number of comprehension questions correctly may be demonstrating literal comprehension but not much inferential comprehension ability. This distinction is valuable for subsequent instruction. When students are encouraged to immediately follow their oral or silent reading with a retelling of the passage, we can determine their sense of the text, including their understanding of the text's content and structure. Retellings also allow students to answer the comprehension questions that accompany commercially published reading inventories spontaneously, without the prompting provided by questions.

Students answering a minimum acceptable number of comprehension questions continue with the reading inventory, while a score below the cutoff suggests that continued reading at the present or more difficult text level will not be fruitful. Should a student need to answer 7 out of 10 comprehension questions correctly to be considered for reading text at the next level, we see the importance of an accurate determination of comprehension. Because student retellings may not match the language included in the scoring guide, there may be times when it is challenging to determine if part of a student's retelling answers a particular question. In such situations, asking the question for clarification is important. We must know the parameters for acceptable student responses to the questions that are asked, how to map student retellings onto the existing comprehension questions in the reading inventory, and when a retelling or an answer to a specific question is not counted for credit.

Students' comprehension of reading passages may be influenced if look-backs—opportunities for students to review the text while answering comprehension questions—are allowed. For students, the challenge of answering 5 to 10 comprehension questions may be due, in part, to the fact that memory is taxed. Look-backs help diminish the demand on students to remember all that they have read for answering comprehension questions. Flexibility with the use of look-backs is recommended; successful readers are adept at returning to text they have read to identify and remember important information. In each case, it is important for us to determine the degree to which students' text look-backs on a reading inventory reflect regular classroom practice.

Following oral reading, retellings, and answering comprehension questions, we determine the number of correct responses. We decide if the student continues oral reading at the next level of difficulty or moves to silent reading. Teachers use several sources of information to make this decision, including the student's rate and accuracy of reading and the nature of the student's comprehension of the oral reading passages. Once a performance criterion is not met (i.e., the student exceeds the maximum number of permissible oral reading miscues, does not reach the minimum number of acceptable comprehension questions, or both), oral reading is completed, and silent reading of passages should begin.

Silent Reading and Listening Comprehension

Students often comprehend text at higher levels when reading silently, in contrast to reading orally. Silent reading, which is the normal mode for most readers, is also silent as to the work that readers do while reading. Silent reading precludes gathering information about students' word recognition, vocabulary, and comprehension processes that is provided by oral reading, so our focus is on how well students have comprehended the passages and their rate of reading. Students read silently, provide a retelling, and answer comprehension questions. Progress through the increasingly difficult silent reading passages is dependent on scoring at or above a level (typically 70%) on the comprehension questions.

A third type of comprehension, listening comprehension, can be measured using the reading inventory. With listening comprehension, the teacher reads the selection and the student listens. When the teacher finishes reading, the student is asked to retell the passage and answer specific comprehension questions. The student's listening comprehension achievement level is often a future marker of instructional and then independent reading comprehension levels. The teacher, as the reader, deals with decoding and word identification, fluency, and reading rate, leaving the student with the task of listening, processing spoken language, and constructing meaning.

Reading inventories provide diagnostic information from word lists and in relation to silent and oral reading and listening comprehension. Given the value of this information, it follows that adopting a single reading inventory and learning the texts, questions, and nuances of that particular inventory makes good assessment sense. As we become familiar with the inventory, we are in a good position to critically evaluate and use the information that the reading inventory provides. Sample questions that teachers can ask of reading inventories are presented in

Assessing Strategies and Skills 65

Figure 3.5. If you are interested in evaluating the contents of a reading inventory, you can use the Critical Questions to Ask of Reading Inventory Information reproducible form in the Appendix.

TEACHERS' READING INVENTORIES

As with commercially published reading inventories, students' oral reading can be analyzed via teachers' reading inventories. We can focus on students' oral reading fluency, decoding, sight word vocabulary, frequency and nature of oral reading miscues, vocabulary knowledge, metacognition, self-correction strategies, and reading comprehension strategies. Done well, teachers' inventories are flexible and adaptable; they may be conducted during the course of a student's normal reading routine. Student reading achievement is examined in relation to authentic school texts. For example, we may work with a student during an elective reading period

- Do the word lists and their grade-level designations reflect the approximate achievement levels of my students?
- Are the graded word lists and graded reading passages well coordinated?
- Do the graded word lists help in the accurate placement of students in their first oral reading passage?
- Are there opportunities to examine students' oral reading fluency?
- How do the estimates of students' reading ability that are provided by a reading inventory compare with other reading assessment information and students' regular text comprehension performance in class?
- Are there comprehension questions that do not appear to tap into important aspects of the text (i.e., questions focused on information that is not central to understanding the text)?
- Are there comprehension questions that are vaguely worded and unclear for students?
- Do the text passages contain content that is more familiar to some of my students?
- Are there comprehension questions that are answered correctly by students when other indicators suggest that students have not comprehended well?
- Are there comprehension questions that can be answered because students have much prior knowledge for the text content and not because they understand the text?
- Do the texts and accompanying comprehension questions afford the opportunity to check students' critical and evaluative comprehension?

FIGURE 3.5. Critical questions to ask of reading inventory information.

or while the class is involved in silent reading. Teachers' reading inventories can focus on the text that a student is reading as part of the school curriculum or on a self-selected text. They can include oral and silent reading, along with listening comprehension, and provide valuable information from miscue analysis and the analysis of comprehension ability. Part of the appeal of teacher-initiated reading inventories is that they focus on reading that takes place in the routine of the classroom. Thus, conducting the reading inventory does not disrupt classroom reading.

USING READING INVENTORY ASSESSMENT INFORMATION

As anticipated by Pellegrino et al. (2001), detailed assessment information allows for detailed inferences about students' reading needs and strengths. When reading inventory data are analyzed, teachers can interpret students' work on individual portions of the inventory and on their overall work. Patterns of accomplishment and need can be identified. The results of reading inventories and the inferences we make from these results can be combined with our ongoing account of how and how well each of our students reads. Accomplished reading teachers are continually updating their ideas about students' strengths and needs, and reading inventory results offer an opportunity to add rich and detailed information to a teacher's conceptions of individual students.

I believe it is helpful to consider students' independent, instructional, and frustration reading levels in relation to Vygotsky's (1978) theories of learning and the zone of proximal development. The zone of proximal development is the area in which we can expect student growth, aided by our focused instruction and support. Figure 3.6 depicts the reading levels juxtaposed with a student reader's zone of proximal development. The reading levels help us create boundaries within which we can expect a student reader's independence and success, growth with assistance, and difficulty. This helps us better understand students' reading achievement from a teaching perspective.

The frustration level represents reading and reading-related tasks that are so far beyond the student's current level of competency that there is little chance (save luck) that his or her reading will be successful. This is a level with which students should have only brief experiences: Prolonged work at the student's frustration level may provide little diagnostic information but much grief. Instructional-level reading occurs within the zone of proximal development; it is here that the accomplished reading teacher helps the student build on current reading competencies for new learning and continued reading development. For example, a student reading successfully at an instructional level may receive our occasional help related to vocabulary, word pronunciation, and comprehension. Independent reading

Assessing Strategies and Skills

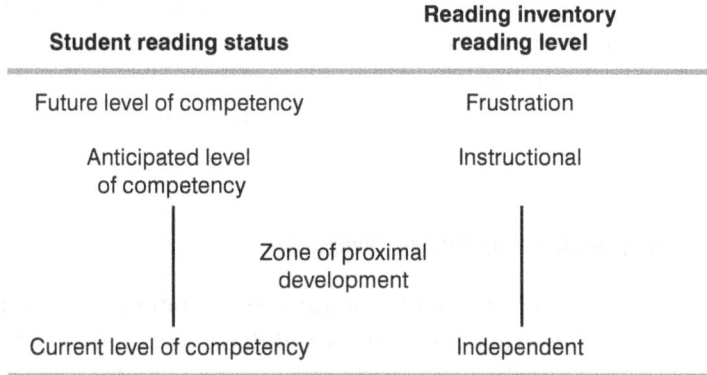

FIGURE 3.6. Independent, instructional, and frustration levels of reading juxtaposed with the reader's zone of proximal development.

signifies student success without a teacher's help because the student is reading at a current level of competency. At this level, the reader is fully capable of constructing meaning and answering questions about the text. Reading inventories help us identify the general range in which students can experience both success and learning, informing our understanding of their zones of proximal development related to reading and providing us with diagnostic details to foster students' reading growth.

READING INVENTORIES IN TASHA'S SECOND-GRADE CLASSROOM

Across the hall from Max's kindergarten classroom, Tasha teaches a diverse group of second-grade students. They vary in their reading experiences and reading achievement levels. Tasha uses a reading inventory to gather detailed information about each of her students at the beginning of the school year. This complex and demanding undertaking is supported by Tasha's building principal and by the school district. Information gathered in MTSS provides a foundation for instruction, and data from reading inventories build on this foundation. All understand the value of the formative assessment information that reading inventories yield. Tasha and her colleagues use a commercially published reading inventory, the Qualitative Reading Inventory–7 (Leslie & Caldwell, 2021), and the teachers' accomplished use of the inventory is supported by professional development that focuses on the procedures involved with administering, scoring, and interpreting the inventory and using the information it yields.

The inventory is a primary source of ongoing information that helps Tasha better understand her students' reading development. Through this understanding, she is in a strong position to provide effective instruction and identify texts and reading situations that are developmentally appropriate for her students. Across the year, Tasha can depend on the reading inventory to provide detailed information on an important range of student reading strategies and skills as they are used to construct meaning.

Consequences and Usefulness of Reading Inventories

Tasha begins constructing her understanding of incoming second graders by reviewing results from universal screenings and diagnostic assessments. Progress-monitoring data from previous years add to this understanding, as well as reading the narratives written by the first-grade teachers at the end of the previous school year. These narratives contain summary information about students' reading strengths, weaknesses, interests, and attitudes. However, Tasha's experience tells her that the summer between first and second grades varies in influence on students' reading. The summer may reflect a student's ongoing growth in reading, indicate that a student is in a holding pattern (i.e., starting second grade with approximately the same strategies and skills as ending first grade), or indicate that a student is regressing to a level below that attained at the end of first grade. Students' independent reading levels, habits, and opportunities to read all influence what a beginning second grader brings to school. Tasha needs to know the current state of her students' reading strategies and skills. She needs a means of considering these strategies and skills on a developmental trajectory for each student. The reading inventory and its designation of student reading levels allows her to do so.

Tasha values the narrative reports provided by her teaching colleagues because they offer a starting point for understanding her new students. Her fellow teachers' insights help Tasha form hypotheses about her students' reading development. Throughout the school year, she strives to collect information through observation and questioning that helps her investigate and refine her hypotheses. She values reading inventories because they provide immediately useful data. The assessment information from reading inventories is a detailed complement to information gathered with other reading assessments. The information provided by the reading inventory allows Tasha to triangulate data—what she has learned about her students through her initial observations, conversations with her students, and narrative reports from the previous year's teacher. With information about her students' reading abilities from different assessment sources, Tasha builds both inferences and confidence in her inferences.

Sam, like his fellow students, begins the school year with a folder that includes teachers' notes from prior years, observations, and an overview of last year's reading instruction, in addition to summative reading assessment information. Prior

Assessing Strategies and Skills

to second grade, Sam demonstrated a commitment to reading. He is "enthusiastic and eager to please," according to his first-grade teacher's year-end notes. He has a sight word vocabulary that is about average for the end of first grade, and he exhibits comprehension that is on grade level. Tasha begins to develop a portrait of Sam as a reader. She uses the reading inventory information to create initial hypotheses about his strengths and needs and to consider suitable reading instruction. Based on Sam's reading of several short passages, Tasha notes that he does not always attend to the ends of words, which contributes to patterns of miscue when he reads. She also notes that he is developing self-correction strategies.

Tasha considers the initial reading inventory information and then compares this with the collected assessment information from previous years. She checks her on-the-fly application of the shorthand for miscues against the tape recording of Sam's oral reading. Her goal is to seek and identify patterns in his reading behavior. The reading inventory reveals that he does well at recognizing short, common words and the beginnings of longer words but that he does not consistently attend to the endings of the words in text. A result is that he substitutes words for those printed in the text, such as *home* for *house* and *fear* for *feat*. A related pattern is that Sam's substitutions are guesses aided by the semantics of the passage. That is, he substitutes words after meaning, which indicates that he is reading with an overall goal of constructing meaning. Rarely does he substitute or insert nonsense words. Tasha believes that the reading inventory provides converging evidence that Sam is consistently focused on self-correction.

Tasha is adept at using the information gained from the reading inventory to plan instruction for Sam and his classmates, double-checking with beginning-of-year diagnostic assessment information. Within the reading program, she builds in exercises in which he is encouraged to attend to the ends of words, processing the visual information to determine words instead of guessing, as he did before. Tasha also helps Sam maintain his healthy focus on reading as meaning-making by encouraging him to ask himself, "Does that make sense?" at the end of sentences and paragraphs.

Across the school year, Tasha blends commercial reading inventory materials and procedures with running records to establish a consistent opportunity to gather information about Sam's reading. This information is fresh—analyzed and used within days, if not minutes or hours, of being collected. She uses assessment results to inform the teachable moment, focusing her instruction on Sam's zones of proximal development. With precious and limited time, it is imperative that she and her colleagues choose their reading assessments wisely. Tasha is convinced that her time and effort with reading inventories are well spent. They provide detailed information about the strategies and skills, and processes and products, of Sam's reading.

Roles and Responsibilities Related to Reading Inventories

The effective use of reading inventories requires teacher expertise with classroom-based assessment. Tasha's path to becoming a reliable user of reading inventories is arduous, but she is convinced that no other reading assessment can so closely inform her instruction. The carefully crafted, administered, and interpreted reading inventory provides her with valuable accounting of how reading develops in relation to the cognitive strategies and skills and the metacognitive routines of reading. Gathering and using reading assessment information with reading inventories is particularly demanding of Tasha's teaching expertise. Reading inventories work well when we are familiar with their contents and structure and when we are expert at giving and interpreting reading inventories. The reading inventory is an assessment with much potential, and Tasha puts much effort into developing her ability to conduct and use the reading inventory in a consistent and accurate manner. Thus, a prime responsibility is the provision of professional development that helps teachers become familiar with reading inventory materials and processes and then master the components and sequences.

Because successful reading inventories hinge on close interaction between the student and the teacher, it is imperative that we attend to the nature of this interaction. If our typical oral reading interactions with students include providing occasional words that pose problems for the students, we must be aware of how doing so during a reading inventory changes the information we get. For example, a student's inability to recognize and say a key vocabulary word as it appears in text might, in another scenario, pose a major block to comprehension. Tasha understands that if she provides the word, following adequate wait time on her part and thinking time on the student's part, she has changed the very reading process that she seeks to assess. This is an example of how the authenticity of the assessment can influence the validity and reliability of the assessment.

Her regular use of the Qualitative Reading Inventory–7 (Leslie & Caldwell, 2021) increases Tasha's familiarity and facility with the inventory's materials and procedures. Over the years, the inventory is increasingly helpful and powerful because Tasha becomes fluent in how she understands and uses it. She has learned and practiced the components and procedures, including using the shorthand for designating particular miscues; understanding the sequence of graded word list reading, oral reading, silent reading, and then listening comprehension; and using guidelines for determining independent-, instructional-, and frustration-level reading for each student. Tasha and her colleagues are fluent in combining the information gotten from reading inventories with assessment data from MTSS to create effective instruction.

Tasha also pays close attention to her students' speech and pronunciation. The interpretation of oral reading depends on a clear understanding of what, exactly, students are saying. Given the language diversity in her classroom, the array of students' accents, dialects, and manners of speaking, Tasha has the responsibility to accurately determine what students are saying. As noted earlier, the use of a tape recorder helps Tasha revisit her students' spoken words and better understand them.

Throughout each administration of the reading inventory with every student, Tasha uses the opportunity to examine her use of wait time and her attitude toward the different students in her class. She is especially sensitive to those students for whom reading is a regular struggle. Her hoped-for balance is to provide enough wait time to allow all students the opportunity to use their existing skills, strategies, and knowledge while she is there with helpful information and support when needed. Wait time is related not only to student reading but also to Tasha's stance toward her students.

Tasha believes that the questions that follow each passage provide good coverage. The questions focus on main ideas and details and require students to demonstrate literal and inferential comprehension. Having used the inventory for three years, she believes that it should be supplemented with her own questions that focus on author purposes, students' critical evaluation of the text, and how students use what they learn from reading. Tasha creates questions that help her understand student comprehension and that can influence her instructional decisions. The reading inventory passages contained in the QRI are relatively short and not exceedingly complex, so Tasha develops additional questions and tasks linked to the passages that allow her to further examine students' growth and needs.

Reading inventories are comprehensive assessment instruments that demand attention and effort on the part of the student. The time on task required during a comprehensive reading inventory means that teachers must be alert to student fatigue. The reading inventory experience may be novel to the student—in form and length of texts, in reading word lists, in the demand for consistent, on-task behavior with little downtime between assessment segments. As teachers develop familiarity with the reading inventory materials and procedures, this knowledge is useful in making decisions about continuing a particular segment of the inventory, moving on to another part, or taking a well-advised break. For example, if a student completes three oral reading passages with few miscues and excellent comprehension, moving to silent reading rather than continuing until a too-difficult oral reading text is encountered makes sense.

Administrators can assume responsibility for making sure that teachers are supported in their work to develop working expertise with reading inventories. This expertise comes from practice and support as teachers learn to administer inventories, code the resulting reading data, and use the detailed information that reading inventories provide. Professional development that focuses on how, when, and why to use reading inventories is important.

Reliability of Reading Inventories

The reliability of reading inventories depends on our expertise in collecting, coding, and interpreting the results of the inventory. Talented teachers know how to make accurate initial placements of students, the appropriate challenge levels for student readers, the shorthand that allows for accurate records of reading behavior, and the means to analyze and diagnose students' reading. Without this working knowledge, the reliability of the reading inventory is reduced, and the inferences drawn from the reading inventory information may be inaccurate.

Tasha's experience with the inventory helps her understand its strengths, weaknesses, and idiosyncrasies. When she was first learning to use reading inventories in a reading diagnosis course, Tasha was encouraged to tape-record her students' reading so that she might have a backup to her initial record of student reading behaviors. The tape recordings allowed for a return to each oral reading and word list performance so that Tasha could scrutinize her original notations of students' oral reading miscues, retellings, and answers to comprehension questions. Tasha has reduced her reliance on referencing the tape-recorded reading of her students over three years. Yet, she continues to make recordings because she believes that it enhances the reliability and consistency of her interpretation of her students' reading behavior. In turn, this strengthens the confidence she has in her inferences made from the assessment. The tapes give permanence to students' performances, and having them allows Tasha to examine in fine-grained detail some student reading performances that were difficult to interpret in real time or were misinterpreted in the first place.

Tasha develops her ability to listen, observe, and record student reading behaviors. She also builds knowledge of the tasks, reading passages, and comprehension questions that accompany each reading inventory selection. As the commercial reading inventory is developed, piloting helps focus attention on the difficulty of the passage, the accompanying questions, and the prior knowledge that a student needs to answer questions correctly, independent of reading the passage. Tasha views her work with the reading inventory as her personal piloting project, as she finds questions that are unusually easy or difficult for her students to answer. She also is comfortable making inferences about what students comprehend, based on their retellings of the passages they read. In each of these instances, Tasha adds to the reliability of the reading inventory by bringing her professional knowledge into the process of conducting and interpreting the inventory.

Published reading inventories consist of preselected reading passages and comprehension questions. Recall that the reading passages are selected using a method that seeks to mediate the amount of prior knowledge that students may have for particular passages. In general, commercially published reading inventories aim for a middle ground of texts with content that will be somewhat, but not overly, familiar for most students. This aspect of the inventory can introduce measurement errors related to readers' prior knowledge for the reading passages and the degree to which comprehension questions can be answered with or without reading the text. For example, consider the student who is asked to read a passage that discusses farm life. The 10 comprehension questions that follow focus on literal and inferential comprehension of the text. Given what we know about the constructive nature of comprehension, will all students in Tasha's class have equivalent prior knowledge to construct the meaning that is anticipated by the questions? Will students who live on farms and are familiar with farming have an advantage in answering the questions?

Validity of Reading Inventories

The goal of reading is the construction of meaning, and an assessment that allows us to better understand the processes by which student readers construct meaning is valuable. How does the reading inventory help us understand students' development in relation to the construct of reading? Reading inventories can provide valuable information about each of the five target areas identified by NCLB: phonemic awareness, phonics, fluency, vocabulary, and comprehension. The inventories can do so in a developmentally appropriate manner. When we read, we use reading strategies and skills in a coordinated effort to construct meaning (Afflerbach et al., 2008). Skill and strategy work in concert, not in isolation. The reading passages and routines in reading inventories are designed to help us observe such: We build understanding of readers' strengths and needs in reading as the students are actually reading. The reading inventory focuses on both reading processes and reading products and thus gains high marks for construct validity.

Commercial reading inventories vary in their ecological validity. The graded reading passages may or may not reflect the type of reading that students do in the classroom. This is especially so with the advent of challenging reading standards and related text complexity. The reading passages contained in most reading inventories are relatively short. Similarly, the retelling and comprehension-question segments of commercial reading inventories may or may not reflect the daily routine and work of the classroom. Commercial reading inventories permit the observation and assessment of reading in a holistic sense. We can gather information about decoding and word recognition, fluency, vocabulary, and comprehension within the same assessment session, and we may be able to better understand how each is contributing to the construction of meaning of text. Or, we may develop an understanding of the areas that are preventing students from constructing meaning.

The materials and procedures used in teacher-developed reading inventories and running records may contribute to high ecological validity. Running records, conducted as students read text that they would be reading anyway, reduce the distance between assessment materials and the classroom routine. Also, reading inventories conducted as students read and use texts as part of their normal school day minimize the differences between reading done for assessment and all other reading that students do. Running records and reading inventories are often strong examples of authentic assessment: reading assessment with texts that are typical in the classroom, and assessment procedures that are minimally invasive.

SUMMARY

A goal of early reading instruction is helping students practice and learn strategies and skills so that they can construct meaning from text. The assessments described here provide detailed descriptions both of readers' strategies and skills and of how these act in concert to help readers make meaning from text. Universal screening and subsequent diagnostic assessment identify and detail students' areas of need, and progress monitoring provides regular check-ins on students' learning. Summary assessments describe students' attainment of unit, marking period, and academic year goals. Meanwhile, classroom-based assessments—especially reading inventories—provide details about student reading in relation to specific reading grade levels and independent, instructional, and frustration reading levels. Furthermore, the inventories help us focus on the processes and products of student reading: the meaning that is constructed and the tools that students use to construct this meaning. Together, the different components of the assessment system give good guidance to teachers and results in students' reading development and achievement. The alignment and integration of assessments is demanding of teachers but yields valuable return on their efforts.

Enhancing Your Understanding

1. Explain the strengths and limitations of diagnostic assessments of discrete skills and strategies.

2. How can you complement the information from a test of discrete skills with information you gather in the classroom?

3. Practice making initial placements for students in word lists, oral reading, silent reading, and listening comprehension passages in a reading inventory, based on your students' assessment information.

4. For a classroom-based reading inventory, choose reading selections that can accommodate the range of student reading achievement in your class. Next, develop appropriate comprehension questions that you can ask students following their reading.

Reading Assessment Snapshot
TECHNOLOGY AND READING ASSESSMENT

Advances in technology influence how we assess. We know that effective classroom-based assessment includes the ongoing collection of information. Talented teachers gather data on each of their students and then use them to make teaching decisions. In general, having copious student assessment information is helpful—until it isn't!

Classroom assessment involves collecting, integrating, synthesizing, and accessing assessment information. While these tasks can be daunting, technology offers a means to efficiently process assessment information. When teachers circulate around the classroom with a handheld device that contains up-to-the-minute profiles of each student's reading needs and strengths, this information can contribute to enhanced teaching and learning. The assessment information is immediately available anywhere in the school or classroom. When the handheld makes it easier to input, store, and combine reading assessment information, technology is making a tangible contribution to our education efforts. Such approaches to classroom assessment help teachers conduct progress monitoring and triangulate related assessment information from different sources. So, too, do software programs that help educators synthesize assessment results.

The timely collection of data is paramount in successful assessment. Technology can reduce the time needed to input, retrieve, analyze, and synthesize the assessment information of our student readers. Likewise, digital portfolios allow students to create copies of reading-related work that otherwise would be challenging to store and display. Digitized copies of students' writing, quizzes and worksheets, video-recorded performances, artwork, and multimedia projects serve as rich assessment sources and indicators of students' learning. Software that yields voice and handwriting recognition and text analysis is poised as an assessment-changing technology. Student development in phonemic awareness, phonics, and fluency can be accurately gauged. Student written and spoken responses to assessment prompts can be quickly scored and reported. In sum, technology can and should be a game-changer for reading assessment.

CHAPTER 4

Teacher Questioning as Assessment

Questions are deeply ingrained in the routines of the school day, and they serve a variety of functions. Questions help us understand what students learn from traditional or internet reading, how they critically appraise texts, and how they use what they learn from reading. Our questions can yield an understanding of students' comprehension of text, metacognitive development, reading progress, and where we may help that progress. Questions help us model good assessment practices for our students. In each and every case, we must be sure that we are asking the right questions and making full use of the student responses that our questions elicit.

A BRIEF HISTORY OF QUESTIONING

Throughout history, questioning has been associated with teaching and learning. Socrates developed a method of rigorous questioning in the fourth century B.C.E. that used questions (1) as a guide to inquiry and thinking and (2) to determine what the person answering them knows. A teacher poses questions that encourage students to think and that provide the opportunity to assess students' learning from text. For example, after a fifth-grade class reads a textbook chapter on immigration, the teacher uses Socratic questioning to help students focus on their family histories of immigration and then how the reasons for immigrating as described in the chapter apply to these histories. The Socratic method also serves as a challenge: As teachers, we should pose questions that assess different types of learning, provoke thought, and are worthy of response.

How we think about reading, the purposes of reading instruction, and the development of the students we teach influence the questions we ask. A century ago, behaviorists posited that readers read with the text acting as the stimulus, and that readers' verbatim recall of the text indicated full comprehension (Watson, 1913). Such a view suggests that "giving back" what is stated in text when responding to questions indicates an accomplished reader. Literal comprehension questions suitably serve this conceptualization of reading. However, our evolving understanding of the mind and reading (Huey, 1908; Snow, 2002; Thorndike, 1917) necessitates an evolution in the types of questions we ask of student readers. Cognitive psychology has demonstrated that readers use prior knowledge, combined with strategies and skills, to construct meaning (Pressley & Afflerbach, 1995). We also know that students' construction of meaning can involve higher-order thinking. We should ask questions that honor these understandings. Moreover, our increasing understanding of the socially situated nature of cognition (Lave & Wenger, 1991) and the increasing demands on students to develop complex literacy abilities for success in life should influence our theory and practice of asking questions (Afflerbach et al., 2011).

Assessment questions are frequently used to evaluate and describe student knowledge. Stevens (1912) observed questioning in classrooms and found that roughly two-thirds of the questions focused on recitation and memory of facts. In this case, and in line with Watson's (1913) ideas of what reading "is," students are expected to memorize text information and then use it to answer low-level comprehension questions. Durkin (1978) examined fourth-grade classrooms and interviewed teachers about their reading comprehension instruction. She found that many teachers equated reading comprehension instruction with asking questions about text, as if posing a question somehow taught students how to answer it. In fact, Durkin's study signified the need for rethinking how reading is taught and making clearer the relationships between reading, teaching, and answering questions. Durkin also concluded that because questions are not an adequate means for teaching, there is a need for the explicit instruction of reading strategies.

Questioning is prominent in present-day classrooms but often occurs in the initiate–respond–evaluate (IRE) discourse form. With the IRE, teachers initiate classroom talk by asking questions, students respond to the questions, and then the teacher evaluates students' responses (Cazden, 1986; Mehan, 1979). Following is an example of the IRE form:

Initiate (Teacher): What is a compass rose?
Respond (Student): It's the part of a map that shows directions.
Evaluate (Teacher): Yes, that's correct.

IRE discourse often focuses on known-answer questions, in which part of the students' task is to figure out what response the teacher is seeking. In reading lessons, IRE questions often focus on literal and simple inferential comprehension of text. It is not that such comprehension is not important—it is critical. Yet, failure to move beyond basic comprehension questions is a missed opportunity to both promote and evaluate students' higher-order thinking. Moving beyond known-answer questions helps us teach students the importance of questioning texts and authors and prompts complex thinking.

CATEGORIZING AND CLASSIFYING QUESTIONS

Good question asking is informed by theories of learning. These theories help us conceptualize how our questions may tap particular types of knowledge that students gain from reading. For example, Bloom's (1956) taxonomy of learning and more recent revisions (Krathwohl, 2002), as well as depth of knowledge (Francis, 2021; Webb, 2002), support the proposal that learning can range from a relatively simple understanding to a complex evaluative understanding. This learning can be assessed with a literal comprehension question and questions that focus on students' critical appraisal of what is learned, respectively (McNamara et al., 2016). If we believe that our reading instruction should help students learn to critically question the authors of the texts they read and apply what is learned from reading, these theories offer a means to categorize our reading assessment questions in relation to these instructional goals. From relatively simple to increasingly complex, the above taxonomies chart possible outcomes of students' reading and associated learning. Thus, the taxonomies can help guide our efforts to develop an array of questions. Table 4.1 focuses on the different types of learning in Bloom's taxonomy and suggests the focus of our questions that can help us understand the nature of students' learning in relation to each level of the taxonomy.

TABLE 4.1. Different Types of Questions Related to Different Categories in Bloom's (1956) Taxonomy of Thinking

Category of Bloom's taxonomy	Questions can focus on . . .
Knowledge	Recognizing, remembering
Comprehension	Understanding
Application	Using, applying
Analysis	Determining attributes, comparing and contrasting
Synthesis	Making hypotheses, planning, speculating
Evaluation	Rating, judging

THE INFLUENCE OF TESTING ON CLASSROOM QUESTION ASKING

High-stakes tests (Afflerbach, 2002b) are a major influence on questioning practices in classrooms. Unfortunately, the cost of scoring students' responses to questions often dictates the type of questions that are asked. Compared with students' constructed responses to questions, machine-scored student responses to multiple-choice questions (e.g., when students must choose from answers A-B-C-D) are cheaper and more easily scored. Furthermore, these tests restrict opportunities for students to answer extended constructed-response items and divergent-thinking items. Such items are useful when we are interested in students' understanding of text and when we acknowledge that there may be more than one correct answer to the question.

From a high-stakes testing perspective, there are promising developments from the Partnership for Assessment of Readiness for College and Careers (PARCC; 2010) and the Smarter Balanced Assessment Consortium (SBAC; 2010), which developed assessments that align with the CCSS. As the CCSS focus on increasingly complex thinking and achievement goals, related assessments must follow suit. Assessment questions and related tasks that are capable of prompting and describing higher-level student performance are required. Examples of items from PARCC and SBAC are examined here.

Consider the following sample test item from SBAC (2014) in which fourth-grade students read three sources (complete articles) related to animals. After reading the texts, students are asked a series of questions. I use two of the questions to illustrate the complexity of the required response and the demand for higher-order thinking that is built into the assessment. The first prompt is as follows:

> Source #1 discusses what some animals do to survive in their environment. Explain how the information in Source #2 adds to the reader's understanding of what some animals do to survive in their environment. Give **two** details from Source #2 to support your explanation.

This is the related question and prompt:

> *Which source would **most likely** be the most helpful in understanding how plants and animals work and live together to allow the place where they live to continue to grow?* Explain why this source is **most likely** the most helpful. Use two details from the source to support your explanation.

I note that the second question and prompt (above, italicized) are an example of how directions to a student may present a reading comprehension challenge in and of themselves. Consider students who understand both texts. These same students may have trouble understanding this complex prompt, and their responses may reflect the confusing nature of the prompt, rather than their actual comprehension of the two texts. Later in this chapter we will examine how the wording of our questions can add to our students' comprehension tasks.

The PARCC (2017) has fourth graders read a short story and a poem, both on a related topic. The related PARCC prompt for students is as follows:

> Identify a theme in "Just Like Home" and a theme in "Life Doesn't Frighten Me." Write an essay that explains how the theme of the story is shown through the characters and how the theme of the poem is shown through the speaker. Include specific details from the story and the poem to support your essay.

The preceding examples of test items from SBAC and PARCC demonstrate that inroads are being made with the types of items (and related, necessary student thinking) that tests are now using. Test questions are changing, and moving to a place where they better represent and prompt the different types of thinking students may do when reading. These advances are promising, but it is important to note that when it comes to asking questions, we are creatures of habit. Assessment practice may be more a reflection of tradition than of principled decision making. Teachers not only ask questions but are also surrounded by questions. We receive a steady diet of questions: those that follow reading selections and those on quizzes, unit tests, and year-end examinations. This diet is often restricted, lacking examples of alternatives to traditional test-like questions. Unfortunately, as tests monopolize assessment, classroom practices that help prepare students to take and succeed on high-stakes tests focus on question types that appear on tests. Why would we ask middle school students to develop a theory of why poverty persists in East Africa when the high-stakes test question requires choosing, from alternatives, the capital of Somalia? Teaching to the test may be teaching to an impoverished notion of what questions can tell us. Perhaps the new generation of assessments can improve this situation, where teaching to the test is better associated with high-quality questions.

CATEGORIES OF QUESTIONS

More than four decades ago, Pearson and Johnson (1978) characterized questions as textually explicit, textually implicit, and scriptally implicit. Each of the characterizations is important for us to understand because they describe the types of reading, thinking, and answering that students must do to be successful. Consider the following paragraph:

> Rowan smiled with satisfaction as her horse vaulted her over the last jump. She knew that the prize would be hers. After crossing the finish line, she did a celebratory gallop past the spectators. The judges awarded her the trophy for First Place, Steeplechase. The trophy was silver with a young rider and horse jumping over a fence. As Rowan got into the car with her parents, she thought of the shelf in her room where she would proudly display her award.

Textually explicit questions require students to locate answers that have exact wording in the texts they read; the answers are right there in the text. For example, the question "What trophy did Rowan win?" can be answered, "First Place, Steeplechase." Textually implicit questions require students to gather information from at least two different parts of the text to successfully answer the question. Here, a representative question is, "Why did Rowan gallop past the spectators?" and an acceptable answer is, "She was celebrating winning the trophy." Scriptally implicit questions require students to integrate information from the text with information in their prior knowledge to successfully answer questions. A representative question is, "Do you think Rowan's parents are proud of her, and why?"

The distinctions of the three question types help us determine the ongoing development of students' reading, thinking, and understanding. This ranges from giving back verbatim information from text to manipulating knowledge contained in different parts of the text to combining text information with relevant prior knowledge. The question types may also provide information about the prior knowledge a student possesses for a particular text. The preceding examples also help illustrate how a student with little prior knowledge for the text content may be at a disadvantage in answering the questions.

The work of Bloom (1956), Webb (2002), Pearson and Johnson (1978), and others offers us frameworks for thinking about our questions. The frameworks help us understand what exactly we are asking students to do with our questions. The frameworks encourage us to consider what kinds of questions we ask and the frequency with which we ask them. Reading questions most often focus on the content of what is read, but the different frameworks remind us that questions can evoke verbatim responses, generalizations from text, reading between the lines (as when we try to determine a text's purpose or intent), evaluations of the content and form of the texts we read, and critical appraisal of an author. Each type of question plays a valuable role in helping us understand the important ways in which student readers develop.

INSTRUCTIONAL PERSPECTIVES ON QUESTIONING

Over the past four decades, we have seen approaches to questioning that serve the double duty of helping teachers gather assessment information about their students while helping students learn to ask important questions themselves. These programs and models include the KWL strategy (Ogle, 1986), question–answer relationships (QARs; Raphael & Wonnacott, 1985), and questioning the author (Beck et al., 1997). Ogle (1986), working with theories of cognition and metacognition, developed the KWL strategy, which requires students to ask themselves the following questions:

- What do I *know* about the topic of the text?
- What do I *want* to learn from the text?
- What did I *learn* from the text?

For example, fourth-grade students reading the first book in a unit on dinosaurs might have responses like these:

What do I *know* about the topic of the text?

- Some dinosaurs ate plants, and some dinosaurs ate other dinosaurs.
- Dinosaurs are extinct.
- Dinosaurs are scary, like in *Jurassic Park* and *King Kong vs. Godzilla*.

What do I *want* to learn from the text?

- When did they become extinct?
- Where did Tyrannosaurus rex live?
- Can dinosaurs really be made in a laboratory?

What did I *learn* from the text?

- Tyrannosaurus rex lived in parts of what is now the western United States.
- We can take a deep breath! So far, no one has used dinosaur DNA to create new dinosaurs!

KWL is popular not only as a questioning routine but also as a means of helping students develop strategic approaches to reading. In fact, the KWL strategy is an example of questioning that guides further student strategy use, promoting text-based comprehension. Thus, the KWL strategy can help us assess both students' learning from text and their strategic approaches to reading. Having asked the question, students can monitor their understanding. Our knowledge of how students think and learn should privilege particular types of questioning practice, especially as we consider the complex curricular goals and sophisticated student thinking that are hallmarks of high-quality instructional programs.

QAR strategies (Raphael & Wonnacott, 1985) help students understand the connections between questions that are asked and the answers that students give in response. In effect, the QAR approach helps students become metacognitive about the relationship of the meaning that is constructed through reading with the comprehension questions we ask them. The approach is built on the assumption that it is important for student readers to know where their answers come from and the suitability of using different sources of information for answering different types of questions. The four categories of QARs are right there, think and search, author and me, and on my own. *Right there* means that students should find the content for their answers to questions from one source in the text. *Think and search* means that student readers should find information across a text. *Author and me* requires students to use information from the text in combination with prior knowledge related to the text to generate inferences about the text. Finally, *on my own* means that although the question is related to the text, the student's answer may or may not be related, and answers emanate from students' prior experiences and knowledge.

Questioning the author (Beck et al., 1997) is a means for students to learn good questions to ask of authors of the texts they read, and for teachers to gauge the development of students' ability to read critically. Questioning the author helps the reader approach texts from a purpose-driven perspective—with the purpose being one other than answering multiple-choice questions. Students may ask themselves the following:

- Why did the author write this?
- What is the author trying to tell me?
- How well does the author succeed at the task of writing well?
- What are the strong and weak points of the author's writing and argument?
- Are there alternative approaches to the author's portrayal of the issue?

One result of questioning the author should be that students better understand authors' approaches to writing, which in turn may influence students' own writing. This approach also helps students make accurate attributions for their comprehension of text. Challenges to comprehension may be the result of poorly written text, and students who understand this and can identify such texts when they are reading them are in a good position to make the correct attributions for their own performance.

Many questions that are asked of students focus on literal and simple inferential comprehension. Such questions will always play an important role in reading assessment. However, they do not fully represent the types of questions that are important to ask of students, nor do they help us assess reading, learning, and thinking at more complex levels. Consider the critical and evaluative questions that we may ask of students.

While a variety of question types in classrooms helps us understand the full range of student learning, there are further benefits to derive from questions that focus on students' higher-level thinking. Students and other citizens in democratic societies must be able to ask questions about the accuracy and trustworthiness of texts. For example, students' ease of access to internet texts—texts that may have dubious origins and sketchy relations to facts—reminds us that critical questioning is an essential reading skill. Outlandish claims stated without evidence, opinion posed as fact, and texts skewed from truth to lying are readily available and must be evaluated.

Student readers should determine the obvious and hidden agendas of the authors who create texts (Jewett, 1940; Muspratt et al., 1997). Advertisements, editorials, political campaign documents, and other forms of persuasive text must be addressed with critical questions. Such questions help us determine if students understand the different purposes for authors writing particular types of texts, the apparent accuracy of accounts of factual information, the strength of an author's argument and claims, and the form and content of the text (Bråten et al., 2009).

CHARACTERISTICS OF EFFECTIVE QUESTIONS

When we envision success for our students in and out of school, does this success revolve around their ability to answer literal comprehension questions? Does it involve a student's ability to read between the lines, stand in critical judgment of authors and their works, and use what is read and understood in tasks and performances? The answers to these questions should influence how we conceptualize and use questions in our classrooms.

Questions are used to determine what a student has learned from reading a text and the thinking and reasoning that students do in relation to their reading. If we ask students to read so that they can give us back information from the text, then factual questions are suitable. If we want students to demonstrate that they know facts and opinions and know when an author is being persuasive, then we need to ask questions that reveal the students' knowledge related to persuasive writing and content learning.

Appropriate questions result from careful analyses of the important components of teaching and learning. First, good questions relate to the text. They seek to identify student learning that occurs as a result of reading. Good questions represent an inquiry into student learning. We want our questions to focus on important points of learning and attainable goals. Our questions should reflect an understanding of how students learn and develop, how knowledge is constructed in particular content areas, and how reading operates.

A checklist for constructing effective questions should focus on both the content and the form of our questions so that they are appropriate, accessible, and answerable. If you are interested in evaluating your questions, you can use the reproducible Checklist for Constructing Effective Questions in the Appendix.

The questions that students encounter related to their reading can shape their stance toward reading and knowledge and their very beliefs about the authority of the text. Just as important, the questions we ask of students consistently communicate what we value. Low-level questions asked across an entire school year send students a consistent message that memorization and retrieval of information from text are the most important goals for reading. More challenging questions invite students to problem solve, problem find, and partake in complex thinking. Across the school career, our questions, whether high level or low level, shape students' epistemologies. This is because questions are proxies for how we view knowledge—they communicate to students a specific perspective on the nature of knowledge and what is important in the texts they read.

Assessment questions model different manners of thinking about learning and knowing. Our questions can teach students about particular stances that they may take toward knowledge (Bråten et al., 2009; Kuhn et al., 2000) and contribute to the development of their epistemic knowledge. Consider the following five questions. Each could be asked as students complete a chapter on the American Revolution in their social studies textbook:

1. Where did Colonial troops defeat General Cornwallis?
2. What is the theme of this chapter?
3. Why did the author choose these examples to illustrate the main idea?
4. Was the author successful in his strategy?
5. How do you judge your performance on these questions?

The perspective that students should learn and memorize historical facts informs the first question. Information resides in text and is to be learned and remembered by the reader. The second question asks students to synthesize a theme based on their literal understanding. The perspective that readers should be inquisitive about the things they read, and be aware of authors' strategies and intent, informs the third question. The fourth question asks students to make a critical judgment about the author's ability. Finally, the fifth question asks student readers to look inward and provide an account of metacognitive processes. Each question is worth asking, and each yields responses that inform us of a student's reading development. A challenge is to balance our question asking so that in relation to texts and our teaching goals, there is no surplus of one type of question and a lack of others.

Examining Different Types of Questions

In this section, we examine the types of questions that we may ask in relation to students' reading. It is common to think of reading assessment questions as focused on comprehension because this is a primary role of questions. However, how we measure and describe students' comprehension of text should not be limited to a series of literal and inferential comprehension questions. We should consider questions that help us understand if students are able to apply what they learn from reading, generalize from what they read to their lives, and adopt evaluative stances toward texts and their contents.

Introduced earlier in this chapter, the IRE approach to questioning and assessment can inform us of the different types of student learning. For example, we can ask students questions like "What is the capital of Kansas?" and "What is a tectonic plate?" and evaluate their responses. A more complex IRE question might be, "How is the French Revolution like the American Revolution?" As our questions and the learning they probe become more complex, so must our assessment. In fact, IRE questions can be used to assess student learning and performance at diverse levels of thinking and understanding.

There are caveats related to the use of the IRE structure in questioning routines. First, IRE is teacher dominated: The teacher determines what questions will be asked and then asks them. If we ask an array of questions that revolve around what is understood from reading, using that which is understood in reading-related tasks and reacting critically to texts that are read, it may well be that students are getting a healthy sampling of the important types of questions to ask. However, if we continually ask lower-level questions (i.e., those that require students to only identify literal information and make simple inferences), this does not help students better understand how different question types encourage different types of thinking. Second, the IRE pattern establishes the teacher as the arbiter of the appropriateness of students' responses. The teacher is the single person with the correct answer to the question. Over time, the IRE routine and the approach to knowledge that it represents can suggest to students that their literal understanding of text is all that matters, that divergent thinking is not appropriate, and that there is a single arbiter of students' answers to reading questions. Third, the IRE pattern represents a teacher monopoly on assessment. When we do all the question asking and oversee all the answers, there may be missed opportunities for students to learn to do question asking, peer evaluation, and self-evaluation. If the teacher generates the questions and then evaluates student responses, there are missed opportunities for students to learn these important reading-related strategies.

Questions That Are Spontaneous or Planned, Divergent or Convergent

Classroom assessment questions can be spontaneous or planned, and divergent or convergent. Spontaneous questions follow the flow of reading in the classroom, prompted by teachers' observations and insights. They help teachers determine the degree to which students have read, understood, and learned from text. Student responses help the teacher decide to reteach, elaborate and enrich, or move ahead during the reading lesson. Spontaneous questions provide useful information in the midst of teaching and learning. For example, we do not plan for students to encounter difficulties when reading an introduction and explanation of plate tectonics, but we should plan questions that guide us to a detailed understanding of individual students' developing knowledge and current needs. These contingent and spontaneous questions fuel our ability to identify and capitalize on teachable moments.

Conversely, planned questions focus on goals of the lesson: We ask questions to evoke expected student learning. Key vocabulary, main ideas, and supporting details are all examples of appropriate foci for planned questions. Planned questions can also prompt critical thinking. Students' responses to these questions help us determine their understanding of important concepts. When our students read an article about plate tectonics, we are interested in their understanding of earthquakes, the Richter scale, and the San Andreas Fault, as well as the tectonic plates themselves. As teachers, we may determine aspects of the curriculum that pose challenges. For example, we note that students' understanding of how tectonic plate movement leads to earthquakes is elusive. Our attention to these challenges allows us to build a repertoire of planned questions, informed by our observations of student performance, that focuses on the relationship between tectonic plates and earthquakes. In summary, student readers will benefit from a mixture of spontaneous and planned questions. Talented teachers assess with both.

Convergent questions are posed with the understanding that different students' responses, when accurate, will be similar or identical. There is often one correct response expected for convergent questions. For example, we can ask, "Where is the San Andreas Fault?" and be confident that there is a single correct answer to the question. In contrast, divergent questions are posed with an acknowledgment that students' answers to the same question may be different *and* acceptable. We can ask, "Why would people live near the San Andreas Fault?" Determining the quality of the responses may be more difficult with divergent questions because the questions can invite different responses, different paths to solutions, different explanations for phenomena, and different criteria for explanation. Thus, the means to evaluate responses to divergent questions should be developed with the understanding that answers may vary and still be appropriate.

Question Comprehensibility, Wait Time, and Passage Independence

When we ask questions, we are most often interested in how well students have comprehended the text. Our questions are texts themselves, and we must query, What is the comprehensibility of the questions we ask? We must scrutinize the questions we ask to determine how well students will understand them. A difficult question can confuse students who, through more appropriate questions, might demonstrate comprehension of what they read. When we construct questions, we should consider the vocabulary of the question and the complexity of the prompt. If the vocabulary demands of our questions are greater than, and in addition to, the vocabulary demands of the learning we seek to investigate through questioning, then we need to revise our questions. (For more on making accommodations, see Chapter 7.)

Between a teacher's posing a question and a student's response to that question exists wait time. Every question that we ask may warrant wait time, from a seemingly simple literal comprehension question to a complex critical and evaluative one. We should not expect that comprehensive answers spring fully formed from students' minds. Thoughtful answers require thought, and thought requires time.

Wait time will vary from question to question and from student to student. The amount of time needed to answer a question is influenced by several important factors, including the focus of the question, students' comprehension of the text, the comprehensibility of the question, the complexity of the thinking required to give an adequate response, and students' individual differences. The wait time we give for students' responses to questions should vary based on our best estimate of these factors. In effect, it is our responsibility to probe the question and understand the demands that it creates for students so we can develop legitimate estimates of how much time a student needs to adequately think about and answer the question. This estimate will have parameters so that we have a general sense of what a question demands and what our individual students require in terms of time to respond.

Students can sometimes answer questions without comprehending the related text. This situation is prominent in multiple-choice question situations in which students with no idea of the correct answer respond correctly, without any understanding of the text: The lucky guess helps. Also, students may come to a correct answer by faulty reasoning. Students can answer correctly by using their prior knowledge related to the text's topic rather than their comprehension of the text. Consider the following question sentence:

Emma rode down the hill on her shiny, red _____.

If asked to complete the sentence, almost all readers will use their prior knowledge of syntax and semantics to determine that *bike* or *bicycle* is the correct word. Prior knowledge fills in the blank. Similarly, if we change one letter in the above sentence (*i* for *o* in the preposition), most readers will determine that *wagon* is the correct word. Thus, our questions should be vetted for text independence—this allows for confidence in our determination of whether or not a student has understood and adequately responded to our question. Asking students to provide reasons for their answers serves as a check on their responses and helps us best understand what a student was thinking when giving a particular answer.

Students' responses to our questions may be written, spoken, or chosen. The response format must be considered as questions and sets of questions are created. Multiple-choice questions require the reader to choose the correct answer, often from among four or five possible answers. A well-developed multiple-choice question can provide valuable information about things students learn. Alternately, our questions may prompt students to provide constructed responses. Brief constructed responses require students to provide short answers, typically ranging from one to three sentences. Extended constructed responses can demand that students provide sentences, paragraphs, or sets of paragraphs. In each instance, our determination of the item format that will best provide useful information is important. Like oral responses, written responses may have considerable wait-time demands for the students to not only find and retrieve information from their long-term memory but also draft, revise, and construct the response to the question.

Good questioning technique evolves over time because teachers who ask the questions pay attention to how students respond. A question and answer that seem excellent from our teaching perspective must be checked against students' performance and perspectives on the same. As questions are introduced into the classroom routine, we must ascertain that they work. We cannot be content with determining if a student's response to a question is correct or incorrect. If we uncover the student thinking that led to the response to the question, it allows us to determine if what we anticipate as a typical thought process and question response is what students actually do when responding to the question.

ASSESSING RESPONSES TO QUESTIONS IN RETELLINGS AND DISCUSSIONS

We can assess students by listening to their retellings and discussions of the texts they read. We gain insights into students' understanding of text when we consider the following:

- As a prelude to systematic questioning, what can a reader who is unprompted tell about what was read?
- Do students discuss their understanding of stories and informational texts?
- How do students give retellings that help us fill in the gaps of our understanding of their comprehension?

There are considerable benefits from student discussions of the things they read (Ivey & Johnston, 2023; Tullis & Goldstone, 2020). As we become sensitive to the content and structure of students' discussions, we can find answers to our questions without asking them. Of course, this requires that teachers listen to, observe, and analyze students' discussions in relation to a set of questions. Task analysis of the important things that students do when they read, practice with listening to students, and matching discussion to questions can make this an important part of the classroom assessment routine.

Teachers who are knowledgeable about questioning and have the time to do so can create a series of questions for the texts their students read in class. More often, questions are included in commercially produced curricula, and it is important to scrutinize those questions. When questions are developed far from the here and now of reading in our classrooms, there may be a reduced chance of a particular question being the best one. Questions can guide or follow thought. The questions that accompany textbooks in social studies, science, music, art, and literature are an estimation of what is needed to focus students on important content and elicit their responses. The questions tend to track how well students learn predetermined content. The questions are based on anticipated student work and outcomes, which may or may not be close to the work of students in our classrooms.

Careful examination of the questions that accompany commercial reading materials can help teachers make decisions related to the questions' suitability. A question, or a set of questions, may be all that is needed by the teacher to determine that important learning is being assessed in an appropriate manner. In such cases, questions can be used as provided in teachers' manuals. In other cases, questions may focus on only part of what the teacher considers to be important learning related to the reading. Such questions should be augmented by the teacher's quest for more information. There may be questions that are directed toward eliciting important information, yet they do not present the best question for a particular student in a particular context.

QUESTIONING IN JOAN'S FOURTH-GRADE CLASSROOM

Throughout the school year, Joan pursues the personal professional development goal of being a good question asker. She regularly asks herself, "What is the *right* question?" For Joan, the right question is determined by a complex set of factors: a student's developmental level as a reader, the content of the text, the type of thinking that is important to model and then require of the student, and the testing landscape in the school and district. Considering all these factors is, at first, demanding. Yet, the result is confidence that her questions are worthwhile assessment for her students that reflect important teaching and learning. Her fourth-grade students are in their last year in a largely intact classroom, with few pullouts, which allows Joan to use her question-asking strategies across the school day and across content domains. She observes students reading and thinking in science, social studies, mathematics, and English, which provides her with a continual source of information related to her students' current state of development. This information helps her with corresponding instruction. She has the luxury of knowing her students across the school day and the responsibility of attending to the detail of their development so that her teaching and accompanying questioning are appropriate.

Joan is a strategic question asker. She knows that good question-asking practice requires a range of questions that evoke different types of student thinking and reveal different types of comprehension and learning. Good questioning is also dependent on the interactive dynamics between the teacher and the student, and the question and the answer. For example, in leading up to a relatively complex question that requires students to propose an explanation (e.g., "Can global warming be slowed while people continue to use electricity and automobiles?"), Joan knows that her students must demonstrate a literal understanding of the scientific findings related to global warming research. Assuming that this understanding exists without first questioning the students to ascertain if this is so could render the subsequent questions worthless.

To reach her goals for questioning, Joan relies on an arc of questions, in which "simple factual inquiries give way to increasingly interpretive questions until new insights emerge" (Wolf, 1987, p. 4). The questions help her address her students' learning about global warming, and the questions are complementary, building on one another. While the set of questions is intended to help students demonstrate their knowledge and thinking at increasingly complex levels, it also has a diagnostic feature. More simple questions (e.g., "What is one cause of global warming?") are asked prior to more complex questions (e.g., "How can global warming be slowed or stopped?"). This sequencing allows Joan to tailor her questions to individual students. She finds it useful to think about an arc of questions in relation to her students' current levels of reading ability and content-area knowledge, along with Bloom's (1956; Krathwohl, 2002) levels of thinking. Table 4.2 contains examples of questions that Joan includes in her arc of questions and indicates their increasing complexity and relationship to Bloom's taxonomy. This arc of questions represents Joan's comprehensive questioning routine and demonstrates her attention to using questions to help shape and assess her students' thinking. If you are

TABLE 4.2. **An Arc of Questions in Relation to Bloom's Taxonomy and Joan's Classroom**

Scenario: Students are reading from different texts to learn about global warming.

Bloom's taxonomy category	Joan's question to her students
Knowledge, or recalling data or information	"What is one cause of global warming?"
Comprehension, or understanding the meaning, translation, interpolation, and interpretation of instructions and problems; stating a problem in one's own words	"How does global warming occur?"
Application, or using a concept in a new situation or unprompted use of an abstraction; applying what was learned in the classroom to novel situations in the workplace	"What might happen with global warming as the number of automobiles increases?"
Analysis, or separating material or concepts into component parts so that the organizational structure may be understood; distinguishing between facts and inferences	"What proof of global warming is offered by those people who claim it is a potentially deadly problem?"
Synthesis, or building a structure or pattern from diverse elements; putting parts together to form a whole, with emphasis on creating a new meaning or structure	"What would you include in a comprehensive plan to reduce global warming?"
Evaluation, or making judgments about the value of ideas or materials	"Are the alternative explanations for global warming that are given by those who are opposed to taking action against global warming credible, and why?"

interested in developing a sample arc of questions for use in your classroom, you can use the Developing an Arc of Questions: From Relatively Simple to Increasingly Complex reproducible form in the Appendix.

Consequences and Usefulness of Questioning

Joan believes that it is important for students to apply what they learn from reading to identify and solve problems, to engage in generative thought, and to be critical consumers of the information contained in the texts they read. She surveys questions and determines those that tap literal and simple inferential comprehension. As she categorizes her instructional goals in relation to Bloom's (1956; Krathwohl, 2002) taxonomy, she can determine the degree to which the questions she asks of students focus on the different types of learning within the taxonomy. A result is robust questioning. Students need to construct accurate literal understanding of text and to complement that understanding with the ability to answer questions about authors' motives and the degree to which claims in the text are supported with evidence. A more typical approach of using literal and inferential questions would not provide assessment information that is as rich as that provided by robust questioning.

There are several critical consequences and uses of the questions that Joan develops for her students. First, the questions help her understand how well students learn course content. The questions tap students' literal, inferential, and critical understandings of the texts they read. Second, the questions, having checked on students' literal and inferential comprehension, then require students to demonstrate diverse approaches to thinking and increased sophistication in their thinking. Questions help Joan understand how students use that which they comprehend. Importantly, questions serve to both provoke thinking and assess it. For example, Joan asks how students might adopt different perspectives (e.g., a research scientist, a climate change denier, and a student who drives) to comment on the portrayal of global warming in their science text. Without the question, it is unclear how many students would be moved to this type of thinking. With the question, Joan also has a means for judging students' approaches to the thinking. Her questions provide process and product information about students' reading development, information that can be used in both formative and summative assessments. (See Chapter 9 for more on formative and summative assessments.)

The consequences for Joan's students are substantial. They are regularly asked an array of questions that target literal and inferential understandings. These questions describe students' text comprehension and serve as practice for the high-stakes tests at year-end, which are heavily weighted to measure students' literal and inferential comprehension. Provided with diverse types of questions, the students in Joan's class get consistent models of thinking and learning to ask questions of themselves as they read. These questions fall into two broad categories—comprehension and metacomprehension—and help students independently determine the degree to which they understand the texts that they read.

Over time, the variety of questions that are asked in Joan's classroom (and in other grades) have a further serious consequence for students: The students learn that what they read is often worthy of investigation and challenge. Questions model for students different ways of thinking and stances toward reading and knowledge. As fourth graders, these students are bombarded with advertisements and other types of propaganda encountered on the internet and social media. Questions that uncover a hidden intent of text, an author's strategy for being persuasive, and the trustworthiness of the text help students navigate their personal lives as they learn to read critically.

Roles and Responsibilities Related to Questioning

Across a school career, the type and frequency of questions used in classrooms can have a profound influence on students' thinking and their engagement with learning. Consider the student who receives an exclusive mix of literal and inferential comprehension questions across elementary school. This student may become adept at giving back specific pieces of text to answer literal comprehension questions, and at combining literal information from text with prior knowledge to achieve inferential comprehension. Unfortunately, this student may not have the opportunity to begin to question the authority of the text, challenge an author's claims, or determine the subtext that underlies an author's explicit or implicit arguments. In societies where there is pervasive intent to convince people that they need to buy things and where truth is evasive among particular political leaders, our students must be able to ask questions of texts so that they are in a powerful, and not powerless, position as readers.

Joan is convinced that good teaching in fourth grade results not only in students' content-area learning but also in further development of students' ability to think and reason. Future grades' curricula in middle school and high school will demand mastering literal and inferential comprehension of texts so that students may critically evaluate the texts. Joan knows that the application of what is learned from reading is demanded in the upper grades and central to much of the reading that students will do outside of school. She is responsible for certifying that her students learn from text in each of the content areas and can apply the knowledge learned. She is responsible for helping her students prepare for high-stakes tests that will determine their futures. She is also responsible for instilling the idea that good questions beget more good questions: Students who are asked diverse questions learn new ways of thinking.

For Joan, asking, "What's the right question?" sets the parameters of her roles and responsibilities. Joan's questions are informed by her ideas of good practice. She makes sure that she provides adequate wait time for all her students to construct appropriate responses and that her questions are comprehensible for her students. She analyzes student responses to her questions. Joan resists the idea of questioning becoming a comfortable habit in her classroom. She knows that questions can lead to the establishment and reinforcement of power relationships in classrooms. Questions can be used to acknowledge students' contributions or lack of contribution to the class. She is focused on determining how and to what degree students are learning content from their reading. She regularly asks questions that focus on what students understand from the textbook chapter on earthquakes, the primary source texts in social studies, and the short stories in English. She also checks for her students' ability to understand math word problems.

Joan continually monitors her questions: She believes that most good questions need a tryout period. To refine and polish her questions, Joan pilots them in her classroom, which allows her to apply her knowledge from a task analysis to help troubleshoot those questions that she believes are important but seem to be causing difficulty for her students. She structures her question-asking routines so that they include opportunities for her students to learn how to ask important questions of themselves. She models, explains, and discusses with her students why we ask questions, where questions come from, and how they then connect to our learning goals and tasks. She explains to students how their responses to questions are evaluated. In addition, she amends the questioning routine that accompanies the commercially produced materials to include questions that direct students to the nature of questions, knowledge, and power.

Reliability of Questioning

Joan uses different types of questions for her students, and she follows a detailed routine for ascertaining the reliability of her questions. At the heart of this routine is a task analysis of what exactly students must do to understand and respond to the questions. (For more information on task analysis, see the Reading Assessment Snapshot, "Task Analysis," at the end of Chapter 2.) This task analysis allows Joan to examine the thinking that her questions will demand of her students. She considers first the comprehensibility of the question: Will her students understand it? Is this literal question more challenging than the text that students must read to answer the question? Next, she examines the fairness of the question: Does it privilege certain students who already know something about the content of the assigned reading? Is the question straightforward and not confusing? Is the language used in the question confounding for EL students? Can the question be answered without reading the text? Next, Joan checks for confounds. (For more information on confounds, see the Reading Assessment Snapshot, "Confounds in Reading Assessment," at the end of Chapter 7.) Will a student's speaking or writing ability influence Joan's interpretation of that student's reading achievement? Joan examines each question to determine the things that students must know and do to answer the question well. She considers the complexity of the question in relation to her students' development and estimates the necessary wait time for each to answer.

The reliability of her assessment also depends on her interactions with the students during questioning. When asking questions during a lesson, Joan can discuss, model, and suggest things that lead students to insights and correct answers. This is a regular part of her question asking during class. In contrast, she is consistent in her treatment of students when asking summative assessment questions. She does not provide hints or clues when questions are related to unit tests because she knows that students must be best prepared to take consequential, high-stakes tests.

Validity of Questioning

Joan's questions must pass three stringent tests related to construct validity. The first test focuses on her conceptualization of reading comprehension as including literal, inferential, and critical comprehension. She makes sure that her array of questions honors the construct of comprehension by asking questions that provide students with opportunities to demonstrate these different levels of thinking. The typical arc of questions in Joan's classroom reflects her knowledge of what it means to understand text. Students must construct literal and inferential meaning of the things they read while understanding why texts are written, authors' acknowledged and unspoken agendas, and how the contexts in which we read can influence what we take from a text. Second, Joan's questions must be accurately mapped onto the information contained in the text. She checks the content and form of the texts that students read, and this allows her to construct appropriate questions and to vet existing questions contained in commercially published reading materials. Joan's scrutiny of the texts her students read helps her determine if detail and main idea questions are appropriate, if there is evidence enough of author intention to ask students to identify intention, or if an argument has sufficient evidence provided to support claims made throughout the text.

The third test relates to the thinking done by students as they answer questions. Related taxonomies (Bloom, 1956; Krathwohl, 2002; Webb, 2002) describe increasingly complex and sophisticated thinking, and the array of questions in Joan's classroom reflects this construct. Thus, her questions serve the dual role of providing detail on what her students learn and providing a model of diverse and sophisticated thinking. They also reflect ecological validity, in that Joan strives to instill further inquisitiveness in her students by posing and modeling good question asking.

SUMMARY

There are many types of questions to ask when we assess our student readers. These questions should be informed by theories of thinking and learning, our students, strategies, cognitive development, the role of the reader, and the curriculum. Across history, questions have been central to reading assessment. We ask questions because we want to know about our students' learning and progress—specifically, their reading development and reading achievement. We ask questions related to phonemic awareness and phonics of students supported by MTSS. Later, we ask questions related to critical inquiry and judging authors and texts. Questions are central to assessing and evaluating students' reading comprehension, yet many questions do not reflect our detailed understanding of the suitability of questions for particular learning goals and reading curricula.

Our questions should reflect the nature of learning and thinking that we expect of our developing readers. Effective questioning practice reflects our attention to factors that include wait time, the questions' relation to retelling and discussion, and the development of a series of questions that represent a range of comprehension levels and the range of content that we are interested in assessing. Finally, the care we give to our question asking can help develop students' habits of mind and expand their thinking.

Enhancing Your Understanding

1. Video-record a reading lesson. Examine your questions: the type of question, the comprehensibility of the question, the wait time needed, students' options for answering the question, and the relation of the question to different learning goals. Who asks questions, and who answers them? How much class time is involved? Is there a balance of types of questions in relation to your different students and lesson goals?

2. In relation to the information in this chapter, would you characterize the types of questions you ask during reading as optimal? Why?

3. Create an arc of questions in a particular content area that helps you understand student achievement from the level of literal understanding through critical analysis and application of what is understood from reading.

4. Think of a recent, personal learning experience. How did you know how you were doing? How did you know how well you did upon completion of the task? What can this teach you about good questions to ask of students' reading, assessment, and self-assessment?

Reading Assessment Snapshot
PROCESS AND PRODUCT ASSESSMENT

Useful assessment revolves around the quality of the inferences we can make about students' reading. The accuracy of these inferences is influenced by the relationship of the assessment to instruction and student learning. With this in mind, it is important to consider how assessments focus on the processes or products of student learning and achievement.

Process assessments help us examine the means by which students learn and achieve. These processes might involve determining the match of the letter *B* with the spoken sound /b/, reading fluently, or the strategies used to comprehend text. For example, teacher observation provides detailed and immediate assessment information related to the processes that fourth graders use as they work with the KWL procedure (Ogle, 1986). The teacher observes students, making note of the things they know and the things they would like to learn from the text to be read. The teacher observes students monitoring their work so they can effectively answer the *L* section of the KWL exercise: What did I *learn*? The teacher's observation is process centered, so the inferences made about students derive from a more direct view to those processes.

In contrast, product assessments are removed from the acts of instruction and learning. These assessments focus on learning that is assumed to be, in some sense, complete. This means that our inferences about students and their learning may be limited to the nature of the products that are the end result of the processes. We may consider completed performance assessments, students' final drafts of writing, or correct or incorrect responses to test questions. In these cases, our inferences are necessarily backward-looking; that is, we can determine that learning occurred or did not occur, based on the student's response, but from that point on, we may have little or no information to understand how the product was created. We may lack the understanding of how, what, and when particular processes were or were not used. Thus, we are not often in a position to use product assessment in a diagnostic manner. We are also not in a position to use product assessment for formative assessment because product assessment has little explanatory power to guide our inferences and instruction.

It is important to become familiar with both product and process assessment and the types of inferences that we are required (and permitted) to make, based on the assessment information. Whatever the nature of the assessment, the quality of the inferences we make from product or process reading assessment must be high—a suitable result of our understanding of the nature of the assessments we use and the inferences that are justified from the data they provide.

CHAPTER 5

Performance Assessment

We are surrounded by performances related to our reading. When we read instructions to assemble a toy, a recipe to make dinner, or a set of directions for taking medicine, reading and action are intertwined. In school, students read earth science articles downloaded from the internet and craft a three-dimensional diorama representing plate tectonics. They create a dramatic skit based on their interpretation of characters in a short story. They read history texts that pose conflicting accounts of the origins of the American Revolution and determine which are accurate and trustworthy. Students read math word problems that require them to determine rainfall averages for each month of the school year, and science texts to help them interpret their firsthand observations of the schoolyard ecosystem. Texts and reading are central to many problem-based learning projects, and these students are using the knowledge they gain through reading to perform important tasks.

Starting in elementary school, performance assessment can help us determine not only what students understand from reading but also how they use what they understand. Performance assessment helps describe student development in relation to complex curricular goals. The knowledge that students gain from reading is not inert, and reading assessment should not treat it as such. Performance assessments situate students' reading in relation to other important work in school, as students read to construct meaning and use it. Performance assessment is demanding of resources and teacher expertise but has many possible benefits.

A BRIEF HISTORY OF PERFORMANCE ASSESSMENT

We read to understand, but also to use that which we understand. The close connection between reading and performance tasks is as old as reading itself. However, current interest in performance assessment is attributable to several converging factors. First, ongoing research on how people read, think, and learn describes the complexity of reading and areas of student growth and achievement related to reading (Ahn, 2023; Cho, 2014; McNamara & Magliano, 2009; National Assessment Governing Board, 2023). Second, the reading standards developed by professional organizations, states, and school districts in relation to this new research knowledge require assessments that capture and describe complex student achievements (CCSSO & NGA, 2010). Third, traditional reading tests do not give a full account of how students use what they understand from reading (Wiggins, 1998). Finally, performance assessments can be used in the teaching and learning of course content and to help students learn to self-assess (Black & Wiliam, 1998).

There is a considerable disconnect between the breadth and depth of students' learning in a high-quality reading curriculum and the narrow focus of many reading assessments (Davis, 1998). The gap between how students read and learn and the assessments used to measure this complex development must be reduced. As we expect reading standards to reflect our most current understandings of reading, we should expect the same of the assessments used to measure student progress. It is difficult to understand the detail of a student's achievement when reading assessment results are a letter grade of B, a raw score of 53, or a ranking in the 82nd percentile. Performance assessments provide useful and educative details that complement the general statement made by such single, summative assessment markers.

Performance assessment has been the focus of broad initiatives to improve teaching and learning in U.S. schools. For example, individual state reading standards and the CCSS (CCSSO & NGA, 2010) represent ambitious student learning outcomes. A major focus of these standards is students using what they understand from reading in content areas. Thus, the standards represent a challenging curriculum that requires a new generation of reading assessments. These assessments include those developed by PARCC and SBAC. Assessments developed by these consortia require student performances that are gauged to the complexity of learning that is demanded by the complex learning standards.

The SBAC (2010) describes general criteria for reading assessments (i.e., criteria that align with performance assessments): "Assessments must be carefully structured to improve teaching and learning. This means establishing summative assessments that reflect the challenging CCSS content, emphasizing not just students' 'knowing,' but also 'doing' " (p. 37).

As this book goes to press, 41 states, as well as the District of Columbia, continue to use the CCSS for English/language arts.

CHARACTERISTICS OF PERFORMANCE ASSESSMENT

Our knowledge of reading is continually evolving. Reading research conducted in the past several decades has added much to our understandings of how reading works, how reading ability develops, and the place of reading in the lives of students (Berkeley et al., 2011; Moje et al., 2004). Performance assessments offer opportunities to describe student reading and learning across the curriculum. In the domains of science, social studies, math, English, and the arts, effective performance assessments share important characteristics. Performance assessments help us understand student growth and learning. They describe student achievement in detail. They are developed in relation to comprehensive analyses of what students must do to understand and complete a specific performance. Effective performance assessment uses scoring rubrics and guides that inform teachers and students as to the nature of the performance and gradations of accomplishment related to the performance.

Task Analysis

Effective performance assessment is enabled by a detailed task analysis of the performance. As the performance task is created, it is imperative that we establish an informed, a priori understanding of what the assessment requires of students. Task analyses involve a detailed accounting of what students must do in order to perform an assessment task satisfactorily. What exactly are we asking students to do when they read the following prompt in an American history performance assessment: "Based on your understanding of the two primary source texts, develop an account of the challenges faced by the Jamestown colonists"? Later in this chapter, we observe that responding to such prompts can involve different types of comprehension (literal, inferential, and critical), knowledge of source text cues, and the ability to take a critical stance toward authors and their work. Using task analysis, we can determine the details of student work required in the combination of reading and using what is read.

The grounding of performance assessment in relation to reading research and task analysis informs the development of a performance assessment's core features, including task demands or prompts, rubrics, and scoring guides. The development of a performance assessment is facilitated by attention to the assessment's specific purpose and goal. Thus, task analysis is complemented by the following questions:

- Why are we asking students to do this?
- What will the assessment describe in terms of student development and achievement?
- How do students demonstrate their accomplishment of the goal with observable products and performances?

The goal here is building a performance assessment in which we have high confidence and from which we can make accurate inferences about students' development and achievement.

Popham (1997) provides two caveats related to performance assessment. First, the performance that is being assessed must be worthy of the time and effort that are needed to develop and use effective rubrics. Performance assessment development must be approached with the knowledge that there are limits to how many assessments might be developed, given the intensive work they demand. Performance assessment tasks must reflect consensus on important student learning. Ideally, these assessments will focus on performances that represent convergences of student learning—incorporating skills, strategies, and the content-domain learning that are the goals of effective instruction.

Effective performance assessments are designed in relation to rubrics and scoring guides. A rubric is a description of how a student performance may vary in terms of quality and achievement. There are three essential features of valid rubrics: the criteria used to evaluate student work, the specification of differential quality of student work, and the means to consistently and accurately score student work. An examination of Table 5.1 illustrates how these three factors operate with a rubric. In this case, the performance assessment focuses on two interrelated history reading goals, or performances: (1) Students read history texts to identify cues in text to determine source text status and then (2) use this source text status to evaluate the trustworthiness of the text. The specification of different quality of student work is apparent in the different descriptions of performance. Following this rubric through the levels of student performance, we are able to trace how students might move from "Not Apparent" to "Developing" to "Proficient" to "Exemplary" levels of performance, earning respective scores of 1 through 4. The means to consistently and accurately score student work is tied to the clarity of the category, the detail of specification of student work of differing quality, and the assignment of that specification to particular scoring points.

Benefits of Performance Assessment

Andrade (2000) describes several possible benefits of using rubrics and performance assessment. Well-structured rubrics communicate to students our expectations for learning. In effect, they tell the student what is needed to earn a particular grade. Rubrics can also provide students with detailed feedback about their learning. By comparing their work with the set of expectations that a rubric presents, students can determine what has been achieved and what remains to be accomplished. Rubrics provide teachers and students with a clear and consistent means for judging student work. A rubric may also be used to help teach important aspects of the required student performance because the rubric focuses our attention and efforts on key curricular goals. Detailed performance assessment rubrics offer opportunities for scaffolding instruction. Teachers can use the different levels of the rubric to teach in reference to students' zone of proximal development

TABLE 5.1. **History Performance Assessment Rubric: Identifying Cues to Determine Source Text Status and Using Source Text Status to Evaluate Text**

Category	Levels of student performance			
	Not apparent (1)	Developing (2)	Proficient (3)	Exemplary (4)
Identifying cues to determine source text status	There is no attempt to identify and use cues to determine source text status.	Student identifies and uses one or more cues to determine source text status. For example, student uses archaic spelling and author voice to attribute source text status. However, identification of type of text cue is inaccurate, and/or determination of source text status is erroneous.	Student identifies and uses one or several cues to correctly determine source text status. For example, student uses archaic spelling and author voice to correctly determine text status as primary source.	Student identifies and uses all possible cues to correctly determine source text status. For example, student uses each and every cue contained in text to correctly determine text status as primary source.
Using source text status to evaluate text for trustworthiness	There is no apparent attempt to use understanding of source text status to evaluate the text. There is no apparent attempt to connect source text status with an evaluation of the trustworthiness of text.	Student attempts to use understanding of source text status, demonstrating connection between source text status and evaluation. However, designation of source text as trustworthy or not is erroneous.	Using understanding of source text status, student demonstrates connection between source text status and evaluation. Evaluation of text's trustworthiness is accurate and appropriate.	Using understanding of source text status, student demonstrates connection between determination of source text status and accuracy of evaluation. Evaluation of text's trustworthiness is comprehensive and appropriate, and use of source text status to evaluate text is elaborated.

Note. Adapted from "Teaching and Learning Self-Assessment Strategies in Middle School" by Peter Afflerbach and Kevin Meuwissen. Copyright © 2005 Lawrence Erlbaum Associates. Reproduced by permission of Taylor and Francis Group, LLC, a division of Informa PLC.

(Vygotsky, 1978), helping one student move from a level 1 ("Not Apparent" in Table 5.1) performance to level 2 ("Developing") and helping another move from level 3 ("Proficient") to level 4 ("Exemplary"). Indeed, Popham (1997) characterizes well-designed rubrics as "instructional illuminators" (p. 75): They shine a light on important content for students to learn.

The effectiveness of performance assessment is enhanced by sharing examples of student performances that clearly signify accomplishment at specific levels. These sample performances should indicate specific levels of achievement for both the scorers of the assessment and the students who create the performance. For example, a scoring guide can be accompanied by samples of student work that provide students with a target for their performance. These samples help students develop a refined sense of what work scored as a 1 and work scored as a 4 look like and how they differ. These samples can provide students with consistent guidance as they build their performance toward successful completion. The examples in Figure 5.1 reflect the ability to locate and use different cues to determine the primary or secondary source status of history texts and then evaluate the trustworthiness of the text to earn a score of 3, thus providing useful guidance to students who are learning this strategy. Over time, our use of rubrics and sample performances contributes to students developing specific schemata for what good work looks like, strategies for progress, and the ongoing self-assessment of their progress toward performance goals.

A further characteristic of performance assessments is that they often require an expanded administration time frame. Many standardized assessments, including reading tests, are administered in a relatively short time. However, performance assessments require time—for learning to use a rubric to support learning, conducting the performance, using self-assessment, and describing and measuring

---

Text excerpt that contains cues used by a student:

> As a citizen of Jamestown verginia I do my demesticall work each day. Yet, there remains little food for us, the poore distressed subjects. We are in dandger of losing our bretheren to hunger, this hunger that hath no seeming end.

Using cues to determine that it is a primary source text, the student writes:

> This appears to be a primary source text because it has old spellings like "poore," "dandger," and "hath." Also, I get a good feel for the author of this text as he speaks in the first person—this makes the description more real for me.

Using determination of source text status to evaluate the text's trustworthiness, the student writes:

> I believe that this is a primary source text because of the archaic spellings and the nature of the author's voice. Therefore, I believe that the text is trustworthy and that it reports an eyewitness account of some of the suffering that the Jamestown colonists experienced.

FIGURE 5.1. Example of a proficient (level 3) performance assessment score: Student reading history text, using cues to determine source text status, and evaluating text for trustworthiness.

student learning. Performances take more time than answering simple questions. Performance assessment done well is a result of the consideration of the time needed to undertake the performance, as well as the provision of a time frame that is appropriate for eliciting students' performances.

PERFORMANCE ASSESSMENT IN IVAN'S EIGHTH-GRADE HISTORY CLASSROOM

Ivan teaches eighth-grade history and has used performance assessment for five years. His enthusiastic use of performance assessment is guided by the strong conviction that students who are about to enter high school must be able to understand complex texts and then apply the things they learn from reading. This belief dovetails with the intent of contemporary learning standards to help prepare students for success in college and their careers. Ivan's students read history texts with competing, and sometimes conflicting, accounts of historical events and characters, from which students must construct an understanding of history and how it is created (Monte-Sano et al., 2022; National Council for the Social Studies, 1994).

Students learn to analyze historical documents, assess primary and secondary source status of texts, and combine diverse sources to construct accounts of history. Students adopt a questioning stance toward texts and authors. Students read critically, considering competing accounts of history and discerning fact and opinion. In this curriculum, students learn how history is written, the materials that are used by authors to write history, and how one can critically read history to try to determine the reliability and trustworthiness of texts. This learning complements students' understanding of historical facts about people, places, dates, and events. These tasks and learning goals reflect reading standards for literacy in history and social studies in grades 6 through 12.

The Nature of the History Performance Assessment

The performance assessment in Ivan's colonial American history class requires students to understand and evaluate history texts like historians. Research demonstrates that historians have specific strategies that help them determine the primary or secondary source status of history texts (VanSledright, 2013). Primary source texts may include original newspaper articles, diary entries, letters, maps, cartoons, and other documents that are contemporary with the historical period being studied. Secondary sources include history textbooks, historical novels, and works representing syntheses of other texts.

Students are required to read three different texts about the same historical events (in this case, the founding and survival of the Jamestown colony). The texts include a diary excerpt from a Jamestown colonist, an account from a work of fiction of how Jamestown changed the lives of Native Americans, and a newspaper article that describes how the arrival of a second group of colonists saved Jamestown from extinction. The performance assessment prompt reads as follows:

> Read the three texts on Jamestown. For each text, identify and use as many cues as possible that help you determine the status of the source text. Once you have identified the cues, determine text status and then evaluate each text for trustworthiness based on these determinations.

Students must locate and use cues in the three different texts to determine when the texts were written, who wrote them, and why the texts were written. Ultimately, students must determine the status of these source texts. Students use particular cues to make critical evaluations of text, including the trustworthiness of the historical account and the reliability of the author. The different types of cues, including vocabulary, spelling, syntax, author voice, type of text, age of text, and header material (i.e., where the text comes from), derive directly from research on reading history and are then built into the curriculum and assessment (Afflerbach & VanSledright, 2001). Cues that students can use to help determine source text status include the following:

- Age of the text
- Type of text
- Header material in text (displays author attributions)
- Author presence and voice in text
- Spelling in the text
- Syntax
- Vocabulary
- Combinations of two or more of the above cues

In the year-end performance assessment, students are responsible for identifying cues and using them to determine if the texts read are primary or secondary source documents. Next, students evaluate the texts for their trustworthiness, based on students' determination of primary or secondary source status. Ivan believes that consistent use of performance assessments to measure complex student learning and help students better understand assessment is well worth the time and effort spent. He knows that performance assessments describe important student learning and help students build an appreciation for both their accomplishments and their increasing ability to self-assess.

Consequences and Usefulness of Performance Assessments

Ivan uses performance assessment for several reasons. First and foremost, it allows him to assess his students in a manner that honors the complexity of their learning and his teaching. This understanding moves our expectations for assessment in history beyond the traditional inventory of students' memory of historical dates, places, people, and events. Learning goals and performance assessment converge as students demonstrate their knowledge about why history is written, how it is written, who writes it, and how it is read. Performance assessment allows students to demonstrate their understanding that history in school includes stories of particular people, places, and events and excludes others. It allows students to identify equity and inequity in the recent and distant past, as well as in the current day. The assessment does not discount the importance of historical dates, places, people, and events but seeks to describe how students learn and understand history. The performance assessment used in Ivan's classroom demonstrates not only students' understanding of the content of history texts but also students' ability to determine the primary or secondary source status of those texts.

Second, the use of this history performance assessment provides Ivan with a window on his teaching. The performance assessment provides Ivan with detailed information about his students' progress toward major goals of schooling. For example, the source text status assessment helps him understand students' critical reading development within history and critical reading in general. Ivan is able to infer, with high confidence, what his students learn and the effectiveness of his teaching.

Third, the performance assessment provides formative and summative assessment information on student learning in relation to the rich construct of reading history. Ivan uses class time to focus on each cue that readers can use to determine the primary or secondary source status of the history texts they read. He constructs related assessments, based on the unit-end performance assessment, that describe each student's ability to recognize and use the different cues. These assessments provide formative feedback on the effectiveness of Ivan's instruction and the extent of student learning. Across the school year, he knows each student's achievement in relation to learning the different cues that help the reader determine the source text status.

A fourth use of performance assessments is their means for teaching important content and strategies for reading like a historian. The detailed information included in Ivan's performance assessment rubrics, scoring guides, and sample student papers is useful for communicating to students what they must do to receive particular performance assessment scores. The rubrics and scoring guide help him focus on important curricular content, materials, and processes. A task analysis of locating cues to determine the status of history texts is used to build the performance assessment, and this analysis also reminds Ivan of the level of detail that is necessary in his instruction. The close match between instruction and scoring rubrics allows Ivan to focus on helping students develop strategies for reading like historians. The rubric itself focuses on the particular means for students to demonstrate their learning and is utilized as an outline for learning.

A further use of the performance assessment is teaching students self-assessment. Independence and success with increasingly complex reading performances are foci of contemporary reading standards. As students develop their performances, they learn to self-check their work against the detailed information in the rubric. Here, the rubric provides the necessary scaffold for students who are learning to self-assess and judge their performances. Ivan prepares a checklist that matches each of the particular cues that students may use and that is tied to the rubric. Students are required to use the checklist to determine if a particular type of cue is present in the history texts they read. Figure 5.2 is a checklist used by Ivan and his fellow history teachers to help students learn and attend to the different text cues in primary and secondary source texts. By using checklists, Ivan is helping his students build a useful schema for conducting self-assessment. Ivan's goal here is to help students practice using the teacher-provided checklist

---

The texts we read in history class may be primary or secondary source texts. Use the following checklist to help you remember particular cues and practice using these cues to determine if a text is a primary or secondary source.

Does this text contain cues that are normally found in primary source texts?

☐ Yes

☐ No

Check the following cues as you find them in the text:

☐ Spelling

☐ Vocabulary

☐ Author voice

☐ Print material attribution

☐ Combination of two or more of the above cues

Based on your reading and search for cues in this text, which do you determine it to be?

☐ Primary source text

☐ Secondary source text

FIGURE 5.2. Sample checklist for cues used to signal primary and secondary source texts.

on a regular basis so that they eventually internalize the criteria it contains. This provides students with the means to read and critically evaluate history texts independently.

A final use of performance assessments relates to their communicative ability. Performance assessment helps Ivan portray the nature of student learning and the quality of his teaching. As described previously, the assessment is used regularly to communicate to students and their parents both the goals of instruction and the means to reach these goals. Seeing the benefits of performance assessment and the ability to describe in detail student learning and teacher accountability, teachers and administrators become supporters of performance assessments. These assessments demonstrate to parents and other school community members the complexity of learning and the success of teaching. The parents who fully understand the importance of their children developing as critical readers appreciate how the history performance assessment helps them move toward this ability. The detailed examples provided by performance assessment help parents understand the advantage of performance assessment relative to more traditional reading tests.

Roles and Responsibilities Related to Performance Assessment

Ivan has four priorities when using performance assessments, and each reflects his school district's commitment to performance assessment: (1) conducting reliable assessment using rubrics and scoring guides, (2) using rubrics and scoring guides as teaching tools in history, (3) using scoring guides and rubrics to help students learn self-assessment, and (4) helping others learn and appreciate the value of performance assessment. The teacher who demonstrates how performance assessments assist instruction, guide student work, and provide a rich measure of students' accomplishments converts parents to this manner of assessment. Each of these priorities creates a series of roles and responsibilities.

Useful performance assessments derive from the careful consideration of what exactly students do as they undertake a performance. As described earlier in this chapter, Ivan uses task analysis to create a detailed account of what students must know and do to perform assessment tasks. Teachers should check to determine the alignment of their instruction, learning standards, and the performance assessment and should be alert to the many different components of student performance. A performance assessment intended to describe students' content-area learning may also involve reading skills and strategies, prior knowledge, motivation, and social interactions. Should the performance assessment be assumed to measure only reading and content-area knowledge, the possibility of mismeasuring student achievement increases.

Performance assessment tasks and student performances are not necessarily transparent. For the student, parent, or teacher who does not understand how the score was derived, a score of 3 on a performance assessment is no less opaque than a score of 78 on a standardized, norm-referenced test. Students must have guidance in the process of conceptualizing and doing the performance so that they are working in the direction of the goal of the performance assessment. Ivan wants both the sample performances and anchor papers (i.e., papers that illustrate the essence of a particular score and are used by scorers to guide their work) to provide details to students about the differences in performance, or what determines a score of 4 and what determines a score of 1. In addition, the samples should help describe the "space between," or the zones in which students can work and develop their abilities toward a better performance. Thus, a key responsibility for Ivan is to learn to use rubrics, scoring guides, and example papers productively; to teach performance; and to help uncover the "black box," or the relatively unknown ways and means of assessment, for his students (Black & Wiliam, 1998, p. 139). He works with performance assessments across the school year and has developed the ability to teach *with* the assessment and not *to* it. That is, the rubrics and examples of student work become tools for teaching in Ivan's hands. As the performance assessment mirrors important classroom learning and achievement, teaching with the assessment is an important daily routine.

Performance assessments often assume student reading ability, rather than directly assessing this ability. Although some assessments, such as standardized reading tests, can provide information about the degree of development of students' decoding, word recognition, reading comprehension strategies, and vocabulary, performance assessments may take this development as a given. Thus, performance assessments most often require an existing level of reading proficiency for entry into the task. This special aspect of performance assessments in reading demands that Ivan place his students in performance situations where they can succeed at the reading work. Students asked to perform complex tasks when they do not have the appropriate reading ability will experience prolonged failure. This undesirable scenario reminds us that task analyses should be conducted to determine what a particular performance might demand of students. Ivan does not want to misunderstand the information that is provided by the performance assessment. The fact that the history performance assessment requires that students read at grade level is incentive for Ivan and his colleagues to keep a close watch on individual students' reading ability. This helps prepare students for the assessment and allows for the allocation of class time to help build reading skills and strategies that are prerequisites to adequate performance on the history reading performance assessment.

Over time, students who are involved with performance assessment should experience growth in their ability to self-assess their reading. Performance assessment rubrics provide a degree of transparency to the assessment and represent an opportunity for students to gradually take control of the assessment of their work.

Performance Assessment

The gradual assumption of control contributes to students' increased independence and success, which can stimulate motivation and engagement with reading (Barber & Klauda, 2020). Ivan provides opportunities to model, discuss, and demonstrate self-assessment for students in the daily routines of the classroom. As his students master using different cues to detect source text status, he introduces checklists that help students build toward independent and reliable routines for assessing their knowledge.

Ivan is fortunate to have colleagues with whom he can discuss and plan performance assessments. The performance assessment group uses a list of performance assessment goals and objectives (Moskal, 2003) that describes the responsibilities related to developing and using these assessments effectively:

1. The statement of goals and accompanying objectives should provide a clear focus for both instruction and assessment.
2. Both goals and objectives should reflect knowledge and information that is worthwhile for students to learn.
3. The relationship between a given goal and the objectives that describe that goal should be apparent.
4. All of the important aspects of the given goal should be reflected through the objectives.
5. Objectives should describe measurable student outcomes.
6. Goals and objectives should be used to guide the selection of an appropriate assessment activity. (p. 2)

In addition, the school district designates administrators' roles and responsibilities that contribute to an effective performance assessment program. Administrators help develop a detailed assessment framework in concert with assessment resources. Detailed guidelines for performance assessment development in relation to administrators' and teachers' roles and responsibilities are presented in Figure 5.3. Any school or school district that sees the value in performance assessment and is planning performance assessments as part of classroom practice needs to examine each of these points carefully. Without attention to each, the best intended performance assessment program may fail. If you are interested in examining performance assessments for use in your classroom or district, you can use the Guidelines for Developing and Using Performance Assessments reproducible form in the Appendix.

Performance assessments often represent a significant change for students, given the passive nature of many student–assessment relationships. Students must be involved with and invested in performance assessments. To do so, students must learn the assessment. The history performance assessments in Ivan's classroom present a set of responsibilities for his students. The responsibilities are framed

- Determine why the performance assessment is needed.

- Specify the important reading knowledge and outcomes that will be assessed by the performance assessment.

- Propose a specific performance that is composed of the reading knowledge and outcomes and conduct a task analysis.

- Based on the task analysis and in relation to research findings, specify the performance that allows students to demonstrate their learning and achievement.

- Specify the aspects of the performance that will receive assessment attention and enable the identification and determination of student success.

- Determine the degrees of students' performances that will be identified using rubrics.

- Set performance levels and different levels of proficiency in relation to instructional goals and standards.

- Use the performance assessment to evaluate student learning and work, perhaps using checklists geared to important (i.e., "must have") aspects of the task, using rating scales that represent the continuum of expected student performance. Note that piloting helps fine-tune scoring guides to best cover and represent what students might do.

FIGURE 5.3. Guidelines for developing and using performance assessments.

by students' developing understanding that performance assessments are helpful and that they hold no surprise in how students and their work will be evaluated. The students know that they must attend to the detailed rubrics to guide their work, that this attention provides guidance on the detail of good performance. For example, the students know that superior performances in the history performance assessment will involve the use of different cues to determine source text status and the evaluation of the text in relation to this determination. The students are familiar with taking responsibility for knowing where they are in a task and how they are doing. They are comfortable with the assessment, providing their own feedback to ongoing efforts. Ivan's students appreciate the control and agency that result from this involvement. They understand that responsibilities taken and met can bring tangible rewards.

Like students, parents should understand the special features of performance assessments and their benefits. When parents are introduced to a new assessment and learn of its benefits to their children, they can become supporters of the assessment (Shepard & Bliem, 1995). The development of appreciation for performance assessment and advocacy for it depend on the ability of the teacher and student to demonstrate its usefulness.

Reliability of Performance Assessment

The complexity of performance assessment creates a set of reliability issues. Teachers and students must attend to the special nature of student performances, work to develop consistent routines for evaluating performances, and be aware of the numerous types of confounds that are possible with performance assessments. Performance assessments may not restrict student answers to a single correct response. Rather, the assessments reflect the fact that student performance may be individualistic. Performance assessments set the parameters for appropriate student performances, but they do not dictate a single acceptable response. When there is more than one acceptable answer, response, or performance, it is imperative that Ivan and his colleagues develop the ability to reliably score them. Here, teachers' knowledge of the parameters of acceptable performance must be well developed. The scorer of a performance assessment must be able to interpret students' varied responses to a single prompt, accommodate variations on a theme, and consistently evaluate these diverse responses in relation to a scoring rubric.

There are potential confounds in a performance assessment. Performance assessments, by definition, demand performances. We must be clear about what skills, strategies, and knowledge are involved in student performances so that we can anticipate how student work related to reading may influence the performance. For example, a performance assessment that requires students to write an account of history based on their understanding of primary and secondary source texts introduces writing ability into the performance. A laboratory procedure that requires students to read instructions and then perform a series of measures using a balance beam involves both mathematical ability and fine motor skills. The creation of a diorama to portray what a student learns from reading about the culture of the Iroquois involves a creative, artistic component. Each of these performances not only demands successful reading but also engages other aspects of students' learning and ability. In each case, our ability to identify and anticipate the non-reading aspects of a performance assessment will provide the opportunity to evaluate students' performances in an accurate and useful manner and contribute to the reliability of the assessment. (For more on this issue, see the Reading Assessment Snapshot, "Confounds in Reading Assessment," at the end of Chapter 7.)

Validity of Performance Assessment

Effective performance assessment programs result from the careful alignment of standards, the curriculum, and assessment. Performance assessments offer the possibility of a rich representation of a construct and related student learning. For example, when we determine that reasoning about the trustworthiness of a particular history text and its author is important, we must invest in assessment that accurately describes the effectiveness of our teaching and students' learning. A performance assessment allows us to create a situation in which students can demonstrate their learning in close relationship and alignment with the construct of reading as a historian. In contrast, we would be hard-pressed to make such inferences from multiple-choice assessment items. The ability of the performance assessment to honor the construct of student learning provides the possibility of attaining high construct validity.

Earlier in this chapter, we examined rubrics, scoring guides, and sample performances. We determined that they can serve as tools of teaching, learning, and assessment. The close proximity of teaching and learning to assessment is a hallmark of performance assessment. When Ivan's students use the rubric to guide their independent work and when he teaches critical history reading strategies in relation to the rubric, these important classroom routines anticipate the end-of-unit performance assessment. The assessment tasks that students engage in to demonstrate learning are the very tasks that they have been engaged in as part of the learning process. The performance assessment's rubric and sample performances serve as a scaffold and superstructure for learning, and when assessment is this involved in teaching and learning, ecological validity is high.

SUMMARY

Performance assessments are especially effective in describing how students use reading within the content domains of school learning. Performance assessments reflect the complexity of learning and using knowledge in school and anticipate students' uses and applications of reading beyond school. These are two of the reasons for the investment in performance assessments shown by curricular and assessment reform efforts (e.g., CCSSO & NGA, 2010; Texas Education Agency, 2017). Effective performance assessments reflect a clear and detailed understanding of the things that we would like students to learn and do. This understanding is established through consultation with relevant research and task analyses that promote detailed understanding of proposed student performances.

Performance assessment can promote excellence in teaching because it presumes our attention to important curricular goals and a detailed understanding of how to reach those goals. Performance assessments come with user's guides, or rubrics, that present students and teachers with clear goals and paths for attaining those goals. Rubrics provide a means for scoring performance assessments in a consistent manner in relation to students' complex learning. Rubrics also provide a means for making transparent our curricular and assessment goals. Teachers can use rubrics during instruction because they help direct attention to important learning goals. Teachers also establish consistent and reliable scoring of student performances with rubrics.

The promise of performance assessment is accompanied by different challenges. Performance assessment demands teacher and student involvement in assessment that may be unprecedented. Although performance assessments have the potential to measure and describe student growth in complex reading tasks, they must be supported by substantial commitments of school resources. We must complement our understanding of how to do a performance assessment well with the sustained commitment of resources that promote the development and use of successful performance assessment programs.

Enhancing Your Understanding

1. Identify important school performances that may be the focus of a performance assessment in relation to your personal goals for students and state and district goals.

2. Conduct a task analysis of your proposed performance assessment. What is demanded of students? What types of reading behavior are expected? What related behaviors, such as writing, creating, and discussing, are also involved?

3. Develop a rubric that delineates at least three different levels of student achievement on a selected performance.

4. Create a lesson that focuses on how students can use performance assessment rubrics to learn to self-assess their reading and reading-related work.

Reading Assessment Snapshot
ADVOCATING FOR ASSESSMENT

Advocacy for reading assessment is important because high-quality assessments do not always find their way into classrooms. For example, many reading assessments require that students answer simple multiple-choice comprehension questions. This represents a level of familiarity and comfort for many who use assessments, but it may also lead to reading assessment conducted by habit rather than by informed choice. Thus, the most appropriate reading assessment for measuring student and teacher accomplishments may be overlooked. When a new reading assessment can contribute valuable information, we need to advocate for such assessments. It's important to match 21st-century learning goals with 21st-century assessments!

The advocacy process presents an opportunity to educate those whose support is needed to implement assessment change: parents, administrators, and others in the school community who have the voice and energy to advocate for change. This process may be difficult when we deal with assessments and rationales that are firmly entrenched. However, our advocacy may be welcomed. Parents who learn that performance and portfolio assessments serve the dual purpose of describing their children's achievement while supporting it may be enthusiastic in their support of new assessments. Administrators who understand that a new reading inventory provides detailed, immediately useful information that helps to both support and describe student growth will support the reading inventory.

Detailed knowledge of the different types of assessment and clear communication of their strengths and weaknesses is required to advocate for a new reading assessment. Advocacy succeeds when we are able to describe how the advocated-for assessment represents an improvement over—or an addition to—the existing assessments. The requirements of advocacy must be anticipated and included in any plan that seeks to engage the school community and change an existing program, implement a new program, or maintain a successful one. Advocacy is a critical part of a thriving reading assessment program.

CHAPTER 6

High-Stakes Reading Tests

Tests are high stakes when their results are used to make important educational decisions. The power and pervasiveness of these tests are matched by the controversies related to their use and intended and unintended consequences. Current high-stakes tests focus on cognitive skills and strategies that are important components of students' reading success. High-stakes tests are the coin of the realm, and test scores are the most frequently used vocabulary to describe student and school reading achievement.

A BRIEF HISTORY OF HIGH-STAKES TESTS

The phenomenon of high-stakes testing is more than a century old. The creators of the first high-stakes tests wanted to create a means to rapidly sort test takers into groups based on their scores. Early large-scale tests were intended to help identify "slow learners" in the general student population and place them with appropriate instruction. Tests were perceived by some as contributing to a just and efficient society, based on the premise that scores could help determine students' future vocation and employment. Large-scale testing became commonplace for college admission and the sorting of military personnel, and this testing had high-stakes consequences: determining whether one could attend college, or one's role in the armed forces.

The past 70 years are marked by increased large-scale testing of students. These tests are most often used to give a general description of student reading achievement at the school, district, and state levels. Government initiatives, including NCLB and the CCSS, require more frequent testing and testing at all grade levels.

In the 1960s, the inception of the National Assessment of Educational Progress marked the beginning of regular, nationwide assessment of students' reading achievement (Hamilton et al., 2002). The NAEP, also called "the Nation's Report Card," is administered to representative samples of 4th-, 8th-, and 12th-grade students to describe reading achievement in the United States. NAEP results allow for a comparison of students' reading scores and for examining trends in reading achievement across the years. NAEP results describe reading achievement in relation to students' gender, ethnicity, and socioeconomic status.

Concurrent with the development of the NAEP, many states developed minimum competency tests, which are administered in later grades and used to determine if students have attained a basic reading level (Supovitz, 2009). In 1983, *A Nation at Risk: The Imperative for Educational Reform* (National Commission on Excellence in Education, 1983) portrayed schools in the United States as severely deficient in preparing students to succeed. The alarmist tone of this publication provided policy makers with a rationale for increased individual testing of students.

The report contributed to the popular perception that students' reading test scores are a direct reflection of teacher and school quality, and that more testing leads to better schooling. The NAEP (to provide general descriptive data on reading achievement), statewide testing (to describe student achievement at the elementary, middle school, and high school levels), minimum competency testing (to pinpoint failing students and demonstrate teacher and school accountability), and accounts of the dire state of student reading in the United States all contributed to increases in the use of high-stakes reading tests (Afflerbach, 2002b).

If this was not enough, school accountability movements value single, high-stakes test scores as the trustworthy measure of students' reading achievement. The mandated testing of reading in grades 3 through 8, required by NCLB to demonstrate adequate yearly progress, furthers the use of high-stakes tests in reading assessment. Concurrently, international comparisons of student achievement, accomplished with tests such as the Programme for International Student Assessment (Organisation for Economic Co-operation and Development, 2021), are gaining in popularity and influence. Tests developed in relation to the CCSS (CCSSO & NGA, 2010) are intended to assess students' comprehension of text and higher-order thinking skills. Due to a host of factors, the last 40 years have seen an unprecedented increase in the use of high-stakes testing of reading (Kober et al., 2008). A study conducted by the Council of Great City Schools (Hart et al., 2015) determined that students were administered more than 112 tests, on average, from the start of formal schooling through grade 12, and that the average time devoted to testing in eighth grade—the grade in which testing time was highest—was 4.22 days. The study also found no correlation between the amount of time spent testing students and their reading scores on the NAEP.

The use of tests is also increasing in the early grades. These tests focus on aspects of reading related to phonemic awareness, phonics use, letter-naming speed, nonsense-word pronunciation, fluency, and knowledge of vowels and consonants. The results of these tests are often used for screening and placement, as in Response to Instruction, so that children might receive instruction appropriate to their levels of reading development. However, professional groups that advocate for young children question the developmental appropriateness of such tests for particular children (International Reading Association, 1999; National Association for the Education of Young Children & National Association of Early Childhood Specialists in State Departments of Education, 2003; National Council of Teachers of English, 2000).

CONTROVERSIES WITH HIGH-STAKES READING TESTS

The use of high-stakes tests in reading is both strongly supported and strongly resisted. Why do high-stakes tests enjoy such popularity, and why do some people place great faith in them, while others mistrust them? First, many people believe that high-stakes tests treat all students fairly. Under typical standardized testing conditions, no student receives preferential treatment. The possibility of teacher bias and teacher favoritism entering into the act of assessment is minimized. However well a test achieves a sameness of treatment of each student, we should not confound that with the fact that students in high-stakes testing situations are different. Students' lives at home and in school, opportunities for test preparation, familiarity with testing, and familiarity with the language of testing all vary. We should not make the erroneous assumption that a standardized test levels the playing field for all students because no test can do so.

A second reason for the popularity of high-stakes testing is the belief that tests are scientific. The majority of high-stakes reading tests are created with considerable expenditures of time and effort. The development teams for high-profile, high-stakes tests, including most popular commercial tests of reading and many statewide reading tests, often consist of trained and experienced measurement professionals whose sole task is to create tests. (I note that there are recent examples of high-stakes test items whose lineage and connection to such expertise is not apparent. Such items can be found by using a search engine to locate *critique of reading test questions*). Test development team members specialize in locating or creating suitable reading passages, developing test items, reviewing passages and items for potential bias, and choosing items based on their ability to discriminate among readers. Most tests exhibit rigor in relation to psychometric formulas and guidelines. Through adherence to what are for most people abstract notions of validity and reliability, tests create an aura of science as being rational, logical, and inscrutable. Tests have the ability to reduce and summarize the complexities of reading to single raw scores and percentile rankings, and in doing so, tests appear almost magical (Afflerbach, 2002b).

In addition, test scores are the frequently used outcome in "scientific" studies of reading. Experimental research designed to investigate reading instruction effectiveness uses test scores as the primary, and often only, measure of students' reading development and achievement. Test scores are the dependent measure in many studies, figuring largely in meta-analyses of reading program success and in the derivation of effect sizes attributable to instructional programs. Thus, the means to "proving" that a reading program is effective involves comparing high-stakes test scores. This insinuates high-stakes reading tests as the arbiter of reliable judgments related to reading achievement. Related, the science-of-reading evidentiary base rests solely on test scores.

Finally, high-stakes tests are familiar. There are few adults who have not experienced firsthand testing in schools. Throughout elementary, middle, and high school, high-stakes tests have been part of our lives. That our current generation of students receives at least as much standardized testing as we did is unsurprising. Testing appears natural, a core experience of schooling, given our assessment traditions. The familiarity of high-stakes tests contributes to their ongoing popularity and often unquestioned acceptance of their use and power.

It is clear from the current debate around high-stakes reading tests that many educators would not make these tests their first choice in reading assessment. Given this fact, why are they used so frequently in schools? To explore this question more deeply, we must consider reading assessment in the context of U.S. society. Teachers and students are largely left out of the educational policy-making process that mandates standardized, high-stakes reading assessments. Teachers are rarely consulted about the types of reading assessment that would best serve their purposes. An example of this lack of teacher input into high-stakes testing initiatives can be found in the passage of NCLB, which was supported in the U.S. Senate by a vote of 91 to 8. This legislation demands that each student be tested in reading for six consecutive years (grades 3 through 8), as if there was not enough testing taking place prior to the passage of NCLB. The tests and their results are intended to communicate adequate yearly progress and to hold teachers and schools accountable.

In contrast, it is possible that politicians, business leaders, and the general public too often focus on test-based accountability without full accounting (and full funding) of the educational programs that would help schools help students become better readers (Berliner & Biddle, 1995; Kohn, 2000, 2015). Is it also possible that high-stakes test results are used to deflect attention (and responsibility) toward schools and away from the greater society of which schools are a part? For example, nearly 38 million people live in poverty in the United States (Shrider & Creamer, 2023). The U.S. Census Bureau (Shrider & Creamer, 2023) set the poverty level for a family of four at $30,000 (annual income). Children of poverty often want for the nutrition, health care, personal safety, reading materials, and models of literacy that help prepare and support them for school success (Bhattacharya, 2016; Moore et al., 2009). That an economic and political system cannot help provide, or guarantee, these things for every child may be considered by some a failure of that system. By this standard, society in general could be assigned a failing grade for neglecting to support the reading development of all students.

The designation of any reading assessment as "high stakes" should cause us to pause and reflect. Who is assigning that label, and what are the high stakes when it comes to teaching and learning reading? From my perspective, an assessment that has the potential to contribute to students' reading development should be considered high stakes.

For example, our knowledge of students' interests and hobbies, gained through classroom discussions or the use of an interest inventory, can help us guide students to recreational reading choices that contribute to increased motivation for reading. In turn, this may contribute to increased reading fluency, content-area knowledge development, and student self-perception as a successful reader. Likewise, we may determine that a reader is struggling with a *cl–* consonant blend based on our ability to accurately observe and record oral reading miscues during diagnostic reading instruction. We help the student become adept and confident in using the *cl–* blend using our assessment knowledge. This may have a further effect of boosting the student's self-efficacy. In addition, our assessments can describe students' motivation and engagement, metacognition, and attributions for their reading performance. This certifies our work as high-stakes assessment. The point here is that our focus must be on reading assessment that has consequential, positive outcomes for our students. If we regularly ask the question, "What are the high stakes related to this assessment?," we will be in the position to make the most of the assessments we use. In any case, the designation of a reading assessment as high stakes should cause us to scrutinize the assessment for the usefulness of the information it may provide.

CHARACTERISTICS OF HIGH-STAKES READING TESTS

High-stakes reading tests are exceedingly familiar to most adults and children. As adults, some of us can reflect on experiences with tests from our student careers. These include teachers' admonitions to sleep well the night before the test, eat a good breakfast, and have strong fingers for keyboarding (or two no. 2 sharpened pencils). We listened carefully to the instructions as the teacher read them. We worked quietly and independently. As we worked through the test, the teacher provided updates on the time elapsed and the time left. We encountered a stop sign when we came to the end of a section. Upon finishing, we submitted our answers and were praised for our hard work.

Reading assessments that match the most popular conceptualization of high-stakes assessments in reading often share the characteristics of being standardized, norm referenced, and administered to large groups of students at a particular grade level. These tests are typically composed of a series of short reading passages accompanied by multiple-choice items that are machine-scored with occasional short fill-in or constructed-response items. In addition, these tests may contain vocabulary items that require the test taker to determine word meanings in isolation and as they occur embedded in text. The arrival of tests related to the CCSS and independent state standards brings some change. Longer reading passages, multiple passages, multimodal texts, and both multiple-choice and constructed-response items are necessary for these tests to exhibit construct validity and allegiance to such standards.

Standardization of Tests and Norm Referencing

High-stakes reading tests are standardized; they are intended to be administered to all student test takers under the same conditions. Sireci (2004) notes, "The idea behind standardization is to keep the measurement instrument and observation conditions constant so that any differences observed reflect true individual differences, rather than measurement artifacts" (p. 7). Standardization conditions typically include time allowed to take the test (i.e., each student has the same amount of time to complete the test) and a scripted interaction between the administrator of the test (sometimes the classroom teacher) and the students. Certain students with special needs may receive accommodations during high-stakes testing. (For more information on accommodation in assessment, see Chapter 7.)

It is assumed that students will take the test in an environment that is quiet, well lit, of appropriate temperature, and free from distractions. Each student test taker interacts with test items that are identical or psychometrically determined to be of similar focus and difficulty. No talking is allowed, nor are students' questions during testing regarding the form, process, and content of the test. A teacher's response to a student's question would invalidate the standardization of the test. These procedures and regulations are regarded by many as proof that all students are treated the same when taking the standardized high-stakes test.

The majority of high-stakes reading tests are norm referenced, or developed in relation to a sample, norming population of students. The tests are developed to portray students' reading achievement scores in relation to one another. In the test development phase, pilot versions of the reading test are given to sample groups of students who are demographically representative of the general student population. Based on these students' performances in pilot testing, particular scores are assigned places along a normal curve distribution. This practice allows test results to be reported as both raw scores and percentile rankings, and for students to be rank ordered. It is important to note that one student's performance on the test influences the characterization of another student's performance. In contrast, a small proportion of high-stakes reading tests are criterion referenced and mastery oriented: Students' performances are scored in relation to a criterion task. With criterion-referenced testing, students' scores are representative of reaching a particular performance level in the reading test task and are not contingent on the scores of other students who are taking the test.

Test Contents and Formats

The content and format of high-stakes reading tests are predictable. Vocabulary is a staple of reading tests, as it correlates highly with reading achievement and general intelligence. Separate vocabulary items include words of varied frequency and difficulty. The vocabulary words included on high-stakes reading tests are often chosen in relation to their relative frequency of occurrence in written language, and the more difficult vocabulary items focus on words that are not commonplace. Other vocabulary test items focus on words that are central to understanding and passage comprehension. Particular vocabulary words may be chosen more for their ability to discriminate among test takers and allow for rank ordering students than for their importance in the reader's understanding of a passage. These vocabulary items may focus on the usage and meaning of words as contextualized in a particular passage.

Comprehension items typically measure students' literal and inferential reading comprehension. Students read the passages, which may or may not be available for students to access as they respond to questions. Text availability status influences whether the test is focusing on readers' comprehension, memory, search ability, or some combination of these. The comprehension items allow for making inferences about how well students understand the reading passages included on the test. Some tests include items that focus on students' critical reading comprehension, but this enterprise is made difficult by tests' relatively short reading passages, a lack of reading passages with content that supports asking truly critical questions, and the time allotted for reading. Items may be constructed for students to demonstrate their ability to determine key aspects of comprehension, including identifying main ideas, themes, and author purposes; summarizing text; determining supporting details; and making inferences. Many reading comprehension items are multiple choice or short constructed response, which often restricts the ability of tests to tap into complex comprehension processes. Such processes include those at work when students bring considerable prior knowledge to the reading act, read more than one passage on the same topic and must synthesize an understanding across texts, and engage in critical and evaluative reading tasks.

The advent of complex reading standards is accompanied by increasingly complex assessment items and tasks. Consider the following fourth-grade standard and the type of assessment necessary to gauge student progress at the standard:

CCSS.ELA-LITERACY.RI.4.6

Compare and contrast a firsthand and secondhand account of the same event or topic; describe the differences in focus and the information provided. (Common Core State Standards, 2024a)

Reading Passages on Tests

Until recently, the reading passages found on high-stakes tests were generally short, although the length and complexity of reading passages usually increases with the grade level of the test. Regardless of grade level, there may be a discrepancy between the type and length of passages that students read in and out of school and the average length of texts contained in the test. The texts on tests are generally of two types: narrative and expository, or informational. This duality of text type is intended to reflect the types of texts that students read in school. In the last decade, the percentage of expository text passages on many standardized reading tests has increased, reflecting the idea that students must become increasingly adept at constructing meaning from informational text as they progress through school (National Assessment Governing Board, 2023). There is increasing attention to a third text type, the hybrid text, reflecting the fact that students read texts that are not easily categorized as either narrative or expository, such as biographies. Other hybrid texts may be composed of integrated textual, graphic, or visual information, combining narrative and expository characteristics within a single text. Finally, tests may include online and hypertext reading experiences for students, in which the ability to find, select, comprehend, and use particular texts is assessed (Leu et al., 2016).

Test Items and Tasks

High-stakes reading tests typically use sets of multiple-choice items and brief constructed-response items to measure vocabulary and comprehension. Multiple-choice items have standard components, including prompts, distracters, and correct answers. Prompts are the questions, demands, or statements that require student thinking and responses. Distracters are plausible yet wrong responses that are provided to student readers in any multiple-choice item. Examples of multiple-choice items, brief constructed-response items, and extended constructed-response items are provided in Table 6.1. Multiple-choice items include a correct answer that is presented along with several incorrect answers. Other test items present students with questions that demand a student-constructed response. In general, constructed-response items are regarded as more demanding because they require the student to devise an answer rather than choose the correct answer from given alternatives.

Test items are typically sequenced in an easy-to-hard order. The items encountered earlier in a test are, in general, less challenging than those encountered later in the test. This ordering of items by difficulty is intended to provide more students with success experiences early in the test in order to support motivation and to decrease the number of students who experience failure early in the test. Item difficulty is established relative to other test items and particular levels of student reading achievement. Computer-adaptive testing allows for the sequencing of test passages, items, and tasks in relation to a student's ongoing performance on the test. For example, if a student obtains a perfect score on the first two reading passages, computer-adaptive testing may automatically revise the test so that the third reading passage is more challenging than had the student performed poorly on the first two passages. Or, a student who has struggled through the first two test items will next encounter an item that is relatively easier.

TABLE 6.1. **Sample High-Stakes Reading Test Items**

Test item	Sample question

Multiple-choice item with a prompt, a correct answer, and distracters	What year was the Jamestown Colony founded? (prompt)
	    A. 1577 (distracter)
	    B. 1607 (correct answer)
	    C. 1776 (distracter)
	    D. 1637 (distracter)

Brief constructed-response item	What was one reason that colonists sailed to what is now known as the Jamestown Colony? (The test form provides six lines for the student's response.)
Extended constructed-response item	Describe one theory for why the Jamestown colony ceased to exist and provide at least three details that support your response. (The test form provides 12 lines for the student's response.)

Scoring and Reporting of Tests

Scores may be reported as individual and group raw scores and percentile rankings. Raw scores represent the actual number that is assigned to an individual student's performance (or a school's or a state's average performance). Percentile rankings, a feature of norm-referenced tests, allow for raw scores to be represented in relation to a normal distribution curve. The raw score indicates the performance of the student in relation to the high-stakes test itself, whereas the percentile ranking indicates the performance of the student or a group of students in relation to other students. A score in the 57th percentile means that the test taker performed greater than or equal to 57% of all other students taking the test.

All high-stakes tests have a decided product orientation. This means that the information yielded by high-stakes tests, typically answers to questions, is one product of the student's reading and thinking processes. From these products, we must try to infer the processes that the student used to construct meaning. As is the case with all product assessment information, we must use what I refer to as backward inferencing to try to determine students' areas of strength and challenge in reading. In essence, we try to reconstruct the process of reading from a score to understand how the product, represented by the score, was created.

Testing and Technology

Technology informs promising aspects of high-stakes testing. First, a refinement in handwriting-recognition software and movement toward student keyboarding to respond to open-ended questions encourages test items that maintain ease of scoring while allowing for test items that demand complex responses. The development of more sophisticated means of machine scoring may contribute to items that better represent the kinds of questions (and related student thinking) that we want to ask in relation to reading. In the coming years, we may witness such beneficial changes to high-stakes testing items and their scoring.

CONSEQUENCES OF HIGH-STAKES READING TESTS

One of the greatest challenges in using high-stakes reading tests is to fully anticipate their consequences. For example, increased performance on high-stakes reading tests will earn a school more money in some school districts, while decreased performance will have the same effect in other districts. In some states, if a school does not meet adequate yearly progress targets for several years, students can move to other schools, including public and private charter schools. This effectively reduces the funding available to the school with low scores. In this section, note that I assign more negative consequences to the use of high-stakes tests because (1) they are mandated from outside the classroom; (2) they are hardly ever a teacher's first choice for a reading assessment that provides useful information; (3) most high-stakes tests reflect an outdated conceptualization of reading and how to measure it (i.e., short reading passages with a single, predetermined correct answer to be picked in a multiple-choice format); and (4) high-stakes tests may be clumsily paired with political rhetoric about the necessity for accountability, rhetoric unaccompanied by sufficient education funding levels to help schools approach nationwide standards of universal literacy (Afflerbach, 2002b).

Possible Positive Consequences of High-Stakes Testing

One positive aspect of high-stakes tests is that they can describe the performance of particular subgroups of students. This means that if we are interested in how students of different genders, ethnic groups, socioeconomic status, or geographical regions fare on a test, we can so designate the scores of students from these different groups, disaggregate these scores from all scores, and then analyze the disaggregated scores. We may determine that subgroups of students are performing well and that others are not as a result of using such disaggregation. For example, the NAEP determines that there is a significant and consistent gap between the reading achievement levels of poor students and other students. This finding might be used to argue for increased funding to support poor students. An example of how high-stakes test results can be disaggregated to provide comparisons between groups of students—in this case, eligibility for the National School Lunch Program, a proxy for socioeconomic status—is presented in Figure 6.1.

To the extent that we use this information to inform educational decision making, including school funding decisions, we may claim positive consequences from a test. The funding of reading instruction initiatives for particular groups of students who have demonstrated histories of underachieving (in comparison with other students) may contribute to their increased reading achievement.

High-stakes tests may also serve a large-scale diagnostic function. As tests are administered over the years, the results provide administrators with a regular and standardized description of some of a school district's reading and literacy program strengths and weaknesses. For example, high-stakes test results may demonstrate that a reading program helps students develop vocabularies of frequently used words but does not work as well in preparing students to determine the meaning of less common vocabulary as encountered in the complex texts. With this information, adjustments to the reading curriculum may be made at the school district level. In addition, an individual teacher's close attention to annual scores may show patterns of student achievement and suggest particular instructional foci related to the results and the use of particular reading instruction materials and

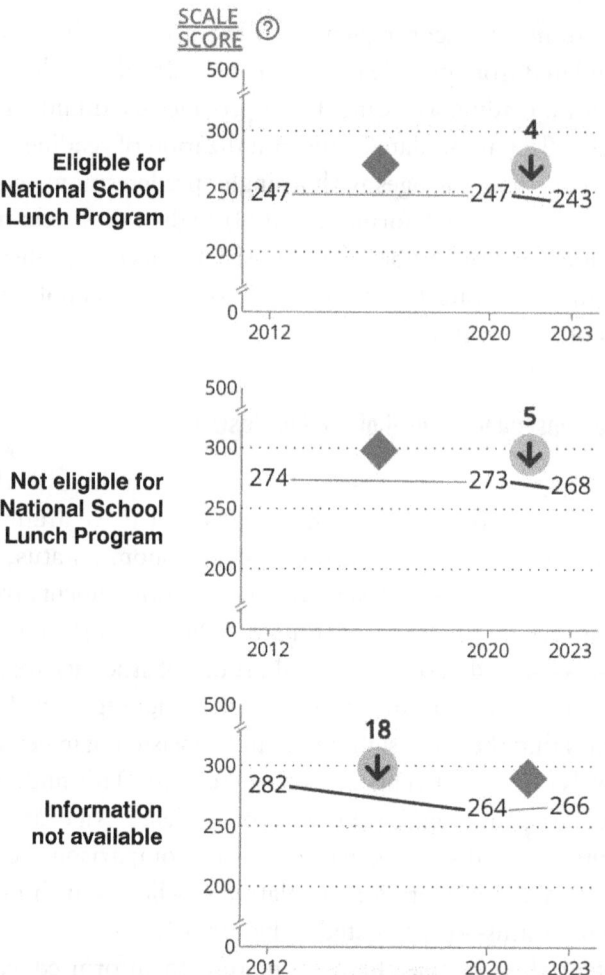

FIGURE 6.1. Example of disaggregated reading test results from the National Assessment of Educational Progress (2023).

procedures. Consistently high or low student test scores in vocabulary or comprehension can help teachers understand their instructional effectiveness and should signal programmatic strengths and weaknesses.

High-stakes tests may motivate students to do well in school prior to taking the tests. The inclination to work with good effort is increased for some students who know that a major test is awaiting them. However, students' motivations related to reading and testing are complex and emanate from different sources (Guthrie & Klauda, 2016). Tests also provide students with information on their reading achievement and their performance relative to others, and in this sense, tests may provide students an awareness of their accomplishment. Scoring high on a high-stakes test is a good experience for most students.

Community trust and support can be built through the sharing of high-stakes test results. Taxpayers, real estate agents and homebuyers, elected officials, and legislators pay attention to test scores. Given their prevalence and value, scores from such tests have considerable weight with many of those in the school community who are interested in student achievement. Yet, as we determine later in this section, one school's experience with the positive consequences of high-stakes test scores may be contrasted with another school's negative experiences and consequences.

High-stakes test scores can serve as a common vocabulary that is used in decisions related to grouping students and helping set goals for them. When students move from school to school, high-stakes test scores may be the single most stable measure of reading achievement. This is because grading practices, reading program emphases, and expectations for achievement vary greatly. Thus, entry into a new school and related initial placements can be helped with the common information provided by the standardized test score. Being standardized, there may be some degree of faith that these test scores mean similar things for each student. However, this faith must be tempered by the following questions: What does a single standardized, high-stakes reading test score actually mean? How much of the story of reading instruction quality and student achievement can a single high-stakes test score tell, and what other sources provide important information?

Possible Negative Consequences of High-Stakes Testing

Each of the potentially positive consequences of high-stakes testing can cut other ways. The notion that these tests provide diagnostic information about reading achievement and program quality can be countered with the argument that there is very little return of useful information on the massive investment of time and money that is spent on these tests. For each student who is motivated by a good test score to read more, there may be one whose motivation to read decreases because of low test scores. The trust and support of schools that may be a consequence of high-stakes tests in one community may contrast with suspicion and lack of support in another community. Finally, although standardized test scores provide a common vocabulary across school districts, the scores are limited in what they describe.

The possible negative consequences of using high-stakes tests are numerous, including effects on students and teachers, the reading curriculum, and student learning. Some students always do well on tests. In contrast, there are students who never do well on tests. These students are too familiar with the routine of their reading failure made public, as they struggle through hours of high-stakes testing. When a test is norm referenced, a large portion of students taking the test will be determined to be below average. A less able student's improvement in reading achievement, while substantial, may be reflected by a large change in percentile ranking (say, from 27% to 43%) but no change in the "below average" label. Test scores, be they percentile rankings or raw scores, are assigned to individual students, creating communities of haves and have-nots when it comes to reading achievement. It may be difficult for the accomplished reader to comprehend the threats to self-esteem and motivation (Wigfield & Eccles, 2000) for students whose continuing experience with high-stakes reading tests is negative. Yet, current testing practice guarantees that significant numbers of less accomplished readers will face threats to their self-efficacy and future willingness to read. Labels from test results are accompanied with myriad related consequences, such as lowered expectations, differential treatment in the reading classroom (Allington, 1983; Allington & Gabriel, 2016), and decreased perseverance for those labeled as low-achieving readers.

In classrooms everywhere, there is tremendous pressure to improve test scores, which leads to additional negative consequences. A reading curriculum may be chosen on the sole merit of being closely related to the content and form of the high-stakes reading test. In such cases, tests contribute to the constriction of reading curricula (Frederiksen, 1984; Parr, 2018). If the majority of standardized high-stakes reading tests were worth teaching to, this would not be an issue. The point is that most high-stakes tests have narrow foci on reading skills and strategies. These skills and strategies are important to reading, but by no means do the skills and strategies sum up to what is practiced and learned in a broad-based reading curriculum. Nor are they all that students need to succeed as readers. In addition to the negative consequence of high-stakes tests constricting the reading curriculum, they take considerable time away from teaching reading. For every school hour spent on reading test preparation, an hour is taken from the instructional day. Time given to practicing and administering tests is time that could be spent on pursuing diverse instructional goals related to reading. When schools devote time and effort to testing and preparing students to take tests, considerable sums of money are spent to do so. Initiatives to support testing take away from other, worthy initiatives. Money might be spent in other ways, including an enriched curriculum and teachers' professional development related to assessment (Stiggins & Conklin, 2002).

Teachers may suffer numerous negative consequences from high-stakes testing. First, teachers are often conflicted about the stance they must adopt in relation to the test and their students. Consider the teacher who does not endorse high-stakes testing but knows that his or her students must be adequately prepared to take such tests. Consider the teacher who has worked for years to develop an array of engaging reading instruction lessons and is forced to give them up to teach to a test. When testing concerns conflict with teacher professionalism, curricular decisions are made according to a test format rather than teachers' knowledge and prerogatives. A further consequence for teachers is that they prepare students to take the tests, administer the tests, and serve as the conduit to parents and others for test results. Thus, teachers serve a vital role in communicating and interpreting the results of high-stakes tests, whether or not they have faith in them. Each of these comprehensive and time-consuming tasks creates practical and ethical dilemmas for those teachers who do not fully endorse how high-stakes tests are constructed and used.

USEFULNESS OF HIGH-STAKES READING TESTS

The different members of a school community may have starkly different ideas of the usefulness of high-stakes assessments. A state legislator believes that tests provide all the necessary information related to how well schools and teachers are helping students develop as readers. In contrast, a classroom teacher is convinced that the same test consumes precious resources while yielding little instructionally useful information. The building principal appreciates the common language that test scores provide for communicating school progress but is concerned with the amount of time that mandated tests take from instruction. This section examines the usefulness of high-stakes reading tests from such diverse perspectives.

High-stakes tests are used as a tool for demonstrating accountability. Taxpayers pay taxes, taxes are used to fund schools, and schools are held accountable. In U.S. society, the primary means of teachers and schools demonstrating their accountability to audiences outside the school is to have students with good high-stakes test scores. The fact that high-stakes tests are standardized contributes to their use as a measure of reading achievement across states, districts, schools, and classrooms. A problem arises when we find accountability at cross-purposes. Imagine a school with a corps of accomplished administrators and teachers and students who have a history of achieving. Their high-stakes test scores are a consistent source of pride for the school and the community. Recent mandates at the national, state, and district levels result in nontrivial forced changes to reading instruction. New regulations require that significant blocks of time be dedicated to test preparation exercises for all students. The teachers and administrators in this school have a long tradition of accountability to their students—and to themselves as professionals. This attention to accountability is lived out each school day through the respect, caring, and attention to students' individual differences that characterize teaching and learning in successful schools. The imposition of test preparation, in the name of accountability, is in opposition to what the teachers believe is best for their students. There is a conflict in the use and usefulness of reading assessment.

High-stakes test results are used for making comparisons. Whenever high-stakes reading test scores are released in counties, school districts, and states, we find corresponding color-coded maps on the internet and in newspapers that take compilations of student scores and present them to the public. Blue-shaded schools did better than the yellow-shaded schools, which did better than the red-shaded schools. The comparison of schools and districts may be used by governmental agencies to provide funding for those schools, reward them in other ways, or take punitive action. The NAEP provides scores for different groups of students by geographic region, gender, ethnicity, and socioeconomic status (National Assessment Governing Board, 2023). In doing so, the NAEP can guide federal legislation and funding that is directed at helping groups who demonstrate consistent underachievement when compared with other groups. These comparisons are also conducted at international levels. The Programme for International Student Assessment and the Progress in International Reading Literacy Study (Mullis & Martin, 2015; Organisation for Economic Co-operation and Development, 2011, 2014) are conducted to compare the reading and literacy achievements of students across countries. International comparisons may be used to suggest that reading initiatives in particular countries are successful or needed.

Classroom teachers may use high-stakes reading test scores as one piece of evidence that describes student achievement and contributes to the decision-making processes of a talented reading teacher. In the meetings held to determine whether students would benefit from placement in a particular remedial reading or gifted and talented program, high-stakes test scores can have great influence because they are one form of reading assessment that most students have in common. In the extreme, reading test scores may supersede other important sources of information about a student's reading achievement.

ROLES AND RESPONSIBILITIES RELATED TO HIGH-STAKES READING TESTS

Many talented teachers and administrators resent the incursion of high-stakes tests into their classrooms and teaching routines. For these teachers, class time given to tests (above and beyond the time needed for administration) is folly. Test scores may misrepresent student and teacher accomplishments, yet scores are overused. I acknowledge that for high-stakes tests to change, advocates for change must be supported and have time to do this important work. Yet, working to change the high-stakes testing system will not immediately change the reality of testing for our current students. Thus, understanding roles and responsibilities is critical.

High-stakes tests bring with them an array of responsibilities that require our careful consideration. A first responsibility is for all involved in testing, including teachers and administrators, to become knowledgeable about the strengths and shortcomings of these tests. This knowledge serves several important purposes. It helps us determine our stance toward such tests: how we regard them, how we use them, and how they figure in the life of the classroom. When we are educated consumers of the results of high-stakes tests, we place ourselves in a more powerful position. Teachers' knowledge about these tests influences teaching and classroom environments. This knowledge allows us to interpret the test results and use them when appropriate. It also allows us to deal with the considerable intellectual and emotional challenges that high-stakes tests may present and should help our work as professionals around what are often conflicting sets of assessment issues and agendas.

A second responsibility for administrators and teachers is to educate others, including students and their parents, about the nature of high-stakes tests. Parents' knowledge is often anchored to their memories of taking tests, and media is a second source of information about high-stakes tests. These sources may combine to suggest to parents that test scores are the only measure of their children's reading achievement that matters. Here, our informed explanations of the strengths and limitations of high-stakes tests, especially in relation to other forms of reading assessment, will demonstrate to parents our professional knowledge. Our words may also influence parents' understanding of teaching and testing to the point where parents regularly seek the teacher's opinion on testing-related issues. Our ability as teachers to demonstrate a detailed understanding of high-stakes tests should gain us an appreciative audience when we describe the strengths and shortcomings of these tests, and their appropriate and inappropriate uses.

A third responsibility, test preparation, accompanies the influx of high-stakes tests (Popham, 1997). Teachers and administrators are responsible for determining the value that test preparation may provide, the way test preparation is conducted, and the parameters of ethical test preparation. Teachers must decide the amount of time, if any, that they are willing to take from the instructional day to devote to test preparation. In other cases, these decisions are imposed on teachers and students. Regardless of our personal position on high-stakes testing in reading, our students must take these tests. Students' scores on high-stakes tests matter in consequential ways, and we must communicate the importance of taking tests seriously to both students and parents.

If we believe that test preparation is suitable for our students, it is important to develop an understanding of the ways and means of effective test preparation. Popham (1991) provides guidelines for selecting test preparation materials and procedures that focus on common features of high-stakes tests. We can make the distinction between teaching *to* the test and teaching *about* the test. Appropriate test preparation may include helping students learn how tests work, how test items are constructed, and how to manage limited time frames that characterize most testing. In addition, teachers are responsible for helping students develop a serious approach to test taking. We must never underestimate the influence that our attitudes toward high-stakes tests may have on our student test takers. Students who respect their teachers take them at their word. If we make ambivalent comments about an upcoming high-stakes reading assessment and students do not take it seriously, we may then fail at the task of being responsible teachers, undercutting the effort and attention that students might otherwise give.

A key responsibility for teachers is to provide thorough preparation for students prior to any high-stakes test encounter. This should serve nervous students well. With high stakes may come high anxiety. When a test is featured on the news, when parents talk about it at home, and when the teacher spends considerable class time helping students prepare to take tests, test anxiety is increased for some students. Certain students have considerable anxiety about tests throughout their school careers. A reading test performance debilitated by test anxiety is an unworthy source of information from which to make important educational decisions.

RELIABILITY OF HIGH-STAKES READING TESTS

Tests must be accurate and consistent in their measure of student work. We want all assessments to be designed and conducted so that they place students in the best (and an equitable) position to demonstrate their reading achievement. Developers of tests should ascertain that a test does not favor a particular student or group of students. Test developers must determine that no student or group of students is privileged by a particular reading passage, a specific type of reading test question or item, or the directions that are read to or by students at the beginning of the administration of a high-stakes test. Each of these components of testing can have a subtle or strong influence on student performance and test scores, which renders the test results unreliable. We must be sure that what is measured in a reading test represents students' achievement in reading.

The content of passages used in reading tests represents a continual challenge for test developers. These passages contain content that may be closely or remotely related to students' prior knowledge. Should a reading passage on a high-stakes test contain material that is familiar to some students, they will have an unfair advantage over those students who are unfamiliar with the material, independent of reading achievement level. As noted in Chapter 4, some students may be able to answer questions correctly without having read or understood the reading passage. This phenomenon is known as passage independence, or the ability to answer assessment items correctly without reading. Conversely, the selection of reading passages that contain material with which few or no students are familiar also poses a problem because we know that prior knowledge plays an important role in constructing meaning from text (van den Broek et al., 2016; Wright et al., 2022). This fact of reading makes it difficult to account for the prior knowledge of content that some students possess (and others lack) for a particular reading passage on a high-stakes test, which directly influences the reliability of the tests.

As noted earlier, the standardization procedures for test administration can reduce or eliminate certain types of bias, contributing to a test's increased reliability. However, the notion that standardization of any assessment removes all extraneous factors from the testing situation is misguided. Would we claim that a student who lost sleep the night before a high-stakes test because of test anxiety is on an equal footing with other students who had a relatively peaceful night's sleep? Would we expect two students of similar reading achievement levels who have great and little prior knowledge of trains, respectively, to perform similarly on reading comprehension questions that follow a passage about trains?

VALIDITY OF HIGH-STAKES READING TESTS

High-stakes tests can be examined through several validity lenses, and in this section, we consider ecological, construct, and concurrent validity. Ecological validity helps us consider the relationship between what students are asked to read and do on high-stakes reading tests and the reading and reading-related work that is typically done in the classroom or at home. The nature of reading on high-stakes tests is rarely representative of the types of reading done in school—unless, of course, the reading curriculum consists of the relatively short texts and multiple-choice questions that compose test preparation curricula.

It is important to determine the relationship of test reading to typical classroom reading. One could argue that the steady diet of high-stakes tests makes students quite familiar with what to expect on tests. Indeed, most students have considerable prior knowledge and experience that can influence their performance on tests. The inevitability and familiarity of tests, however, do not create an argument for their validity or continued use. When the content and form of classroom reading and reading instruction differ greatly from the nature of the test that is intended to measure learning, we must question the ecological validity of the test. High-stakes tests that consist of short reading passages and a preponderance of multiple-choice items will be challenged by the following questions, related to the regular classroom and thus ecological validity:

- Do students regularly read entire chapters, documents, or books?
- Do students do so over substantial periods of time?
- Are students encouraged to read critically?
- Are students encouraged to question the author or critique the style of a text and the apparent trustworthiness of the information it contains?

- Do students regularly engage in higher-order thinking in relation to texts and tasks in the classroom?
- Are students reading multiple texts, from which they are expected to synthesize information?
- Are students reading complex texts and performing related, complex tasks?
- Do students read to use what is understood for solving problems?

Construct validity of a test is a judgment of how well the test reflects and measures reading and what are agreed upon as the important areas of reading development. These may include the five target areas identified by the National Reading Panel report (National Institute of Child Health and Human Development, 2000) as well as the higher-order thinking that is associated with "21st-century skills"—the ability to question the author, determine the truthfulness of sources, and monitor one's reading progress are equally important reading abilities (McNamara & Magliano, 2009; Muspratt et al., 1997; Pressley & Afflerbach, 1995). We are the beneficiaries of considerable research that continues to describe the complexity of what it means to read and student development as a reader. Research descriptions of reading continually evolve, and we happen to know much about the cognitive, metacognitive, motivational, affective, and prior knowledge factors that influence each and every act of reading (Afflerbach, 2022; Alexander, 2005; Guthrie et al., 2013). Our knowledge of reading is cumulative, with new research findings adding to our existing understandings of reading.

It follows that reading research evidence should influence how we think about the construct of reading. This construct—representing state-of-the-art accounts of the complex thing we call reading—should guide the development of standards for learning. In turn, standards for reading should influence a reading curriculum. And, this curriculum should be honored by reading assessments that are closely aligned with the curriculum, standards, and constructs.

How do high-stakes assessments relate to our current understandings of the construct of reading? We could conduct a familiarity test to begin to answer this question: To what degree does the high-stakes test used in your classroom this year, whether elementary school, middle school, or high school, resemble the high-stakes tests you took while in the same grade in school?

Scrutiny of a test's construct validity often leads to the determination of partial validity. Tests may focus on lower-level reading skills and strategies (e.g., they help us understand how well a student decodes words or establishes literal and lower-level inferential comprehension) but lack items that focus on more complex reading and higher-order thinking (Afflerbach et al., 2011). We are at an important juncture in the history of high-stakes reading tests. Many high-stakes reading tests continue to represent reading as information processing. Students read short passages and are expected to give back information when answering questions. Passages are chosen with the expectation that students' prior knowledge for the text content is fairly distributed: Either almost everyone knows something about the text topic, or only a few know a little about the topic. This consideration of students' prior knowledge for text content is done with the good intention of trying to ensure that no student or group of students is privileged due to knowledge of content brought to the test. Yet, this very practice works against the fact that reading comprehension occurs when readers combine text information with relevant prior knowledge (Pressley & Afflerbach, 1995). Our current knowledge of the constructive nature of reading comprehension is not fully represented in most high-stakes reading tests.

In contrast, recently developed tests require that students read increasingly complex texts and perform increasingly complex tasks related to that reading. These tests, along with other tests developed in relation to state and Common Core standards, are a step toward bringing high-stakes tests in better alignment with the current understanding of reading. A result is better construct validity.

Construct validity of a reading test may be influenced by the economics of testing. For example, requiring students to construct their own responses to a reading assessment prompt allows for potentially detailed information from which we may infer students' reading accomplishments and achievements. Yet, students' written responses are difficult to score by machine, and hiring people to score reading test items is an expensive proposition relative to the machine scoring of tests. To sacrifice the quality of high-stakes tests by ruling out the use of multiple, longer text passages and extended constructed-response items because of their scoring costs may seem to some indefensible assessment practice—in effect guaranteeing only a partial read of our students' accomplishments.

Finally, concurrent validity influences the nature and popularity of high-stakes reading tests. Most of these tests are developed by for-profit companies. Given the strong tradition of using standardized, multiple-choice reading tests, commercial publishers of tests must always anticipate their market and what will sell. Publishers must present their reading tests as dependable and useful instruments and must make their test sales pitch in particular social and political contexts. In these contexts, familiarity is often more important than innovation. The producers of high-stakes reading tests must explain how their tests measure important aspects of reading and also demonstrate a connection to the current array of high-stakes tests. This leads to the practice of using concurrent validity to demonstrate a test's value. By this, we mean the degree to which a new reading test correlates with or resembles an existing reading test. High concurrent validity between two tests indicates that they measure similar aspects of reading. However, high concurrent validity also means that a new test resembles existing tests rather than reflecting our most recent and detailed understandings of reading.

SUMMARY

High-stakes reading tests are omnipresent. The results of these tests serve many audiences and purposes. Often, test scores are used as *the* single indicator of student achievement, teacher effectiveness, and school accountability. These tests are accompanied by many possible consequences. Some are intended, whereas others are not. Positive consequences from the use of high-stakes reading test scores may include increased funding and the establishment of a common reading measure for most students. That some unintended negative consequences occur with high-stakes reading tests should be unsurprising because most of these tests are mandated and imposed from outside the classroom. This creates a situation in which accomplished classroom teachers must adapt to the high-stakes system in an effort to help their students demonstrate their reading achievement, regardless of the teachers' professional knowledge and values related to the tests.

Enhancing Your Understanding

1. Inventory the high-stakes tests used in your school and create a list of the strengths and weaknesses.

2. Describe how high-stakes tests offer one perspective on reliability in assessment.

3. Determine what teachers can do to help prepare their students to take high-stakes tests, paying particular attention to acceptable and unacceptable test preparation practices.

4. Develop an account of how present-day testing practices influence your teaching and your students' learning.

5. Describe how high-stakes tests fail to measure all that is important in your students' development as readers.

6. Develop an account of how well the high-stakes tests used in your district describe student achievement in relation to the mechanics of reading and higher-order thinking.

Reading Assessment Snapshot
CONSISTENT ASSESSMENT IN SCHOOLS

In schools, instructional programs across the content areas vary. We should expect this—earth science has different learning goals than American history. A related result is variation in the types of assessment used, and it is unsurprising that students encounter inconsistent assessment materials and procedures.

There are considerable benefits that emerge from reading assessment that is consistent across grades and content areas. First, the consistency provides teachers with many opportunities to practice and develop expertise in classroom-based assessment. For example, if performance assessments and rubrics are used in classrooms from kindergarten through high school and across content areas, students and teachers have repeated opportunities to become familiar with the nature of assessment. Second, consistent assessments help teachers understand what their students accomplished in previous grades and classrooms. This affords an understanding of the students' strengths and needs and the appropriate instructional focus. Third, students benefit from the consistency of assessment, which helps them practice how to become independent readers and learners. For example, working with consistent forms of checklists (e.g., What is your goal for reading? Did the author provide evidence to support this claim?) helps students learn the common aspects of reading and self-assessment across content areas. Students are not required to spend extra time learning new approaches to assessment at each grade and in each content area, except when needed.

If you are interested in examining the degree to which assessments in your school or district are consistent across grades, or consistent across content areas, you can use the Creating Consistent Approaches to Reading Assessment across Grade Levels and Content Areas reproducible form in the Appendix.

CHAPTER 7

Assessment and Accommodating English Learners and Special-Needs Students

Accommodation in assessment is intended to help students best demonstrate their reading development and achievement. Students who are ELs, have learning disabilities, or have special needs, among others, may benefit from accommodation, or modification of the reading assessments they take. This chapter focuses on the different types of assessment accommodation, the students who benefit from accommodations, and the contexts in which accommodations are considered, developed, and given.

As defined by the Board on Testing and Assessment of the National Research Council (Koenig & Bachman, 2004), *accommodation* is "the general term for any action taken in response to a determination that an individual's disability or level of English language development requires a departure from established testing protocol" (p. 1). I note that this definition applies to accommodation in standardized testing situations. For our purposes, accommodation includes all relevant reading assessments and is not limited to tests. Different types of reading assessment, ranging from reading inventories to our classroom questions to high-stakes tests, may be modified in relation to students' needs. The guiding principle is that reading assessment accommodation helps students perform in assessment situations to the best of their ability, which results in useful assessment information. Accommodation helps us get the best return on our assessment efforts. The hoped-for result is reliable and valid information that helps us best understand accommodated students' reading development.

ACCOMMODATION IN ASSESSMENT

There are three general types of assessment accommodation. The first is accommodation based on the needs of students who are English learners, and the second is based on the needs of students with learning disabilities. The third type of accommodation relates to how teachers might use their assessment materials and procedures to best accommodate all students, as accommodating student differences is a hallmark of fairness.

Accommodating English Learners

English learners often receive assessment accommodations. According to the National Center for Education Statistics (2024a, 2024b), 5 million students (10.3 percent of the entire public school student population) were English learners in 2022. The percentage of public school students who were ELs ranged from 0.7 percent in West Virginia to 20.1 percent in Texas. I note that the terms used to describe students who are learning to read in English are numerous, and not without controversy. The federal government uses the terms *English learner* (EL) and *limited English proficiency* (LEP). Throughout this chapter, I use the term *English learner*, or EL, and I retain the use of other, related terms as they occur in referenced sources.

English learners are sometimes given accommodation in high-stakes test situations. These accommodated students may have more time to take tests, may be provided a glossary of important terms, or both. Some assessment materials may be translated into a language that is more familiar to the students. The accommodation of ELs focuses on the fact that when the language of assessment is English, and a student's English is not well developed, the information we get from assessment has limited usefulness. Across the United States, the criteria for identifying such students varies from state to state, as do the time frames in which students are expected to learn English and take tests in English, unaccommodated.

Accommodating Students with Learning Disabilities

A second major accommodated group is students with learning disabilities. These students receive accommodation in accordance with the Americans with Disabilities Act of 1990 and the Individuals with Disabilities Education Act amendments of 1997. These bodies of legislation codified both the types of challenges that make students eligible for accommodation and the particular types of accommodation that can be used to meet these students' needs. Accommodations related to this legislation can often be found in a student's individualized education plan (IEP), in which a special education need is described and documented. As with the EL student population, the population of students with learning disabilities is considerable. The National Center for Education Statistics (2023a) notes:

> In 2021–22, the number of students ages 3–21 who received special education and/or related services under the Individuals with Disabilities Education Act (IDEA) was 7.3 million, or the equivalent of 15 percent of all public school students. Among students receiving special education and/or related services, the most common category of disability was specific learning disabilities (32 percent).

Accommodation of students with special needs and ELs is guided by law, but helping each student is considered by many a moral and ethical issue. From this perspective, we want to ensure that all students are given the best opportunity to demonstrate their reading achievements and needs through assessment. I add to this legal, moral, and ethical mix a practical element: We use reading assessment information to make consequential decisions. If our assessment information is unreliable because an accommodation is not made, or an accommodation is inappropriate or ineffective, then we are wasting time and resources on the assessment.

Documentation of a student's needs is required to mandate accommodation, needs so substantial that they earn the "learning disability" or "English learner" label. Stringent criteria are used to make these designations, which leads to a situation in which there are two classes of students in our classrooms: those who are entitled to assessment accommodation and those who are not. This raises a major concern. How many students in our classrooms might benefit from accommodation, be it the extension of time to complete an assessment task, simplifying an assessment prompt, or clarifying an assessment question? The current operating assumption is that within specific but broad parameters, students can be expected to not have major impediments to their performances on assessments because of language issues, disabilities, or both. Thus, these students need no accommodation. This assumption is worthy of challenge. What classroom of 30 students has no students who might benefit from the legitimate accommodation of extra time or the repeating of instructions when taking an assessment?

Although current assessment accommodation is driven by the identification of students as ELs and students with special needs, there is a third group of students who are worthy of consideration for accommodation. These are the students who are not legally entitled to assessment accommodation but who may, nevertheless, benefit from it. These students include those who are near, but not quite close enough to, the designation of being a student with a learning disability or an EL. In addition, other students might benefit from accommodations that include more time to complete an assessment, a repeated explanation of the nature of an assessment, or clarification of an assessment item.

Teachers who are sensitive to their individual students' characteristics and needs strive to accommodate their students during reading instruction and assessment. We use our knowledge of a student's relative strengths and weaknesses to accommodate writing challenges by allowing the student to respond orally to assessment questions. We provide more time for some students to answer our questions. We repeat assessment directions for students who may benefit from that guidance. Our accommodation focuses on providing the best possible environment for students to demonstrate their reading and learning. These accommodations are not intended to help students avoid important aspects of school and learning, such as improving their writing and speaking. Rather, accommodation is provided because we are most interested in finding out how well our students read and understand. We are fully aware that special challenges to our students, unaccommodated, could skew our conception of their accomplishments and continuing needs. Throughout the history of accommodating students on reading assessment, the primary goal has been to change assessment materials and procedures, not to change the construct that is measured as a result of the accommodation.

CHARACTERISTICS OF ACCOMMODATION

Accommodation is a change in assessment materials or procedures based on a recognized student need, without which there will be challenges to the valid assessment of the student's knowledge and skills (Rogers et al., 2019; Thurlow & Bolt, 2001). Accommodation of ELs focuses on aspects of students' language proficiency that may interfere with valid assessment. For example, aspects of testing that demand students' English-language competency include the directions that accompany tests and the items, tasks, and prompts that compose the test. These are primary candidates for modifying or translating the language of the assessment. Students who are accommodated for special needs may have hearing impairments, visual impairments, behavioral and emotional disorders, learning disabilities, autism, intellectual disabilities, or speech and language impairments.

Accommodation with assessment is related to the larger efforts of inclusion and is intended to bring more students into mainstream educational experiences. The accommodation stems from our efforts to be fair to all students and to demonstrate school accountability. Abedi et al. (2000) propose that assessment accommodations can provide a more accurate picture of overall student achievement and growth, as well as diagnostic information for teachers, parents, and school administrators. In addition, assessment accommodation can provide evidence that students have demonstrated progress and, in the case of ELs, demonstrate their development from this initial designation.

An ongoing challenge for those considering a specific accommodation is to "validly combine assessment and accommodation" (Stretch & Osborne, 2005, p. 1; Zhang et al., 2014). The assessment accommodations that we make for our students must have the goal of providing useful information. When accommodation is done well, the assessment is changed to accommodate the special needs and characteristics of students, yet the resulting assessment information remains valid and reliable.

Special needs are addressed in order to allow students to demonstrate their reading ability less impeded by the format and nature of the assessment. Without accommodation, particular reading assessment materials and procedures will not yield accurate accounts of some students' reading ability. For example, a student who can demonstrate full comprehension of text but needs more time than is allotted in a standardized test may have unaccommodated test results that indicate a failure to comprehend at grade level. Here, an accommodation of more time to take the test will result in a more accurate representation of the student's ability because the accommodation conditions meet the student's need for extra time. Furthermore, without accommodation, many students are shut out of consequential assessment experiences (National Center for Education Statistics, 2023a). These students are not accounted for in a school's overall achievements, which can have profound effects when schools, districts, and states contemplate their instructional priorities and funding. Having not taken a test, unaccommodated students are unaccounted for in these decisions.

Federal law (i.e., NCLB) requires school districts to report high-stakes reading test scores for subgroups within each school, including students with special needs and ELs. Assessment and accommodations related to NCLB can help us develop the most accurate account of students' reading achievement. The need for accommodation in assessment is paralleled by the need for ongoing research on the nature and effects of accommodation (Abedi et al., 2000; Cook et al., 2014; Fletcher et al., 2006). A most pressing concern is for research that investigates and describes the influence of accommodations on the validity of the assessment. This research should help answer questions that include "Does allowing students more time to take a high-stakes test change the validity of the test?," "Does the rewording of test items influence validity?," and "Do the assessment accommodations given to particular students result in bias against other students taking the test?" The current situation is one in which the demand for assessment accommodation is extremely high, but the guidance provided by research on the effects of accommodation is developing.

The attention to students with accommodation needs necessitates the development of a knowledge base that helps inform our accommodation: determining how and when accommodations meet the elusive standard of changing the student–assessment interaction without changing the nature of the information yielded by the assessment (Abedi, 2012; Abedi et al., 2000; Vidal Rodeiro & Macinska,

2022). Yet, there remains much work to be done to fully understand the consequences of assessment accommodation on both students' assessment performances and students' overall development in school. A goal for accommodation is what Phillips (1994) refers to as the "differential boost," where the assessment accommodation helps the intended student while not penalizing other students.

Zuriff's (2000) maximum potential thesis posits that unaccommodated students are at their maximum level of performance when they work within the time limits of standardized tests, and accommodated students perform significantly higher on untimed tests than on tests with the standardized time allotment. Yet, many students benefit from extra time (Abedi et al., 2000), whether or not they are deemed legally eligible for extra time accommodations. This raises the issue of "timedness" and why it is an enduring feature of almost all standardized, high-stakes tests of reading. Is timed performance more important than optimal performance? If so, why?

The very consideration of accommodation—in this case, the timed or untimed nature of assessment—can lead us to examine assumptions that underlie our testing and assessment for all students. If we are interested in how we can construct assessment scenarios that allow students to perform to their full potential, then we should examine assessment conditions, including the timed nature of high-stakes tests, for all students.

Research on accommodations in assessment is largely restricted to summative, high-stakes testing. However, given the importance of formative, classroom-based assessment, accommodation should be practiced in all forms of reading assessment. Consider that Response to Intervention (RTI) includes four types of assessment: screening, diagnostic, progress monitoring, and outcome measuring. Each deserves our scrutiny, and as noted by Brown and Sanford (2011),

> Regardless of the tools for screening and progress monitoring used within an RTI model with ELLs [English language learners], these tools' effectiveness will depend significantly on the ability of educators to develop a level of expertise and proficiency in their use along with skill in investigating each child's experiential, linguistic, and cultural background—the very components that form the context within which plans must be made for appropriate instruction and intervention. (p. 19)

A related issue is how we conceptualize and care for our students. We know that continued accommodation of students may create dependencies in students' present and future lives: in the workplace, at home, and in the community. We also know that many students not designated as being entitled to accommodation do better with it. I believe that this set of issues is best addressed as teachers work to develop consistent and dependable approaches to accommodation for their students. Accommodations can be developmental in nature. For example, in our unit tests and classroom questioning, we can adjust the wait time that we provide to students who answer our questions, in effect providing the most appropriate time frame for students to think and respond. Additionally, the reading development trajectory that is expected of our students involves increased speed of doing things, such as using strategies quickly and then automatic skills, and this fact must be considered. Yet, if we are interested in first determining that our students can do things and then determining how quickly these things can be done, then we have created a basis and rationale for providing accommodation for any student in our classroom.

Accommodation for Students with Learning Disabilities

The most common accommodations for students with learning disabilities include extended time to take the test, reading the test aloud to the student, providing a scribe to take dictation from a student, paraphrasing test instructions and contents, and testing in small groups (Shyyan et al., 2016). Specific types of assessment accommodations for these students include where the assessment takes place, when it is given, the setting of the assessment, how assessment materials are presented, the time provided to take the assessment, the assessment materials, and how students respond to and interact with the assessment. Several sources (e.g., Christensen et al., 2012; Thompson et al., 2005) provide helpful guidelines for accommodation, which are detailed later in this chapter. These guidelines focus on standardized testing situations rather than daily, teacher-conducted reading assessments. Nevertheless, the guidelines can help us as we consider accommodations with a variety of assessments.

First, accommodations may focus on the physical space in which the assessment takes place, such as preferential seating, a separate location, or a specialized setting. Preferential seating can accommodate students with vision and hearing needs, including the ability to accurately see, hear, and understand proctor assessment instructions and directions, and sample items. Preferential seating or a separate assessment location may be provided to students who are more easily distracted than others, and a specialized setting can be tailored to the specific needs of the individual student. For example, a student with vision needs may be seated in a brightly lit area of the classroom and receive large-print instructions in order to better see and read the assessment directions and questions. Second, the accommodations may include modification of a single-session assessment to one that is broken up over several sessions, a reordering of particular sections of the assessment, or changing the specific time of day at which a student takes the assessment. Furthermore, providing breaks within the assessment can help students who may have difficulty maintaining concentration, and providing extended time to undertake and complete an assessment can assist students who work at a slower pace than others. In each case, the scheduling accommodation is done in relation to the student's needs, which may be related to a shorter-than-typical attention span or the need for success early in an assessment to motivate continued performance at later stages of the assessment.

A third type of accommodation relates to the presentation of assessment materials, including offering different audio and visual versions of the assessment, reading the assessment items and assessment directions aloud, rereading the directions, providing cues, offering prompts to students, responding to students' clarification questions, supplying templates and markers, securing students' papers and other work materials to the desk or work area, and providing magnifying and amplification devices. Different editions of an assessment can include Braille and large print, as well as answer sheets with large prompt and response formats (for standardized testing) or fewer items per page. Reading aloud both the assessment content and the directions to students alleviates the need for them to do so themselves. A special caveat is that reading the content of the test (e.g., reading aloud to the student the text and subsequent items) will transform a reading test into a listening test and compromise the validity and reliability of the test.

Fourth, providing cues to students is a form of presentation accommodation, in which particular features in the assessment are highlighted. Rereading directions to students accommodates those who may not understand and remember assessment directions the first time. Prompts to students may have them continue with the assessment, pause, or rest, as indicated by the particular student's needs. Clarification accommodations mean that a teacher can answer students' questions about the assessment or give extra examples to illustrate the assessment materials and procedures. In addition, templates, or cutouts that provide a barrier to viewing all the information on an assessment, can be used to accommodate students who may be distracted by the sheer amount of print on the assessment or by a particular graphic layout. Markers, such as a plastic chip, can be used to help students keep their place on an assessment. Students who may be challenged by the amount of paper involved with an assessment can have their work secured to their desks. A further accommodation of assessment materials involves the magnification of printed information or the amplification of spoken information.

Finally, the response format can vary in relation to how students use their assessment booklets, the verbal and written responses, writing instruments, reference materials, and technology. Students who cannot clearly mark and write in their assessment papers can have those answers and responses transcribed by an adult or may respond verbally to questions. When students are responsible for writing in relation to their reading, spelling can be an obstacle that prevents clear communication of thought. Thus, students with special needs may use spell-checkers and dictionaries to help them. Furthermore, some students may be challenged to write with paper and pen or pencil but able to write using a computer keyboard and word-processing program. Students may also be accommodated by being permitted to point to answers when testing involves multiple-choice items.

Accommodations for English Learners

English learners benefit from accommodations (Abedi, 2012) that may include extra time to take the assessment, linguistic modification of assessment items (i.e., making the language of the assessment more easily understood), and providing a glossary of key terms or a translation of text. Abedi et al. (1997) examined ELs' performance on short and long test items and found that they had more difficulty with longer items because of the items' higher cognitive language demands and linguistic complexity. Abedi et al. (2000) examined ELs as they took tests with different accommodations of extra time to take the test, a glossary of key concepts on the test, both extra time and the glossary of key concepts, and linguistic modification, or reducing the complexity of language in the test questions. The single accommodation that reduced the gap in test scores between EL and non-EL students was linguistic modification.

Linguistic modification is aimed at reducing the influence of complex assessment language and making it less of a factor on student performance (Cohen et al., 2017). The means of eliciting student participation and response should be straightforward, vetted for unnecessarily difficult words. Linguistic modification results from analyzing the language we use in assessment situations and working to simplify that language so that it retains meaning, but may be more accessible to EL students (Pennock-Roman & Rivera, 2011). Consider, for example, the following multiple-choice question, with the correct answer and distracters:

What word does the author utilize to describe how Elizabeth feels at the party?

- Dizzy
- Ecstatic
- Frantic
- Solemn

The prompt, or question, has a complex sentence structure and relatively difficult vocabulary. If the question's intended focus is on a vocabulary word that tells about the character's feeling, then the question might be linguistically modified as: "How did Elizabeth feel at the party?"

The revised version of the question is less complex and more straightforward, and will have the probable result of confusing fewer students. Of course, linguistic modification is a valuable strategy to apply to all of our assessments for all of our students. Assessment tasks, items, and prompts can vary in difficulty, according to the student thinking and learning that we seek to describe. (For a discussion of how our questions can vary in complexity, see Chapter 4.) The value of linguistic modification is that it acts as a check on assessment language that is unnecessarily complex. An important caveat is that the complexity of the questions we ask should always be intentional and gauged to the type of thinking and response we are seeking. Thus, we should be vigilant that our attempts at linguistic modification do not change the nature of the information and the indication of learning that we seek from students. If you are interested in examining the means to use linguistic modification with the assessments used in your school or district, you can use the reproducible Checklist for Linguistic Modification of Reading Assessment in the Appendix.

Fairbairn (2007) advocates test preparation as a form of accommodation for ELs. Students so designated may be recent arrivals in the United States and unfamiliar with the materials and procedures of high-stakes testing, facing the dual tasks of understanding texts and understanding tests. Fairbairn (2007) notes, "Familiarizing students with the format of the test or of test questions is not 'cheating'; rather, it is creating the possibility for the test scores to more accurately reflect student abilities" (p. 4). Appropriate test preparation can help students build schemata for these influential assessments, on which many consequential decisions are made.

The accommodations may include reviewing sample test items and sections with students, explaining how and why tests are formatted, and explaining how multiple-choice questions work. This last item involves teaching students that there should be one best answer and that there may be distracters that are legitimate but not the best answers.

ACCOMMODATION WITH CLASSROOM-BASED ASSESSMENTS IN STEPHEN'S 10TH-GRADE CLASSROOM

Accommodation with Standardized and Summative High-Stakes Tests

In Stephen's experience, accommodation of assessment is most often undertaken with high-stakes standardized tests. This is important, as highly consequential decisions are made based on the results of these tests. Standardized tests are just that: standardized. The means to derive raw scores, standardized scores, and percentile rankings on these tests are based on piloting that adheres to standardization criteria. Accommodation in testing undoes the standardization because it violates the premise that all students are treated the same while taking the test. Stephen pays close attention to the tests and testing procedures that involve his students. This provides him with information about how well particular accommodations are working for particular students. It also informs him about students who are not accommodated in testing situations but struggle nevertheless. In the past, Stephen's vigilance has helped him identify several students who were not designated ELs but had little or no experience with standardized testing. This identification allowed him to provide lessons intended to help familiarize the students with tests and testing. In addition, Stephen has determined that numerous students perform well in class, where designated time limits are flexible, as opposed to the shorter time frame demanded of the standardized test.

In efforts to be fair to all of his students, Stephen must ascertain that unaccommodated students are being treated fairly. For example, accommodated students receive extra time in which to take a test, as designated in their IEPs. Stephen is concerned that other students without such IEPs are not allowed to receive such accommodation, as many students benefit from extra time on high-stakes assessments (Zuriff, 2000). Accommodations encourage us to focus on the important issue of why certain students should receive special treatment, and in doing so we may determine that special treatment is deserved by other students. An important question to ask of any possible accommodation is, "Does the proposed accommodation eliminate unfairness in assessment, or does it move it around among other students?" Stephen advocates for accommodation when it is clearly indicated while paying attention to how one accommodation may introduce bias and unfairness to another student or group of students.

Accommodation with Classroom-Based Formative Assessments

Throughout the school year, Stephen conducts formative assessments to help him plan his instruction, gauge the effectiveness of ongoing lessons, and provide feedback to his students. Accommodation in the context of his formative assessments is geared to gathering immediately useful information. Stephen works with ELs and students with learning disabilities, and he follows Abedi's (2012) suggestions for linguistic modification:

- *Use a reasonable number of questions.* Stephen continually checks on how many questions are needed to elicit student responses in regard to the goals of the lesson. This practice helps him eliminate questions that are redundant and questions that evoke responses that are not central to learning outcomes.

- *Write all questions clearly and concisely.* Stephen vets his questions. He is on the lookout for language that may prove too challenging for his students, language that might get in the way of student thinking and appropriate responses. He drafts the questions he will ask students and then revises them as needed. He rephrases assessment prompts and questions that he believes are posing a problem to his students, not because of the students' inability to answer but because of the wording of the question or prompt. The linguistic modification is possible because

Stephen continually questions his questions and analyzes the assessment language he uses.

- *Get feedback from students.* In addition to careful examination of students' written and spoken responses, Stephen seeks student comments and insights into the questions he asks. He regularly asks his EL students if they fully understand what he is asking. This practice helps him keep the essence of his questions while framing them with the most direct and simple language possible.

- *Provide specific feedback to students from formative assessments.* Stephen's work helps students become familiar with the language and processes of assessment. It also teaches students that teacher feedback is a valuable, positive influence on their learning and development. As Stephen explains the nature and purpose of assessment, he is also teaching assessment—focused on the long-term goal of each student becoming independent. Stephen likes to think of his questions as the beginnings of conversations with students. As students provide responses to his queries, he provides detailed feedback as to how and how well an answer meets the question. His familiarity with students' needs for linguistic modification guides not only his assessment questions but also his feedback to students around those questions.

- *Be as specific as possible and avoid general terms such as* good, poor, *or* not adequate. For students who are learning English, general terms such as *good* are not good enough to describe what a student does well. Stephen's feedback to students is positive—and when a student's performance is commendable, he describes why the answer (or test-related performance) is good. The same approach holds for Stephen's review of student work that indicates students' needs—he strives to use simple and straightforward language that helps students focus on learning that is yet to occur.

- *Provide feedback as it relates to the same steps taken in teaching a lesson, such as identification of a goal, direct instruction, guided practice, independent practice, and assessment.* Stephen's assessment feedback to students follows the structure of his lessons. He considers the students' recent (or ongoing) experience with the lesson as a resource—students' memory of the time course and content of the lesson can help them use assessment feedback most appropriately.

- *Provide feedback related to the student's areas of need in each of the four domains—reading, writing, speaking, and listening.* A final area of focus for Stephen's work with linguistic modification is across the language arts. For example, Stephen knows that an EL student's reading comprehension may appear enhanced or diminished based on the student's mode of writing or speaking the answer to comprehension questions. Stephen seeks student answers in each mode, and tries to determine what mode is best suited to helping students demonstrate their reading achievement. At the same time, he is working to help students build competency with English across the language arts.

Accommodation in Daily Teaching and Assessing

Stephen teaches four sections of science each day. His students include several with special needs who have IEPs, and others who are newly arrived in the United States and have little spoken English and limited reading experience. Throughout the school year, Stephen strives to accommodate in relation to the needs of all his students. This means he regularly consults the IEPs of his special education students and considers the language issues of his ELs, along with his knowledge of the other students in his classroom.

A substantial responsibility here is meeting the demands of time and effort needed to build knowledge of students, their assessment history, and their needs for accommodation. Those students designated as having learning disabilities, ELs, or both have clear accommodation for the high-stakes testing that is conducted in the state and school district. As students prepare to take these tests, Stephen helps them by providing practice in test taking with the particular accommodations that the students will have. These accommodations include additional time to take the reading test, timed breaks between sections, and repeating instructions and directions that are not well understood by students in the first place. Stephen also believes that test preparation should involve activities that familiarize students with the materials and procedures of testing, and he accommodates students who lack this knowledge.

Stephen amends Abedi et al.'s (2000) four factors for accommodating ELs. He uses them to consider accommodations in classroom assessment in relation to validity, effectiveness, differential impact, and feasibility. The four points are addressed by the following questions:

1. Does provision of accommodation alter the construct of the assessment? (validity)
2. What accommodation strategies would be the most effective in reducing performance gaps between ELs and non-EL students that are due to language factors? (effectiveness)
3. Which student background characteristics influence accommodated assessment? (differential impact)
4. Which accommodations are more feasible, particularly in large-scale assessments? (feasibility)

Classroom-based reading assessment offers Stephen an opportunity to further his efforts in inclusion. Thus, his classroom-based reading assessment is diagnostic not only of students' developing skills, strategies, and mindsets but also of how particular assessments tell or do not tell a detailed story of students' reading achievement.

Consequences and Usefulness of Assessment Accommodation

Stephen conducts reading assessment so that he may best teach his students. At the heart of accommodation in assessment is attention to the individual differences that students bring to our classrooms. We expect accommodation to be a prominent theme when we assess students with special needs and ELs. Most often there are subgroups of students who have a legal designation as learning disabled and whose IEPs specify and require accommodations according to federal law. Groups of ELs may also have mandated or recommended accommodations for reading tests, although this can vary widely depending on the state in which students live.

Stephen wants all of his students to show their best possible performances on assessments, and he focuses on those accommodations that help students do so. He is concerned about students who lack the designation of "English learner" or "learning disabled" but have clear challenges during assessment situations. The nervous test taker and the slow (but not slow enough to gain special-needs status) processor are students who lack official support for accommodation but deserve it. Furthermore, developing English language users may have no legal designation that warrants accommodation, yet they benefit from an assessment glossary in their stronger language and from extra time to read and respond to comprehension questions.

Roles and Responsibilities Related to Accommodation

Knowing all his students' accommodation needs is a challenging task for Stephen. He regularly uses the guidelines for accommodation that are mandated for some of his students and beneficial for others. That is, he accommodates individual students regardless of their classification as learning disabled or EL so that his assessments provide valuable information that is worthy of the assessment effort.

Stephen first wants to determine if his students can successfully complete assessment tasks and then whether his students can do the tasks under specific time constraints. He needs to know if his students can do something more than he needs to know if they can do it in a short time frame. This has positive consequences, as Stephen may provide more time to students working toward mastery or provide clarification to students who do not fully understand an assessment request or demand. Thus, he views assessment accommodation in his daily classroom routines as closely connected to his understanding of individual students' development and a matter of fairness to all students.

Stephen is responsible for the reliability and validity of his assessments. As much as he strives to accommodate his students, he knows that inappropriate accommodation can render assessment results unusable. His inferences about student reading achievement may not be supportable when the assessment providing information is modified. Thus, Stephen continually performs a balancing act in which his students' accommodation needs are balanced against his need for valid assessment information.

Reliability of Assessment Accommodation

The reliability of assessment is a paramount concern whenever accommodation is used. Recall that reliability focuses on the accuracy, consistency, trustworthiness, and fairness of an assessment. Whatever our intentions and the goodwill that surround our efforts, we must remember that accommodation can result in a change, subtle or overt, of assessment. Stephen does not want his efforts to accommodate students' individual needs to put other students at a disadvantage. He considers the following advice information from the *Standards for Educational and Psychological Testing* for both the summative and formative classroom-based assessments he conducts:

> While test takers should not be disadvantaged due to a disability not relevant to the construct the test is intended to assess, the resulting accommodation should not put those taking a modified test at an undue advantage over those tested under regular conditions. (American Educational Research Association, American Psychological Association, & National Council on Measurement in Education, 2014, p. 105)

Stephen does not want to be caught in an endless cycle of adjusting assessments to help some students only to find that it places other students at a disadvantage. He uses the concept of differential boost (Phillips, 1994) and the maximum potential thesis (Zuriff, 2000) to suggest assessment practice, and it turns out these are valuable but often difficult criteria to meet. For example, Stephen is comfortable providing extra time to students who need it to do their best work, and this provision is included in the IEPs of several of his students. Yet, several of Stephen's students do better work when given more time, even though these students are not accommodated by law. Stephen appreciates that laws designate particular services and accommodations according to students' documented needs. However, he is troubled by the idea that students in the "undesignated middle" are not considered for accommodation.

At the same time, Stephen is required to provide the sameness of experience to students taking standardized, high-stakes tests. He knows that circumventing the standardization procedures will reduce the inferences that can be made from assessment results. Thus, his classroom is marked by two approaches to accommodation. The first is legally required and mandated, and it applies to the high-stakes tests that his students must take each year. The second approach is practiced throughout the year and in relation to the many assessments that Stephen conducts in the classroom. Here, he has no qualms about repeating assessment prompts to help students gain clarity on the specific demands of the assessments, nor does he withhold extra time from those students who achieve more when given extra time.

With formative assessments, Stephen gathers information that can inform instruction—that updates his mental model of the student and describes areas of achievement and need. Stephen's standard for reliability of assessment here is different than for standardized tests. That is, if his reading assessment processes and results yield instructionally helpful information, then he is willing to modify the assessment. For example, when he wants to know that students can ably summarize chapters or articles, he rephrases or repeats an assessment prompt or question. He allows extra time for students who need it. He scrutinizes the clarity of the assessment demand and the time frame in which students are expected to meet the demand. This results in an accurate and reliable account of his students' achievements and needs.

Validity of Accommodation

Stephen approaches validity in assessment with three related goals. First, he wants to be fair to all of his students. Second, he wants the assessment to be worthwhile and considers how accommodations may help him realize this goal. Third, he wants to be faithful to the assessment and the construct that it is supposed to measure. He is sensitive to how certain accommodations change assessment and validity. For example, if he reads passages from a reading test and then asks students to answer comprehension questions, his accommodation changes the reading test into a listening test. Although both are receptive and related language acts, reading and listening are different constructs. Stephen is also sensitive to the fact that while accommodation is of potential help to students in the present, their future within and outside of school may be one that is not so accommodating of them. Thus, he works with students and their parents to consider long-term goals. Stephen is sensitive to the observation that test accommodation typically demands a delicate balance: Standardized tests have psychometric needs to maintain their validity, just as accommodated students have needs that are met through accommodation.

SUMMARY

More than 12 million students in public schools are classified as ELs, learning disabled, or both. Fortunately, there are means of accommodating these students. Ongoing investigation of these well-intentioned accommodations continues to contribute to a research base that informs our use of particular accommodations. Appropriate accommodation helps students give us their best in assessment situations. As we endeavor to include and teach the diverse learners in our classrooms, assessment accommodation is warranted. Would that it were so simple! In making accommodations, we must be certain that all students continue to be treated fairly and that one type of accommodation does not have the unintended consequence of placing other students at a disadvantage. Accommodation is also complex and time-consuming, adding to the already considerable assessment tasks of classroom teachers. Our work with assessment accommodation should be energized by two facts: Accommodation represents our best efforts to treat all students fairly, and accommodation done well yields truly useful assessment information.

Enhancing Your Understanding

1. Reflect on your current assessment routines. Do you make conscious or unconscious accommodations for students in your classroom? What is the basis for making these accommodations? Are these accommodations in the spirit of making the assessment fair while maintaining the validity and reliability of the assessment? What are the possible intended and unintended outcomes of your accommodation practices?

2. Identify an assessment routine, item, or procedure that needs revision in relation to accommodation of a particular student's needs. Conduct a task analysis that focuses on how accommodation is needed and the nature of the accommodation to be made.

3. Analyze your questions and other reading assessment language. Identify language that may be too difficult or confusing for some of your students. Try to simplify the language and develop a plan for keeping track of how you do this. As you simplify the language, determine if it changes the intent of the item.

4. Pay attention to how you accommodate different students in your classroom. Keep a journal of how you come to understand students' individual differences, how you conceptualize them into accommodation, and how you accommodate these students, whether or not they have a legal determination for accommodation.

Reading Assessment Snapshot
CONFOUNDS IN READING ASSESSMENT

Confounds occur when unanticipated factors influence students' performance on an assessment. If confounds are present in reading assessment, our account of a student's true achievement may be inaccurate. We may make erroneous inferences about students' reading achievement because the assessment is influenced by factors other than students' reading ability.

Consider an assessment that requires a student to read and understand a U.S. Civil War–era history text as a prerequisite for a performance. Based on their understanding of the text, students are to create a historical skit that reflects understanding of historical characters' attitudes and beliefs and present the skit to the class. This task promises an authentic assessment opportunity to observe how students use information learned from reading the history text.

However, we must examine how confounds might influence our interpretation or misinterpretation of students' reading achievement. First, the student must be able to construct meaning from the text, which contains numerous references to people, places, and events. A student's relevant prior knowledge for the text content can influence the assessment outcome; students with substantial prior knowledge may do exceedingly well when otherwise their comprehension would be average. The student must also take notes, recording information about historical figures, their interactions, and other details that may be useful in the skit. The student must apply knowledge learned from the text to develop ideas for the skit. Next, the student must be an able writer, for this allows the transcription of knowledge gained through reading into notes and then the written text of the historical skit.

Once the skit is written, edited, and polished, the student is required to present it. Here, the student's public performance ability will influence our interpretation of achievement. The shy student who is uncomfortable in front of classmates may stumble through the skit, but the gregarious student eagerly performs his or her skit for the class. Both students read the history text and established comparable levels of understanding, but the manner of assessment introduces confounds in what is assessed.

The confounds that may arise in assessment should not be a deterrent to complex assessments. Rather, our insights into how reading fits with complex performances allows us to focus on the reading component and design appropriate assessments, while also focusing on the fact that we need to ask students to read and use that which they comprehend. In relation to the above scenario, a performance assessment could include a pure measure of reading comprehension, such as questions that require constructed responses that allow students to demonstrate what they have comprehended. The assessment might also include a checklist for note-taking that reminds students about the type of information that is useful for their purposes. Combined, these assessments enhance our faith in the conclusions we draw from them, fully aware of the confounds.

CHAPTER 8

Assessing "the Other"
Important Noncognitive Aspects of Reading

What are the important and enduring outcomes of effective reading instruction? What are the ways we hope our students grow? Do they include students' understanding that reading is a valuable tool, a means to achieve goals, a manner of relaxing, and a key to personal growth? Do the outcomes include students identifying themselves as readers? Students believing they will achieve as readers? In this chapter, we explore assessment of "the other." That is, important factors that are both contributors to and outcomes of students' reading development, but that are infrequently the focus of assessment. These factors include readers' motivation and engagement, self-efficacy, agency, interests, and attitudes, as well as the attributions that readers make for their performances in reading (Afflerbach, 2022). We consider the factors from a formative perspective, examining how they develop and how they support or impede reading development. We also consider the factors from a summative perspective, as they represent positive or negative outcomes of our reading instruction and students' reading experiences in school. These factors are central to a student's reading success and are interrelated. Yet, they are largely neglected in contemporary reading assessment, thus their designation as "the other."

Consider the narrative report card section in Figure 8.1 and how it describes Jamal and positive, important outcomes of effective reading instruction. Such a report card is possible because administrators, teachers, and parents worked together to help develop an assessment system that acknowledges the importance of factors that influence students' reading, beyond reading strategies and skills. The figure also provides a sampling of things we know to be important yet often fail to assess.

Rowan Mill Elementary School		
Narrative Report Card		
Student: Jamal Turner	Teacher: Ms. Nan Fleming	Date: March 15, 2017
Jamal continues to develop as an enthusiastic reader. He chooses to read when given choices for independent work in the classroom. He identifies himself as a reader, and his self-efficacy is growing. He understands that he is in control of reading and that his effort and persistence influence the outcomes of his work. Compared with the beginning of this school year, Jamal is a motivated reader. I attribute this to the fact that he now understands the value of reading: how it helps him reach learning goals and how it helps him prepare for the future. Jamal's hard work at learning the needed reading strategies is clearly paying off. At the beginning of the school year, he did not believe that he was in control of his reading and had a poor attitude toward reading. Through a series of lessons, hard work, and the development of a positive attitude and motivation, Jamal has learned that understanding text is something that is under his control. He demonstrates the sense of agency that is so important to successful readers. The ability to begin, work through, and complete reading on his own contributes valuable lessons about his hard work and his ability to succeed and act on the world in a positive manner. In summary, Jamal now sees himself as a reader, one who experiences success and values the outcomes of his reading.		

FIGURE 8.1. Sample narrative report card.

A BRIEF HISTORY OF "THE OTHER" AND READING ASSESSMENT

How did we arrive at this point in time, knowing that there are many ways to judge successful reading programs, yet only assessing students' cognitive strategy and skill development and their content-area knowledge gains? For over a century, reading instruction has focused on teaching reading strategies and skills (Huey, 1908; Pearson et al., 2020; Thorndike, 1917). Despite variation in how reading instruction has been conceptualized (Verhoeven & Snow, 2001) and efforts to increase attention to the noncognitive aspects of students' development (Alexander, 2010; Anderson & Bourke, 2000; Athey, 1985; Mathewson, 1994; Peura et al., 2021; Schiefele et al., 2012; Schunk & DiBenedetto, 2020; Soto et al., 2023), there is a lack of assessment attention to "the other." "The other" includes our students' motivation and engagement, their self-efficacy, their expectations for success or failure, and their willingness to put forth effort and persevere.

However, knowledge of these powerful factors and how they influence reading is not reflected in our assessments. The hyperfocus on strategies and skills and the uneven treatment or neglect of "the other" can be illustrated in many ways: through school district curriculum guides, reading programs, and state education standards. Consider how the California Department of Education (1998) characterizes "reading comprehension and writing skills" for grades 3 through 5:

In grades three through five, students are becoming more sophisticated writers and speakers. These skills include engaging in research projects that question what they read and hear, taking information and putting it into their own words, and creating written pieces that follow a structure geared toward a writing purpose (e.g., a narrative story, an informational report, or an opinion text).

With an emphasis on developing comprehension with texts, students are exposed to a variety of literature and informational texts and learn how different genres, or types, of books have different structures. *Students are encouraged to read, read, read* and to expand their knowledge in areas of personal interest or new research topics. (italics added; State of California Office of Education, 2024)

The above description of accomplished elementary school students focuses on the cognitive strategies and skills needed to read and related learning in the content areas. We might assume that motivation and engagement, self-efficacy and metacognition are operating in support of students who "read, read, read." While it is difficult to imagine students who enthusiastically "read, read, read" without motivation, engagement, self-efficacy, or metacognition, there is no mention of these. Nor is there any related assessment.

A further example of the focus on cognitive strategies and skills comes from the introduction to the CCSS (CCSSO & NGA, 2010):

Students who meet the Standards readily undertake the close, attentive reading that is at the heart of understanding and enjoying complex works of literature. They habitually perform the critical reading necessary to pick carefully through the staggering amount of information available today in print and digitally. They actively seek the wide, deep, and thoughtful engagement with high-quality literary and informational texts that builds knowledge, enlarges experience, and broadens worldviews. They reflexively demonstrate the cogent reasoning and use of evidence that is essential to both private deliberation and responsible citizenship in a democratic republic. In short, students who meet the Standards develop the skills in reading, writing, speaking, and listening that are the foundation for any creative and purposeful expression in language. (p. 3)

The above description is notable in that it includes the ideas of readers' engagement with text and that close, attentive reading is necessary for enjoying complex works of literature. However, the focus remains on cognitive strategies and skills. With the CCSS description, we can envision students who "actively seek . . . wide, deep, and thoughtful engagement" with texts, but engagement is not a focus of reading assessment.

Do students become accomplished readers only because they have mastered the mechanics of reading? Do students become lifelong readers simply because of learning cognitive strategies and skills and our careful assessment of the same? Or is there more to student readers' development and more to consider when we assess student development and the outcomes of reading programs? When viewed from the perspective of Pellegrino et al.'s (2001) model of assessment, current reading assessment practice privileges cognition and ignores other aspects and therefore does not account for student growth relative to the full construct of reading development. If we are successful in advocating for attention to these powerful influences on reading development, we may be able to change the status quo in reading assessment.

Successful student readers are motivated and engaged, have high self-efficacy, and can make accurate attributions for their performances. Yet, the centrality of these factors to school success is largely ignored in influential educational policies and documents. These include NCLB legislation, the related report of the National Reading Panel (National Institute of Child Health and Human Development, 2000), and state and Common Core standards. A resultant risk is that reading instruction is conceptualized as teaching only phonics, phonemic awareness, fluency, vocabulary, and comprehension, with less or no attention paid to the affective and conative lives of student readers. Every finding from scientific research and every classroom observation that demonstrates the power of motivation, self-concept, attitude, interest, and attributions in students' reading development should call the question, "Why don't we assess these important aspects of students' reading development?" (Guthrie & Klauda, 2016; Pajares & Urdan, 2006; Zee et al., 2021).

The good news is that research evidence and our classroom experiences can help us advocate for assessing these important facilitators of reading. Likewise, there are assessments that describe student readers' development in relation to self-efficacy, motivation, interests, and attitudes. However, schools and classrooms already overburdened by testing will find it difficult to accommodate another series of reading assessments. School budgets, already placed at risk by mandated testing costs, have little or no money for more assessments. This makes the challenge twofold: We must advocate for the importance of "the other" in how our student readers develop, and we must find ways to assess "the other" in an already crowded reading assessment program.

WHAT ABOUT "THE OTHER" NEEDS TO BE ASSESSED?

How might we conceptualize the successful student reader? Accomplished student readers share important characteristics that are related to, but different from, cognitive strategies and skills. The narrative report card included earlier in this chapter, in Figure 8.1, touches on a number of these characteristics. Successful student readers are strategic, resourceful, and motivated and have beneficial self-concepts.

These students have life interests that can be examined and extended through reading, interests that can influence a reader's stance toward a reading task. These students possess positive attitudes toward reading and identify themselves as readers. Reading fits into the lives of successful student readers in many ways. It helps them achieve school-related goals and investigate areas of personal interest. Reading is something worth doing: It rewards, enriches, informs, and transforms. Many students learn to read, but many choose not to read as they leave school and live their lives. Aliteracy is not the failure to learn to read but a failure to realize the value of reading.

Factors such as motivation and self-efficacy are possible outcomes of becoming a better reader. Each is also a potential facilitator of students' ongoing reading development. Consider a less accomplished reader: A struggling fourth-grade reader may have already experienced five years, or half a lifetime, of below-average reading performance in school. He has a history of reluctant reading, in part because when his reading is on public display, his self-concept and motivation suffer. Thus, he has developed routines that help him avoid reading situations. These routines have mixed effects. He avoids embarrassment but misses opportunities that could contribute to his reading development (Stanovich, 1986). He has a negative attitude toward reading and is not interested in reading on his own. He is not motivated to do things with which he repeatedly experiences failure, which is unsurprising.

That a teacher can influence a student's motivation to read is a powerful form of accountability. A reluctant reader who approaches acts of reading with a history of failure and then learns to build and maintain motivation has accomplished much. The reluctant reader who builds identity as a successful reader and elects to read outside of the classroom demonstrates a possibly life-enhancing change. This change should be assessed and described.

A CLOSER LOOK AT "THE OTHER" FACTORS THAT FACILITATE AND REFLECT BECOMING A BETTER READER

This section provides overviews of the possible contributions of five reader characteristics to reading success:

- Motivation and engagement with reading (For example, moving from a single interest in reading about football to reading in general and having the motivation to read in the face of challenge are learned habits of good readers.)
- Self-efficacy (For example, do students believe they can succeed at reading in general and with specific texts and tasks?)

- Reader attitudes, which can enhance or inhibit reading from the start
- Reader interest, which may be topic specific or general
- Reader attributions (What student readers attribute their success and failure to can have a great influence on their reading.)

One or all of these factors may be enmeshed with reading, encouraging or discouraging students' reading development. These factors may contribute to what Stanovich (1986) calls "the Matthew effects" (p. 360), in which those students who experience success with reading are in a good position to further grow as readers. While Stanovich focuses on cognitive strategies and skills and their relationships, consider the possibility of a Matthew effect in relation to readers' affective and conative characteristics. A reader who experiences success in reading in school may be motivated to continue—there is the inclination to read. In other instances, the factors may present an obstacle to reading growth. These factors can have interactive and additive relationships to reading development. Consider, again, the student who is a struggling reader. He has a history of not reading well, and reading in class is an immediate threat to his self-efficacy and related effort to read. Why would he be motivated to read? Such students may experience a reverse Matthew effect: a deliberate effort to avoid reading, with the result of the poor getting poorer. The task, then, is to describe the potential contribution of "the other" to reading success, the relation of "the other" to reading, and the means to assess these important factors and outcomes.

ASSESSING "THE OTHER" IN NAN'S FIFTH-GRADE CLASSROOM

Nan is a fifth-grade teacher whose instructional focus includes students' motivations to read, their self-efficacy, their interests and attitudes related to reading, and their attributions for reading success or failure. Her focus is determined, in part, by the availability of assessment tools that help her examine and describe each of these important aspects of student reader development. Nan is what I call an opportunistic assessor of her students' reading. She consistently looks for opportunities to assess her students during reading class, listening and observing. This opportunism has led Nan to focus on specific "other" outcomes of reading and on assessments that help her best understand related student development.

Nan uses items and tasks from different assessments: the Elementary Reading Attitude Survey (McKenna & Kear, 1990), the Motivation to Read Profile (MRP; Gambrell et al., 1996), the Reader Self-Perception Scale (Henk & Melnick, 1995), the Reading Self-Efficacy Questionnaire (Carroll & Fox, 1997), the 30-item version of the Reading Self-Concept Scale (RSCS-30; Chapman & Tunmer, 1995), a reading interest survey (Hildebrandt, 2001), and a guide for constructing self-efficacy scales (Bandura, 2006). Each of these assessments is aligned with important aspects of student readers' development. Each assessment has the further appeal of being readily available: Nan and her colleagues are happy to use existing assessment instruments that are well suited to their needs, thus avoiding the demands of having to create a new assessment.

Nan must be judicious with her assessment choices, for her time is at a premium, and a considerable portion of the school district's assessment effort focuses on federally mandated testing. Nan and her colleagues do considerable legwork to identify existing assessments that can help them meet their goal of assessing "the other."

Student Readers' Motivation

Motivations have a subtle or obvious influence on our work. They can be weak or strong, positive or negative. They are often related to our past experiences. Nan is familiar with students whose lack of motivation stems from their prior reading histories: struggles to read, little or no perceptible reward for their efforts, difficult public performances, and unpleasant memories. Nan empathizes with these readers. These experiences create a lack of motivation (Nevo & Vaknin-Nusbaum, 2020) that is similar to her lack of motivation to have a root canal or visit the Department of Motor Vehicles. In contrast, Nan is quite motivated to read. She identifies herself as a reader and can read most things that she encounters and develop an understanding of them. Her prior experiences are positive, and they motivate her to return to acts of reading because they bring rewards.

Nan's experiences and those of her students are related to a robust research literature on motivation (Bae et al., 2020; Finn et al., 2023; Guthrie & Klauda, 2016; Sutter & Campbell, 2022). This research demonstrates that motivation can serve as a facilitator of students' reading achievement and that increased motivation to read is an outcome of effective instruction and learning. Simply put, motivated readers are willing to persevere when reading is challenging, they choose to read in the face of attractive alternatives, and their positive motivation facilitates more reading. Thus, motivation can contribute to the increased reading that in turn contributes to increased reading achievement.

Motivation can turn students toward or away from acts of reading. A related phenomenon, engagement, reflects the combination of motivation and thoughtfulness (Azevedo et al., 2023; Guthrie, 2001). According to Guthrie (2001), engaged readers exhibit four characteristic behaviors: They are well motivated, they approach reading strategically, they are knowledgeable about reading and content areas, and they interact socially in relation to their reading. Engaged readers are motivated as they read to pursue varied personal goals, and they use different strategies and their prior knowledge to construct meaning from text. Engaged readers interact socially as they construct and use meaning.

To better understand their students' motivations to read and aspects of engagement, Nan and her colleagues use items from the MRP (Gambrell et al., 1996). The MRP has two sections: a self-report reading survey, which is administered in groups, and an individual conversational interview. The survey assesses two dimensions of reading motivation—student readers' self-concepts and how students value reading—whereas the interview explores individual aspects of students' motivation to read, such as their personal interests in reading. Nan and her colleagues select a subset of items from the MRP, as shown in Figure 8.2.

The use of the items from the MRP helps Nan and her colleagues combine their classroom observations with focused questions that further describe students' reading motivations. These sources provide valuable information for planning instruction, suggesting reading activities and materials, and focusing on the motivational aspects of helping students become better readers. Nan strives to join cognitive skill and strategy instruction with tasks and activities that motivate and help her students understand their progress.

Student Readers' Self-Concept and Self-Efficacy

Each of us carries with us an extensive set of self-concepts. These are developed as we experience life and think about ourselves in relation to these experiences (Peura

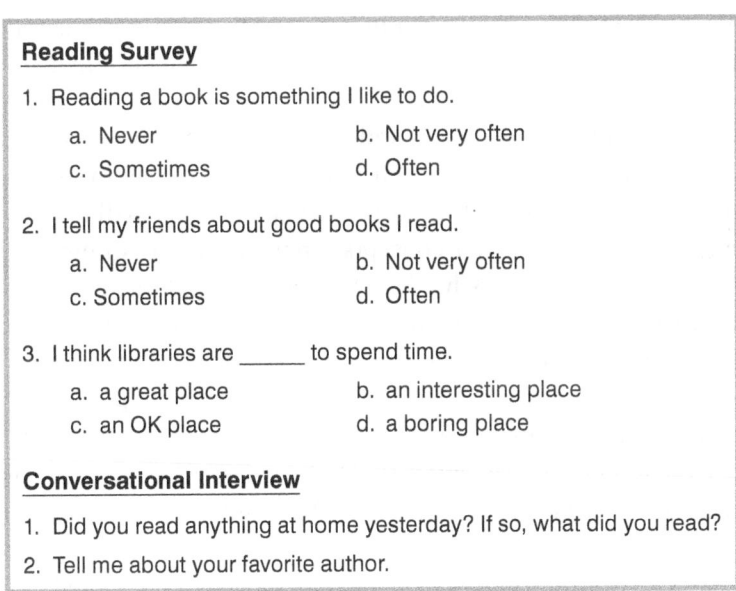

FIGURE 8.2. Sample items from the Motivation to Read Profile, which is in the public domain (from Gambrell et al., 1996).

Competence subscale	• Can you work out hard words by yourself when you read?
	• Are you good at remembering words?
Attitude subscale	• Do you look forward to reading?
Difficulty subscale	• Do you make lots of mistakes in reading?
	• Are the books you read in class too hard?

FIGURE 8.3. Sample items from the 30-item version of the Reading Self-Concept Scale. From "Development of Young Children's Reading Self-Concepts" by J. Chapman and W. Tunmer. Copyright © 1995 American Psychological Association. Reproduced by permission.

et al., 2021). We can also develop a sense of efficacy: the power to produce a desired result. For example, Nan's limited experiences with playing tennis, combined with watching matches from Wimbledon and the U.S. Open, lead her to conceptualize herself as a novice tennis player. She does not have a problem with this self-concept because she believes it to be accurate, and it helps her recognize when she might, or might not, be a suitable tennis partner for another person. Her self-efficacy as a tennis player is suitably humble. She plays with an awareness of her strengths and weaknesses, knowing that playing with effort has helped her play her best.

Nan has other self-concepts that are not so impoverished. For example, her experiences with reading suggest to her that she is a fairly accomplished reader. She understands the vast majority of things she reads. Both of these self-concepts influence the approach that she takes to different aspects of her life. Nan's reading history and her positive self-concept contribute to her high self-efficacy. Nan views herself as a strong and capable reader, and she is willing to take on often challenging reading tasks because she sees herself as one who can meet those challenges.

Research demonstrates that positive self-concepts contribute to students' achievement, whereas negative self-concepts can interfere with or prevent academic progress (Carroll & Fox, 1997; Schunk & Bursuck 2016; Unrau et al., 2018). From this research, we understand that all the effective skill and strategy teaching in the world may not influence reading success if a student's self-concept is negative. To explore the development of students' self-concepts as readers, Nan and her colleagues utilize sections of the RSCS-30 (Chapman & Tunmer, 1995), which includes items that focus on students' self-concepts related to reading competence, attitude, and difficulty. The items selected by Nan and her colleagues from each of these sections are shown in Figure 8.3.

As is the case with information provided by the MRP (Gambrell et al., 1996), Nan uses the results of the RSCS-30 (Chapman & Tunmer, 1995) to complement the information she gathers through classroom observations and discussions with students. For example, she can identify students who appear to possess negative self-concepts as readers. She knows that many students reading below grade level develop a low self-concept from the consistent messages they receive about the nature of their below-average reading and that even above-average student readers may have a weak self-concept because of pressures they receive or place on themselves to do better. Assessing students' self-concepts provides Nan with valuable information. The information from the RSCS-30 helps Nan plan her reading lessons, working to boost students' strategies and skills while also attending to their needs for positive reading experiences and increased self-concepts as readers.

Self-efficacy is closely tied to students' motivation and engagement, as well as self-concept. Bandura (2006) describes self-efficacy as follows:

> Among the mechanisms of human agency, none is more central or pervasive than belief of personal efficacy. *Unless people believe they can produce desired effects by their actions, they have little incentive to act, or to persevere in the face of difficulties.* Whatever other factors serve as guides and motivators, they are rooted in the core belief that one has the power to effect changes by one's actions. (italics added; p. 308)

Students' high self-efficacy leads to increased classroom achievement (Solheim, 2011), and students with high self-efficacy are more strategic (Peura et al., 2019). Students with high self-efficacy make fewer attributions for performance to external causes, such as luck, task difficulty, and teacher help (Fitri et al., 2019; Shell et al., 1995). In contrast, students with low self-efficacy have reduced aspirations for success, have reduced commitments to goals, attribute their poor performance to poor ability, and persevere less frequently when facing challenging tasks. These students attribute school success to external factors, such as luck and task easiness. The research implications for the classroom are stark: Students whose ongoing experiences with reading do not support the development of self-efficacy are at risk of failure (Dweck, 1999; Muenks et al., 2018).

Students' Attitudes toward Reading

Reading attitudes are closely related to reader motivation and reader self-efficacy. Nan thinks of her students: Who has a strong, positive attitude toward reading? Who has a less-than-positive attitude toward reading? How consistent are these attitudes? As Nan develops a mental model of her student readers with a positive attitude, she notes the following characteristics:

- I have a generally good attitude toward reading.
- I expect to find reading rewarding.
- I expect to succeed.
- I know that when I encounter difficulties, I will probably be able to overcome them.

Nan knows that, in contrast, students with a history of failure in reading are often further hindered by a poor attitude toward reading. The less-able students identify reading in school with experiences of failure and public demonstrations of weakness.

To identify students' diverse attitudes toward reading, Nan and her colleagues use the Elementary Reading Attitude Survey (McKenna & Kear, 1990), in which students are asked to circle a cartoon character (Garfield) whose drawn expression most closely represents their own feelings. Sample items are shown in Figure 8.4.

This survey helps Nan further examine her students' attitudes toward reading and sharpen the focus of her instructional efforts. She finds the survey especially useful because it helps differentiate between her students' academic reading and their recreational reading. When Nan finds discrepancies between student attitudes in these two types of reading, she tries to locate an area in which a student has a relatively positive attitude toward reading. For example, when she determines that a student has a very positive attitude toward recreational reading because there is choice involved, she provides the student with choices in academic reading in an attempt to convey the already existing positive attitude into academic reading.

Students' Reading Interests

Nan and her colleagues believe that knowing students' interests to help plan reading instruction can positively influence student reading. Nan is concerned that several of her students are disinterested readers. Assessment that helps her pinpoint student interests within and outside the classroom is worth the time and effort. She googles "interest inventory reading," which leads her to Hildebrandt's (2001) reading interest inventory. This survey seeks information on school reading interests, reading habits, and special areas of interest for each child, as shown in Figure 8.5.

Recreational reading scale	• How do you feel when you read a book on a rainy Saturday? • How do you feel about getting a book for a present? • How do you feel about reading instead of playing?
Academic reading scale	• How do you feel when the teacher asks you questions about what you read? • How do you feel about reading your school books? • How do you feel when you read out loud in class?

FIGURE 8.4. Sample items from the Elementary Reading Attitude Survey (McKenna & Kear, 1990).

> - What are some of the books that you have read lately?
> - List the topics or subjects that you might like to read about.
> - Do you have a hobby? If so, what is it?
> - Put a check mark next to the kind of reading that you like best. (The options provided include history, sports, romance, science fiction, adventure, novels, humor, folk tales, poetry, biography, how-to books, mysteries, and plays.)

FIGURE 8.5. Sample items from the Reading Interest Survey. From "'But There's Nothing Good to Read' (in the Library Media Center)" by D. Hildebrandt. Copyright © 2001 Denice Hildebrandt and the Michigan Association of School Librarians. Reprinted by permission.

Nan compares the information provided by the reading interest inventory with her understanding of her students gained through her classroom listening and observation. For example, Nan determines that a student is interested in science fiction and space exploration and uses this information, with the help of the school media specialist, to develop a suggested reading list for the student—one that focuses on things for which the student has an affinity, so reading progress may occur.

Students' Attributions for Success and Failure

Each of us builds theories about our work in the world: Why did this day go well? What could I have done differently to change things? Why did I get this "B" in reading? Why are my peers better readers? Students, like adults, think about the outcomes of things they do. School performance is important and consequential for most students. High or low grades (and scores) get students thinking about why a grade is high or low, how the grade was determined, and why it is expected or unexpected. This thinking leads to theorizing about performance and the development of attributions for our performances (Berkeley et al., 2011; Hiebert et al., 1984). We can believe that external factors, such as luck, the difficulty of the reading task, or the teacher liking or not liking us, cause our reading outcomes. We can make an internal attribution that we gave much or not enough effort to our reading task, or that we are intelligent or not intelligent. Each attribution has the potential to become a habitual way of thinking about oneself in relation to reading success or failure.

Students' theories of their performances may or may not be accurate, but the theories are powerful. Built on students' prior experiences with reading, these theories—attributions—can influence present and future reading experiences. Students may attribute their past reading performances to not being smart and believe that all future reading outcomes will reflect this fact. Students with such attributions are supremely challenged: "Not being smart enough" is seen by most students as a fixed and permanent attribute. From the perspective of the student, reading is best avoided, and when it cannot be, the student may be resigned to failure (Johnston & Winograd, 1985).

Nan uses a series of questions and observations to determine to what students attribute their successes and failures. The questions reflect Nan and her colleagues' knowledge of the research literature on attributions and their ongoing concerns with students' attributions (Frijters et al., 2018; Van Keer & Verhaeghe, 2005). For example, Nan is interested in the attributions her students make about their reading performances, including scores on a quiz, how they understand and discuss stories, and their detailed portfolio work. She also would like to determine if students' attributions are consistent across all the reading they do or if attributions vary related to the subject matter, the type of text, and the nature of the assignment. The questions she asks include the following:

- Why do you think you got this grade?
- Why do you think you understood this chapter?
- Why is your portfolio structured this way?
- Do you feel that you will be more successful with certain reading tasks? Which ones? Why?

Students can change their ideas about the etiology of reading failure and success, which is called retraining attributions, so that new understandings may include "I worked hard and gave my best effort, and as a result, I read better, learned, and achieved." Nan wants to learn the details of her students' attributions so that she can support the development of positive attributions and help students change any negative attributions they possess into positive ones. Given the potential power of the theorizing that students do about their successes and failures, she asks, "Shouldn't we be in the habit of assessing and understanding attributions?"

ASSESSING "THE OTHER": PORTRAIT OF A STRUGGLING READER

It is not enough that we seek to identify the powerful influences of "the other" on reading and the outcomes of reading. We must have a plan that provides assessment information about these factors and address, in a formative manner, students' individual needs. Nan uses assessments that provide formative and summative assessment information related to "the other" factors. At the beginning of the school year, surveys and questionnaires provide information on aspects of students' lives that are essential for reading development. The questionnaires focus on student motivation and engagement and on self-efficacy. These assessments provide complementary information to the cognitive information gathered with a comprehensive reading inventory. Combined, this formative assessment helps Nan understand the challenges her students face and the strengths they possess, both of which can figure greatly in how well students learn strategies and skills.

Nan talks with her colleagues about their students' motivations, self-efficacy, interests, attitudes, and attributions. Each week, she focuses on a particular group of students in her class, using observation and questions to update her understanding. In addition to the beginning- and end-of-year assessments, Nan writes narrative reports on her students' development, one of which is included earlier in this chapter (see Figure 8.1). She uses checklists and series of questions to keep track of her students' growth. Assessment in Nan's classroom is conceived to yield both formative and summative information about "the other" in reading.

Consider Jesse, one of the less accomplished readers in Nan's classroom. Jesse makes the wrong attributions for his reading performance. The attributions are predictable and logical, but they work against his progress in reading. He believes that he is not in control of the act of reading. Thus, his success or failure in reading is perceived to be at the whim of external forces, including luck and the difficulty of the reading task. Related, Jesse is not motivated to read. He comes to Nan's classroom with a record of not reading to grade-level expectation in previous grades, and he is well aware of his status within previous classrooms as a "low" reader. In fact, there is powerful motivation for Jesse to avoid reading, because it portrays him as unsuccessful. The MRP (Gambrell et al., 1996) triangulates the information that Nan gleans from his prior years' narrative report cards. Using her assessment information, she establishes improved motivation as a key goal in fostering Jesse's reading growth. He has very little that is positive regarding his identity as a reader. He has no discernible, helpful reading habits, and his attitude leaves him with little or no opportunity to practice and learn new reading strategies or stances toward reading. If asked, he might state that across the entire school day, he feels least in control of things when he is required to read. His lack of self-efficacy leads him to give minimal effort when reading.

Nan uses items from the reading interest survey and determines that Jesse is devoted to caring for animals. She notes that he is most motivated to try to read almost anything that has to do with rescuing animals and saving injured animals. Currently, this approach is yielding mixed results: Jesse is showing motivation to read, but he is often frustrated because what he wants to learn from text is inaccessible, too difficult to understand. Nan uses her diverse assessments of "the other" to foster his self-efficacy and attitude related to reading. She finds reading materials on animal care that he can understand and use; helps him understand that his motivation yields good results; and works with him to help him see the connections between his motivation, his reading, and the outcomes of his reading.

The fact that Jesse is fanatical in his devotion to caring for animals is key information for helping him begin to make positive changes in terms of motivation, self-concept as a reader, and reading attitude. It is also the place in which he is able to make constructive attributions for his reading performance. That is, he is willing and able to make the connections between his hard work, his perseverance, and the good that comes from his reading efforts. Nan uses this knowledge about Jesse's love of animals to provide him with reading materials from diverse sources, including veterinarian magazines, websites of organizations that care for animals, books on the lives of animals, articles about pets and wild animals, and brochures from zoos. He also becomes a participating member of an online discussion group that focuses on helping local wildlife.

Nan's years of experience teach her that students carry diverse reading motivations, a sense of self in relation to reading, attitudes, and interests that are shaped by (and can shape) their reading. In fact, her reading instruction is clearly intended to foster positive changes in these characteristics within each learner. These are incredibly important outcomes of reading instruction, for without them, attainment of reading standards and benchmarks is nearly impossible.

Finally, Nan and her colleagues use a Healthy Readers Profile (Afflerbach, 2022) to record information related to these "other" aspects of reading development. The Healthy Readers Profile (Form 8.1) is shared from school year to school year with teaching colleagues, providing an account of how motivation and engagement, metacognition, self-efficacy, and attributions are influencing each student's development and achievement. The Healthy Readers Profile is also presented to parents at school meetings and serves to guide teachers' presentation of students' needs beyond strategies and skills. It also helps communicate teachers' efforts and students' accomplishments related to the "other" aspects of student development.

Consequences and Usefulness of Assessment of "the Other"

Nan knows that her assessments of these "other" factors have powerful consequences. Assessment helps Nan understand her students' often complex mix of motivations, self-concepts, attitudes, interests, and attributions at the beginning of the school year, and with this information, she can develop instructional strategies that directly address her students' diverse needs. Nan can chart the change or maintenance of students' affective factors across the academic year. For example, she can demonstrate that her assessment helped her become aware of Jesse's lack of motivation and poor self-concept as a reader and then address both these obstacles through her instruction. Taking Jesse's high-stakes test scores and the detailed documentation of his growth related to motivation, self-concept, attitude, and attributions, Nan develops an explanation of her success in teaching reading—success through attention to both affective and cognitive student growth.

FORM 8.1 Healthy Readers Profile

MOTIVATION AND ENGAGEMENT

Student name: _____

Classroom observation:

Listening to student conversations:

Student interview:

Informal assessments:

Formal assessments:

From *Teaching Readers (Not Reading)* by Peter Afflerbach. Copyright © 2022 The Guilford Press. Reprinted in *Understanding and Using Reading Assessment, K–12, Fourth Edition* (The Guilford Press, 2025). Permission to photocopy this material, or to download and print enlarged versions (*www.guilford.com/afflerbach2-forms*), is granted to purchasers of this book for personal use or use with students; see copyright page for details.

Nan uses assessment to help her pinpoint factors that will enhance or inhibit her students' reading development, and she charts the outcomes of her instruction that represent positive affective changes in her students. The range of assessments allows her to describe growth in her students. Although Nan and her colleagues feel immense pressure to teach the requisite reading strategies and skills, they are convinced that without detailed knowledge of their students' accompanying motivations, attitudes, interests, and self-concepts, their students' test scores will not tell the full story of learning.

The array of assessments contributes to Nan's detailed communications with Jesse's parents. She describes situations in which parents might expect Jesse to be a motivated reader and situations to avoid. Reading materials in which people help animals are clearly recommended. Nan is especially concerned that his parents understand how his self-concept as a reader is gradually changing for the better and that it is a fragile work in progress. With her assessments of "the other," Nan can describe Jesse's reading interests and work that should contribute to his positive self-efficacy.

Roles and Responsibilities Related to Assessment of "the Other"

Nan and her colleagues have gone the extra mile in relation to using assessments to learn about critically important "other" aspects of students' reading development. In many classrooms, assessment helps teachers develop detailed understandings of their students as information processors—readers seen through the lens of strategy and skill assessments. Adding to this assessment mix is work that must be supported and well planned. For Nan and her colleagues, it is an ongoing project to discuss the ideal student reader, or the characteristics of students they would label "healthy readers." A responsibility here is to continue discussions in which successful readers are defined not only in relation to the cognitive target areas of NCLB and state and district learning standards, but also in relation to motivation, self-efficacy, a positive and accurate self-concept, a good attitude toward reading, and making accurate attributions for reading performance. Nan and her colleagues conceptualize their student readers as more than a conglomeration of cognitive strategies and skills and are committed to investigating and describing "the other": those factors that are both influences on and outcomes of successful reading.

Reliability of Assessment of "the Other"

Consistency in assessing "the other" is a goal for Nan. She works toward this goal with several strategies. First, she becomes familiar with the instruments she uses, the sets of items that are taken from each assessment, and the procedures for administering the assessments. Second, she seeks triangulation of all her hypotheses about students' motivations, self-concepts, interests, attitudes, and attributions. To this end, Nan regularly focuses on single students to update her ideas about their reading progress and the factors that can complement or inhibit this progress. She uses classroom observations and questioning, in conjunction with the results of different assessments, to help her follow up on hunches that she has about individual students' motivations or attributions. The observations and questioning derive from a master list of student characteristics and questions that are designed to seek similar information about each student in a reliable and predictable manner.

Validity of the Assessment of "the Other"

Nan and her colleagues want to expand people's ideas about outcomes of high-quality teaching and student reading development and achievement. Nan's classroom experience and knowledge of the research literature tell her that assessment must be a more comprehensive reflection of student reading than is provided by a year-end test that focuses on reading strategies and skills. To this end, her assessment practice not only provides valuable and valid information but also expands her idea of what reading is. Strategies and skills always matter, but they must be surrounded by a supportive network of motivation, self-concept, and a positive attitude toward reading.

Nan's approach to assessing the more broadly conceived construct of reading provides information about factors that *influence* reading development and factors that are a *result* of reading development. For example, the formative assessment that describes students with low motivation to read is used to create motivating reading experiences, and over time, these experiences have helped create more motivated student readers. Summative assessment allows Nan to capture and describe these valuable products of her assessment and instruction.

SUMMARY

Assessments that focus on "the other" in reading help fill in the gap in our understanding of how students are challenged, how they develop, and how they achieve. The information complements what we know about students' cognitive achievement. A result is the development of profiles of readers that move beyond their cognitive strategies and skills to describe each student's motivation to read and willingness to persevere, self-concept as a reader, reading interests, and attributions for reading successes and failures. In this sense, our understanding of affective and conative aspects of students' reading helps us determine how strategies and skills are best used. Furthermore, the assessments used by Nan and her colleagues best represent the integrity and reach of their reading instruction and their students' corresponding growth and achievement. If you are interested in pursuing assessments of "the other" in your school or district, you can use the Assessing "the Other": Questions for Teachers and Administrators reproducible form in the Appendix.

Enhancing Your Understanding

1. Create a map or graphic organizer of your goals for your students as readers. Next, describe how your assessments map onto this territory. What is covered? What is not covered? What needs attention?

2. Choose one aspect of students' reading development that you feel is underrepresented or missed by current assessment in your school. Determine how you can begin to assess, address, and report on this aspect of reading development. Create, find, and borrow your means to do so.

3. Develop a presentation for your teaching colleagues, administrators, or parents that catalogs the things that are missed with the current reading assessment regimen. Propose the means to assess "the other" in your school, including motivation, self-concept, attitude, interest, and attribution.

Reading Assessment Snapshot
ASSESSING STUDENT COLLABORATION AND COOPERATION

Working and learning often involve collaboration with other people. In school, an individual student's learning and achievement continue as the primary focus of assessment. Yet, what about the school tasks that revolve around students learning and collaborating with one another? How do we assess collaborative group work and problem-based learning? For example, a school assignment that engages students in a group project to learn about a particular country's imports and exports may include specific roles and responsibilities for the members of a collaborative group. The assignment must be matched with an integrity of assessment: clearly defined measures that describe how students read and contribute to collaborative work and how they grow in terms of content-area learning.

Creative solutions to assessment challenges help us make the most of the collaborative experiences that we undertake in our classrooms. One solution is to assign specific tasks within the collaborative learning team so that each member has clear goals whose attainment helps demonstrate the learning and work that take place. Although the division of learning tasks within collaborative groups can be time-consuming work, it is necessary and beneficial. A task analysis of what is to be learned and assessed and how different collaborative group members may or may not be engaged in different facets of the project is important. At least as challenging is the measure of each team member's learning and contribution. We must be able to account for an individual student's particular learning and contribution in relation to an assigned role or task. We must also be able to chart and describe the student's growth and learning in the larger, collaborative task. Collaborative learning may join students of mixed ability levels, interests, and motivations. In each of these situations, we must be careful to clearly specify the work to be done, the division of responsibility, and the means to measure and describe collaborative and individual student contributions to accomplishments. It is important that we have a clear sense of the complexity and magnitude of the work and achievement that we expect in collaborative learning situations so that we can adjust our expectations and assessments accordingly.

Collaborative learning situations provide students with opportunities for social learning. Outcomes may include a newfound respect for classmates and their opinions, understanding work team dynamics, and taking turns. Our assessment efforts will do well to describe these valuable learning outcomes, above and beyond the information that they yield related to reading achievement.

CHAPTER 9

Formative and Summative Assessment

Effective reading programs combine formative and summative assessment. Formative assessment helps us understand students' ongoing reading strengths and needs and informs instruction that fosters students' reading development. For example, a fifth-grade history lesson includes new vocabulary that is central to understanding the text. The teacher's questioning about the concepts represented by the vocabulary indicates that some students struggle to comprehend the text. This formative assessment information is immediately useful to the teacher, who determines that the challenging words should be the focus of further discussion and explanation. Formative assessment captures the students' needs and alerts us to immediate teaching and learning opportunities.

In contrast, summative assessments provide a summary of student achievement. These assessments help us take measure of student achievement in relation to curriculum goals and district and state learning standards. High-stakes tests are examples of summative assessments, as their results are used for comparing students and determining which students meet achievement benchmarks. Unit tests in history and other subjects provide summative accounts of student learning in relation to curricular goals, as do year-end tests. Summative assessments can also be used for comparing students with other students and with actual and expected student achievement levels.

The designation of formative or summative assessment is determined by the way a particular assessment is used. Some assessments can be used in both a formative and a summative manner. For example, consider teachers' questions that follow reading in history. Students' responses to these questions allow us to make inferences about students' learning. Our immediate consideration of students' answers might suggest that we need to reteach and clarify an important concept, such as democracy, or check on students' understanding of a related vocabulary word, such as *citizen*. Thus, the teacher's questions serve as formative assessment. The answers to the questions describe students' understanding of important course content—and their attainment of important learning outcomes. A student's answers figure into the weekly grade and are then used in determining the history report card grade. Here, student responses to the teacher's questions provide summative assessment.

Conducting formative assessment or summative assessment may require different levels of teacher expertise. High-stakes tests are standardized, and the teacher's role in administering these tests is prescribed; for example, teachers read scripted instructions and are expected to present them to students clearly and to treat each student in the same manner. In contrast to such summative assessments, teacher expertise with formative assessment involves keeping close track of the important questions to ask during classroom lessons, interpreting students' responses to those questions, and using those responses to inform instruction.

There is a clear need for a balance of formative and summative reading assessments in the classroom. As students work toward complex reading and related standards, formative and summative assessment should work together to inform us of students' growth and development in relation to attaining the standards. The PARCC and SBAC consortia developed performance assessments that provide measures of cognitive strategy and skill and content-area knowledge gain. The tests are administered at the conclusion of cycles of complex learning and performance. Examples of these summative assessments are available at each website: *https://resources.newmeridiancorp.org* and *https://smarterbalanced.org*.

An examination of the PARCC and SBAC tests, and the reading prowess that students must possess to succeed at these tests, reminds us that success on summative assessments depends on formative assessment.

THE NEED FOR FORMATIVE ASSESSMENT

The ongoing focus on summative, high-stakes tests should not deflect our attention from formative assessment. Indeed, students' adequate performance on these tests depends on effective formative assessment. We do not want students taking challenging summative performance assessments without instruction that is informed by formative assessments and that helps prepare students for the summative assessment. In this sense, formative assessment serves to guide both student and teacher along the path to reading achievement that is demonstrated when meeting a particular standard, as measured by summative assessments.

I believe that juxtaposing formative assessment with zones of proximal development (Vygotsky, 1978) is useful for examining the interrelationships of teaching and learning, and formative and summative assessment. Effective teaching and learning in zones of proximal development revolve around the idea that teachers can determine, with the necessary detail, students' current level of accomplishment and achievement. The determination of "where the student is" is accomplished with formative assessment. With the information gained through formative assessment, the teacher determines what a student needs next, and the instruction and learning that will help move the student through successive zones of proximal development. Over the course of a content-area lesson, unit, or marking period, these teaching episodes contribute to students' learning. Informed by formative assessment, teachers create instruction that helps students progress from their current level to the next anticipated level of achievement.

As readers, we construct meaning by combining new information from the text with prior knowledge, or what we already know. As teachers, we construct new understandings of our students by gathering "fresh" assessment information, updating our knowledge of what a student can do, what learning challenges are appropriate, and what instruction is suitable. Formative assessment provides this information.

CHARACTERISTICS OF FORMATIVE ASSESSMENT

Mansell et al. (2009, p. 10) provide a fine-grained description of formative assessment. In the following section, I elaborate on Mansell et al.'s (2009) list of preferred characteristics of formative assessment.

- *Part of effective planning.* Done well, formative assessment is "built in" as curriculum is developed. It is not patched on after the fact. This demands that teaching and learning and assessment be conceptualized simultaneously, adding to the task of planning effective curriculum. Efforts in this regard are rewarded by the a priori determination of what to assess, when to assess, and how to assess, and the dovetailing of formative assessment with summative assessment.

- *Focused on how pupils learn.* Formative assessment is conducted in the midst of teaching and learning. As such, teachers are privy to what students learn and how they learn. Assessment information helps teachers focus on the processes that students use to learn, as well as the content that students learn.

- *Central to classroom practice.* Assessment is a natural part of the teaching–learning–assessment cycle. When assessment is at the heart of classroom practice, it creates new responsibilities for teachers, and making it so requires appropriate amounts of time and teacher training to develop and use formative assessment.

- *A key professional skill.* Successful teachers gauge instruction to students' individual needs. This accomplishment, of meeting students where they are to provide effective instruction, reflects the skill of teaching. As important is the skill of conducting and using formative assessment in the service of teaching and learning.

- *Sensitive and constructive.* Student learning is influenced by many factors, including prior knowledge for content areas and strategy and skill development. In addition, motivation and engagement, self-efficacy, and attributions have demonstrated influence on student reading. Effective formative assessment is sensitive to each of these and provides teachers with information that contributes to teaching for students' ongoing development.

- *Fosters motivation.* Motivation drives learning. Formative assessment can influence student motivation in several ways. It helps students build the connection between their effort and accomplishment. It helps teachers identify students' zones of proximal development, in which student achievement and related motivation to learn can continue to develop. Formative assessment helps teachers create attainable challenges for students, and students' attainment, in turn, fuels positive motivation to read.

- *Promotes understanding of goals and criteria.* Students may be reminded, through assessment, of the point of instruction. Teachers can provide assessment feedback to students that is framed in relation to the goals of learning. In addition, formative assessment provides the forum in which the means for evaluating student learning can be described and discussed.

- *Helps learners know how to improve.* Formative assessment is developed with curriculum, and this means that assessment information is dovetailed with instruction. The focus of formative assessment is the "nitty-gritty" of learning, and this affords teachers the opportunity to influence both the processes and products of learning. As formative assessment helps students learn how assessment works, it contributes to their metacognitive development.

- *Develops the capacity for self-assessment.* Effective programs not only "do" good assessment, but they also teach students how to do assessment for themselves (see Chapter 10 for more on self-assessment). Formative assessment, conducted as students learn, can serve as a model. Self-assessment involves student mindsets and strategies—and these can be modeled and described by teachers much in the manner of reading strategy instruction.

- *Recognizes all educational achievement.* Formative assessment allows us to note learning as it occurs during lessons and across the school day. It is an "on demand" form of assessment that informs about learning whenever it occurs, and it is not constrained by a predetermined time or place. Thus, formative assessment faithfully reflects the nature of learning—occurring sometimes in small but important increments. If you are interested in examining the nature of formative and summative assessment in your school or district, you can use the reproducible Checklist for Planning Effective Formative Assessment in the Appendix.

In summary, comprehensive formative assessment must be an integral part of any reading program. Formative assessment provides critical information about the status of student learning, and so informs instruction. Formative assessment helps teachers gauge student work in relation to a myriad of learning outcomes, and helps students become mindful about their learning.

CHARACTERISTICS OF SUMMATIVE ASSESSMENT

Summative assessment provides important information throughout students' school careers. Summative assessment helps us determine the nature of students' growth in relation to learning objectives, be they at the end of a teaching sequence, a unit, a marking period, or an academic year. A teacher's question at the end of a lesson, an end-of-unit test, a final examination, and a performance assessment—all can provide summary statements of student achievement.

Summative assessments are often associated with accountability. Test scores are used in evaluations of teachers, reading programs, and schools. Teachers may be judged in relation to their students' performance on summative, high-stakes tests (Gabriel & Allington, 2016). Tenure and salary decisions may rest on the evidence of a single score on a summative assessment. Reading program effectiveness is judged by examining how many students meet (or fail to meet) school district and state benchmark performance levels and standards. Similarly, school accountability is strongly tied to summative assessment test scores. I note that while summative assessment scores are used to demonstrate accountability, accountability is created through the regular use of classroom-based formative assessments.

Summative assessment is typically less flexible than formative assessment in terms of the questions and prompts that are used to evoke student responses. This is because summative assessments are most often tied to preestablished learning outcomes. Examples of these outcomes are national and state standards, reading program goals, and state and benchmark reading performances. By contrast, formative assessment is dynamic and informed by ongoing teacher and student interactions (Mansell et al., 2010).

FORMATIVE AND SUMMATIVE ASSESSMENT IN JORGE'S THIRD-GRADE CLASSROOM

Jorge teaches a class of diverse third graders. His students vary in their reading achievement levels—some are reading at a fourth-grade level, and others are struggling with

Formative and Summative Assessment

developing comprehension strategies and sight word vocabularies. Similarly, there is diversity in students' motivation, engagement, and self-efficacy. Meeting all students at their areas of strength and need is challenge enough. However, all students in Jorge's class are expected to meet the third-grade CCSS at the end of the school year. Such diversity in students and learning outcomes demands a suite of assessments that best samples, supports, and communicates students' development.

The path that Jorge and his students follow toward the attainment of the standards is informed by formative and summative assessment. Meeting standards requires that the third graders engage with complex texts and complex tasks. Embedded in these tasks is an array of reading strategies, skills, and mindsets that must be operating for student success. Thus, it makes sense to take account of all the "parts" of reading that must be operating for student success. The coordination of formative and summative assessment allows for this accounting. It is within this frame that we can consider the nature of formative and summative assessment, their differences, their relationships, and the need for them to work together in support of teaching and learning, and it is a first-order task for the school administration. The allocation of funds helps to chart the path from students' learning individual strategies and skills to the successful coordination of these and their application in increasingly complex tasks, with increasingly difficult texts.

Jorge, his third-grade teacher colleagues, and district administrators analyze the CCSS to inform their decisions about instruction and formative assessment. As part of the districtwide effort to help students meet the standards, they perform a task analysis that allows them to pinpoint the specific knowledge that students must have to succeed at the English/language arts standards. For example, Jorge and his colleagues conduct a task analysis of the following CCSS:

Integration of Knowledge and Ideas:

CCSS.ELA-LITERACY.RI.3.7

Use information gained from illustrations (e.g., maps, photographs) and the words in a text to demonstrate understanding of the text (e.g., where, when, why, and how key events occur). (Common Core State Standards, 2024b)

The task analysis yields information that helps Jorge and his colleagues focus on related formative assessment. Meeting the third-grade CCSS involves students doing the following:

- Constructing meaning from text
- Understanding a related illustration
- Determining related information from text and illustration
- Comparing the two sources for common and unique information

- Synthesizing information from the two sources to achieve multiple source comprehension
- Using metacognition to coordinate all these strategies and skills and monitor the complex task

At the conclusion of this task analysis, the teachers pose a question: "How will third-grade readers succeed at this CCSS, one that includes text complexity and task complexity, without the benefits of ongoing formative assessment and related teacher feedback and instruction?" Because Jorge's class is marked by a diversity of reading achievement levels, formative assessment must inform as to students' reading strategies and skills: what students possess and what they still need. This information helps shape daily instruction.

The task analysis puts Jorge and his colleagues in a good position to understand and appreciate all that a third-grade student must do to meet the CCSS. With this understanding, they can consider the formative assessment that helps them help students learn the different facets of the complex performance. Formative assessment also provides feedback as students progress to the final, orchestrated grand performance that is the attainment of the standard.

The task analysis reveals that students must be accomplished readers in order to meet this standard. They must use all five target areas of NCLB and Reading First in concert to construct meaning from the text. The third-grade students who are struggling must have their needs identified in relation to phonemic awareness, phonics, fluency, vocabulary, and comprehension. The students must also comprehend a related illustration (a drawing, diagram, or photo)—and to do so, must have appropriate prior knowledge. Next, students must be able to determine the common information from the two related sources—that from text and that from the illustration. Students must then synthesize information from the two sources to construct meaning from them. Jorge and his colleagues assume that students use metacognition to coordinate these skills and strategies and to guide the entire reading process.

While a daunting prospect, helping all students progress toward attainment of the standard will be fostered over the course of the third-grade school year. This accomplishment is not possible without the benefits of continuous formative assessment and the instruction that it informs. The detailed task analysis conducted by Jorge and his colleagues helps create the blueprint for both formative and summative assessment. Following are the foci of the formative assessment and how third teachers will gather this assessment information:

- *Construct meaning from text.* Teachers use a combination of questions, student retellings, and observing and listening to their students to make this determination.

- *Understand a related illustration.* Teachers ask questions that require verbal and written responses that demonstrate their students' comprehension of the diagram (or other related illustration or table).
- *Determine related information from the text and the illustration.* Teachers use a template that allows students to list what they learned from each source. From these tandem lists, students then determine what information is shared across the two sources.
- *Compare the two sources for common and unique information.* Students work with Venn diagrams to list the information they learned from each source (text and illustration) to determine the joint or unique nature of the information given.
- *Synthesize information from the two sources to construct meaning.* Students think aloud, describing how they synthesize information from the two sources. Teachers assess students' text syntheses using a scoring rubric that is displayed prominently in the classroom and understood by students.
- *Use metacognition to coordinate all these strategies and skills and to monitor the complex task.* Students use metacognitive checklists that prompt questions including "Does that make sense?," "Is there a problem?," and "Am I remembering the information from the text and the image?" Teachers scrutinize responses to the checklist to check in on students' ongoing comprehension, reading-related task, and development of comprehension monitoring.
- *Develop motivation and maintain engagement.* Students need motivation and engagement to keep them focused and to fuel their effort throughout the complex performance.

The above approach requires frequent formative assessment. Each of the assessments informs Jorge as to what reader strategies should be assessed. The deconstruction of the CCSS allows for instruction that focuses on the strategies and skills that sum to attainment of the standard. We should not expect that students learn all the constituent parts of a complex performance at once or that they are facile in orchestrating the use of these parts. These parts are learned along the path to successful performance, and formative assessment allows us to check student development on that path. Students demonstrate learning (and teachers demonstrate accountability) when a CCSS is met. However, the success at the summative performance (such as the focus CCSS included in PARCC or SBAC assessments) is made possible by a series of detailed and informative formative assessments. If you are interested in examining the nature of formative and summative assessments in your school or district, you can use the Formative Assessment Coverage That Contributes to Students' Achievement on High-Stakes Summative Assessments reproducible form in the Appendix.

Jorge also fosters the metacognitive strategies that students need for success. His careful questioning serves as a scaffold for students' further inquiry and helps them progress to more complex cognitive processing. With this move toward increasing complexity, students may become motivated to monitor their work and progress (Clark, 2012). In addition to the cognitive growth that is hoped for across third grade and demanded as an entry point by the CCSS, Jorge and his colleagues assess students' motivation and engagement and self-efficacy using a combination of observation checklists and published surveys. They listen to their students. This information is combined to yield complex student profiles that inform instruction beyond strategy and skill. (For more on assessment of these "other" aspects of students' reading development, see Chapter 8.)

SUMMARY

It is critical that formative and summative assessment are coordinated. Both must operate, not in opposition or competition, but together to provide teachers and students with useful information. Effective reading programs include both formative and summative assessments, and they reflect the careful consideration of how these two general classes of reading assessment work together. Formative assessment provides information that helps teachers address students' immediate instructional needs, framing students' zones of proximal development. Formative assessment provides details about what students need in a timely manner. Across the school year, well-coordinated formative assessment supports teachers and students in their work toward complex reading achievements. Summative assessment tells us of students' attainment of key learning goals and curriculum outcomes. Over a lesson, unit, marking period, or academic year, summative assessment helps us understand progress over time. Summative assessment should always be coordinated with formative assessment, and the former should offer a measure of student reading that is anticipated by the latter.

Enhancing Your Understanding

1. Choose a relevant reading standard (e.g., a state reading standard or an English/language arts CCSS). With your colleagues, conduct a task analysis that identifies the different aspects of reading that a student must use to succeed at the standard.

2. Next, create a list of formative assessment materials and procedures that will help you best understand the degree of your students' development in relation to each and every aspect of reading identified by the task analysis.

3. Choose a student in your classroom and determine an area of reading development in which the student will benefit from your instruction. Next, consider the student's zone of proximal development: What formative assessments can you use to best inform your reading instruction with the student?

Reading Assessment Snapshot

AUTHENTIC ASSESSMENT

Authentic assessments share at least one of two characteristics. First, such assessments may be embedded in classroom routines of instruction and learning and conducted during regular activities of the classroom. These assessments are clearly related to students' learning and achievement. The inferences that we make from this information regarding student development are more directly connected to the curriculum and student learning. Second, authentic assessments may focus on students' real-world reading as opposed to more typical test-like texts. Here, authentic assessment should involve students' performance on texts and tasks that have important counterparts in the world outside the school. This authentic assessment is situated in contexts that anticipate the use of reading in the lives of students in and out of academic settings, be it for work, personal fulfillment, or academic pursuit. Authentic assessment holds great promise for describing the diverse ways in which students grow and develop in the literacy curriculum.

When district, state, and national standards for reading specify goals of complex student learning, we must use assessments that describe and accurately measure this complexity. Authentic assessments done well provide such measures. Authentic assessment is often centered on the interactions of teachers and students, and because the assessment is embedded in instruction, the teacher must assume the role of assessment expert. Assessment that is focused on important classroom routines can provide results that are immediately useful. Teachers use the results of authentic assessment to shape instruction and provide feedback for students.

When authentic assessment reflects (and anticipates) the manner in which we read and apply knowledge gained through reading, we are able to expand our ideas about student achievement. It is the manner in which an assessment is used, how it connects to the curriculum, and what it demands of students that contributes to authentic assessment.

CHAPTER 10

Promoting Self-Assessment to Help Students Build Reading Independence

Across the school years, assessment provides important information about students' reading development. Formative assessment identifies students' current strengths and needs and informs teaching in the moment. Teachers use assessment to shape their instruction to best meet student needs in their zones of proximal development (Vygotsky, 1978). Formative assessment guides our decisions about what and when to teach. In turn, summative assessment informs about students' attainment of learning goals—at the completion of lessons, units, marking periods, and the academic year. These traditional and valuable uses of reading assessment—to provide ongoing and summary information—might be reward enough for our assessment efforts. However, if we limit our vision, we miss an opportunity for reading assessment to further contribute to students' reading development.

What does assessment have to do with independent and successful readers? Reading assessment can help us teach. When assessment is used in a teaching role, we can model how, why, when, and where to assess (Afflerbach, 2022). We can discuss and explain assessment so that it helps students begin, work through, and successfully complete reading tasks. Eventually, these external assessment models become internalized by the independent student reader. This marks a major difference between developing readers and independent readers. Independent readers set goals, monitor their progress at reading, and determine if they have met their reading goals. Readers who are successful at self-assessment know when they are reading well. When these readers encounter difficulties, they identify problems, address them, and then continue on.

We don't expect early readers to read with a complete repertoire of cognitive strategies, and the same dynamic operates with self-assessment strategies. Indeed, a marked difference between most kindergarteners and successful older readers is the ability to self-assess. Over time, students' growth in self-assessment affords independence and successful reading. Reading independently is a watershed accomplishment for students, and self-assessment is at the center of the achievement. Thus, we do well to confirm that reading assessment not only informs us about the status of student reading but also teaches students how to do assessment for themselves.

THE NATURE OF SELF-ASSESSMENT

Self-assessment, metacognition, self-awareness, mindfulness, executive function—these words help describe students who are progressing toward success and independence in reading. Veenman (2016) describes metacognition as including organizing, directing, and controlling one's learning. To be successful, student readers should learn to set goals, monitor their progress, evaluate their performance, and reflect on their learning. Self-assessment is an aspect of metacognition, and metacognition is at the center of students' independent and successful reading. It promotes academic learning and contributes to reading comprehension (Baker & Brown, 1984). Wang et al. (1990) determined that students' metacognition, including self-assessment, is a strong predictor of learning success. Students who self-assess use their awareness of their own thinking processes, their understanding of what is needed for learning, and their regulation of cognitive strategies, skills, and the learning process to read successfully (Barzilai & Strømsø, 2018; Borkowski & Turner, 1990). Metacognition helps students gain control of their act of reading (Boekaerts et al., 2000; Zimmerman & Moylan, 2009).

Veenman (2016) lists three phases of reading that are impacted by students' self-assessment. First, there is *orientation and planning at the onset of reading*. Here, successful students "size up" the reading task at hand. They make sure that they understand the reading task, whether the task is assigned or self-selected. They check on the resources that they believe are needed to succeed. They may determine that they are ready to begin reading or that they need to consult others (including teachers, peers, and different media). Students also set goals in relation to the reading task, and this goal-setting provides a constant against which students can measure their progress. Without the self-assessment that is needed for orientation and planning work, student readers will not have a foundation on which to judge their progress.

The second important phase of self-assessment occurs as students *monitor and select methods* for processing text during reading. Here, students pay attention to their progress at constructing meaning. They check to see that they understand the information in text—within and across sentences, within and across paragraphs, and across texts. Self-assessing students regularly ask, "Does that make sense?," "Is there a problem?," "What is the problem?," and related comprehension-monitoring questions. These students are flexible in selecting reading strategies, and they check their progress at understanding text with the goals they set at the beginning of reading. Self-assessment helps students manage their reading—from simple to complex reading tasks.

Third, students who self-assess *evaluate after reading*. The completion of reading is marked by students determining the degree to which the goal of reading has been met. Students compare the meaning constructed with the understanding(s) necessary for successful completion of the reading-related task. This end-of-reading evaluation is a final complement in the ongoing assessment that takes place as students work through a text. Evaluation can focus on different reading outcomes. These range from determining that a literal understanding of text is established to the application of what is learned in a performance that reflects students' higher-order thinking. Upon completion of reading, students can review their performance.

THE DEVELOPMENT OF SELF-ASSESSMENT

Self-assessing student readers are mindful and strategic, and they share important developmental characteristics. Self-assessment abilities develop over time and with experience, and the assessment we do with our students can contribute greatly to this development. When classroom reading assessment is planned to both evaluate and teach, we are in a position to garner the greatest benefits.

Consider the following array of strategies and mindsets that operate when students self-assess. Students who self-assess are learning to control their reading. They effectively plan and then begin their reading, consistently monitoring their progress toward their reading goal. They monitor comprehension, checking on the meaning-construction process, noting blockages to the construction of meaning and addressing them. When difficulties are encountered, these readers employ fix-it strategies. Students self-assess and adjust their reading based on what their assessment yields. They focus on near and far goals and related tasks, and they determine if they have met their reading goals. Students not only become aware of their cognitive performance—it helps them make connections between their effort, motivation, self-efficacy, and reading performance. Self-assessment provides insights that help students make accurate attributions for their performances. For example, a student may determine that a better performance could be had through increased attention and effort, or that both were operating to fuel success. In turn, this knowledge contributes to self-efficacy, as self-assessing students understand the connection between their use of strategies and skills, their effort, and their achievement. Self-assessment can contribute to an understanding of the "bigger picture" of learning to read.

The above depiction assumes that students learn to reflect and become increasingly aware of themselves as readers. The benefits of self-assessment come with costs, however. Self-assessing adds to students' tasks as they read. As with the development of reading strategies, we should expect that students who are learning and using self-assessment strategies will place considerable cognitive resources and effort into the process. Consider the second grader who is learning to ask questions like, "Does this sentence make sense?" and "What problem is making it hard to understand this story?" These questions, and the work that they prompt on the reader's part, place demands on what may already be the student's fully engaged cognitive system. To self-assess well, students must give attention to both constructing meaning and assessing it. This adds to developing student readers' cognitive load—and it reminds us that the teaching of self-assessment is best accomplished with incremental, easily learned and practiced assessment routines. Then, self-assessment strategies should be marked by increasing efficiency in use. Later in their reading careers, such strategies can become automatic, operating as automatized cognitive reading skills (Afflerbach et al., 2008).

The implications for instruction are important: Helping students learn to self-assess involves two complex zones of proximal development. The first relates to the student's developing reading strategies and skills (say, fluency, comprehension, or decoding), and the second involves the developing self-assessment system. Our instruction should seek a balance between the two, and should encourage students to work with texts, learning goals, and self-assessment goals that offer them a comfortable challenge. Because both reading and self-assessment are developing, a too-challenging combination may lead to failure and frustration. For example, if students are reading a demanding text that fully engages their cognitive strategies and skills and is on the edge of prior knowledge resources, then a complex self-assessment task may overwhelm the student reader. A demanding self-assessment routine may tax the developing reader's cognitive system to the point where even the literal comprehension is difficult.

Conceptualizing reading assessment as something to teach allows us to plan instruction in relation to the development of students' self-assessment strategies and mindsets. In many schools and classrooms, reading assessment is done *to* students or *for* students. Students respond to teachers' questions and receive feedback as to the accuracy of their response. Often, students are not privy to teachers' reasoning behind the assessment. Students take quizzes and tests that are evaluated and graded, and then returned to the student. The student work is assigned a score, but the student gains no understanding of how assessment works. A result is that assessment is a "black box" (Black & Wiliam, 1998)—students know that important things happen in this black box, but they have no idea what these things are.

A consequence of students being outsiders to the culture of assessment is that they do not learn to do reading assessment for themselves. When we ask questions in class, students will not understand how we evaluate their reading without our explanation of why we ask these questions or how we arrive at our evaluations of student responses. When we evaluate students' performance assessments, students will not comprehend how we determine the grade if we do not explain the dynamics of using rubrics to help evaluate performances. Not sharing assessment with students means lost opportunities for them to learn to do reading assessment on their own. Self-assessment cannot happen when students do not know its workings.

We must create classrooms in which assessment is done *with* students and *by* students. Our assessment should provide students with the means to eventually assume responsibility for assessing their reading. Accomplished readers regularly assess their ongoing comprehension of text and their progress toward reading-related goals, as they are metacognitive. This ability is not innate: It is learned from models of doing assessment that the students eventually internalize. In fact, a hallmark of a successful reader is the ability to monitor reading and conduct ongoing assessment of reading progress (Xie et al., 2023).

In summary, self-assessment is necessary for students' independent, successful reading. Across history, people have learned to self-assess without related, formal instruction. However, instruction in self-assessment strategies makes this learning process more efficient. The teaching of reading self-assessment strategies and routines can help optimize the developing reader's movement from little metacognition to becoming an independent, self-assessing reader. Helping students achieve success with self-assessment requires that we augment assessment done *for* students to assessment done *with* and *by* students. We do so by consistently presenting assessment as a necessary and powerful aspect of reading. We discuss assessment; we explain its value; we model its use; and we think aloud about how it works, when to use it, and the tangible outcomes of self-assessment.

USING ASSESSMENT TO TEACH SELF-ASSESSMENT IN CICELY'S CLASSROOM

Given the centrality of self-assessment to students' reading growth, we should plan to teach assessment. Consider schools in which teachers and administrators are working to bring the teaching of assessment front and center, with the long-term goal of encouraging students' self-assessment, independence, and success. In Cicely's third-grade classroom, assessment plays a major role in helping students build awareness, plan their work, and reflect on their progress. Students' development as self-assessing readers is encouraged by the districtwide curriculum that emphasizes mindfulness, reflection, and self-awareness. The district adheres to Veenman's

(2016) suggestion that self-assessment should focus on students' orientation and planning at the onset of reading, monitoring and selecting methods for being metacognitive, and evaluating themselves after reading. In social studies classrooms, students are learning to self-assess themselves in relation to effectively using cues to determine source text status. In science, students are learning to self-assess their ability to follow written directions as they conduct scientific inquiry. In music and art, students chart their progress in relation to detailed performance rubrics.

As students begin to develop self-assessment mindsets, we can provide self-assessment strategy instruction. The mindset provides a "place" for developing readers to build these strategies. Across the school year, Cicely focuses on three aspects of reading assessment to help her model, explain, and teach self-assessment. Teacher questions, checklists, and rubrics for performance assessments provide ongoing opportunities to show students the means and benefits of building independence through self-assessment.

Teacher and Student Questioning

Teachers' and students' questions, and the discussions surrounding these questions, are a rich resource for the teaching of self-assessment. (For more on questions, see Chapter 4.) Modeling effective questions, explaining the purpose of our questions, examining the "nuts and bolts" of how we decide what questions to ask, and demonstrating how we evaluate student responses to these questions can help students best understand self-assessment.

Cicely models self-assessment questions in accordance with Veenman's (2016) phases of reading. This allows her to present important questions for self-assessment, and to present them in a sequence that fairly mimics the time course of reading. Thus, students get models of good self-assessment questions and when and where to ask them. Cicely's questions are presented in Figure 10.1.

Cicely thinks aloud and explains her questions, and she encourages student discussion about each question. Students' follow-up discussions allow for reinforcement of the what, how, when, where, and why of these questions.

Cicely's attention to teacher questioning results in students' familiarity with questions and an increasing ability to self-assess. The positive influence of these self-assessment questions is not limited to Cicely's face-to-face interactions with her students; as we see in the next section, checklists containing these and similar questions serve as a scaffold to encourage success and independence.

Checklists

Checklists play an important role in helping students learn to self-assess. With checklists, we can help students initiate, practice, and master self-assessment

> **Orientation and planning at the onset of reading**
> - What are my goals for reading?
> - Do I have the needed resources to succeed at reading?
> - What other resources might I need?
> - When will I check on my progress?
> - How will I check on my progress?
> - Am I flexible so that as I read I can revise my plan?
> - Am I flexible so that as I read I can change my goal?
>
> **Monitoring and selecting methods for being metacognitive**
> - When and where am I checking on my progress?
> - Against what standard am I making self-assessment decisions?
> - When my self-assessment alerts me to a challenge, how do I link it with my reading strategies?
>
> **Evaluation after reading**
> - What is my goal for reading?
> - Did I reach my goal?
> - If so, what contributed to my success?
> - If not, what were the challenges I encountered?

FIGURE 10.1. Sample self-assessment questions.

routines. Consider the checklist used by a second-grade teacher in Figure 10.2. When students read, she asks them to refer to the checklist and engage in the self-assessment thinking that it requires. She models how to use the checklist and explains that her students will learn to use it as they read independently.

The checklist makes several contributions to students' developing self-assessment abilities. First, it provides concrete examples of appropriate self-assessment. This is important instructional follow-through from the classroom discussion of self-assessment questions and Cicely's modeling of asking questions.

> ☐ I check to see if what I read makes sense.
> ☐ I remind myself why I am reading.
> ☐ I focus on the goal of my reading while I read.
> ☐ I check to see if I can summarize sentences and paragraphs.
> ☐ If reading gets hard, I ask myself if there are any problems.
> ☐ I try to identify the problem.
> ☐ I try to fix the problem.
> ☐ When the problem is fixed, I get back to my reading, making sure I understand what I've read so far.

FIGURE 10.2. Sample self-assessment checklist used in second grade.

The checklist items in Figure 10.2 focus on comprehension monitoring. Over time, students can internalize these statements and use them as prompts to engage in self-assessment. As students learn to regularly ask such questions, they can move from a printed checklist provided by the teacher to an internal checklist that can be applied as needed. Second, the checklist provides an example of a typical sequence of helpful self-assessment questions. For students, it is a question not only of what questions to ask, but also when to ask them. Third, the checklist can be complemented by teacher talk and modeling—the teacher models the use of the checklist by asking related questions of herself when she reads to the students and thinks aloud about why she asks the questions and her answers to the questions. This predictable presentation of self-assessment routines helps set developing readers on a healthy path to self-assessment. If you are interested in developing a student self-assessment checklist for use in your classroom, school, or district, you can use the reproducible Checklist for Self-Assessment in the Appendix.

Administrators and teachers throughout Cicely's district created a developmental approach to helping students learn self-assessment. Based on their experiences in early elementary grades, there is the assumption that students can grow increasingly sophisticated assessment routines. To this end, the checklists used in the district are adjusted to the content and complexity of instructional goals. Early elementary students focus on comprehension monitoring. Beginning in fourth grade, students use checklists to enhance their critical reading. Checklists for critical reading include the following items:

- ☐ I try to determine what is fact and what is opinion when I read.
- ☐ I check to determine if the author provides evidence to support claims.
- ☐ I compare the text information with what I already know about the topic.
- ☐ I try to determine the author's purpose when it is not explicitly stated.
- ☐ I work to identify the subtext of things I read.

If you are interested in developing a checklist for students' critical reading for use in your classroom, school, or district, you can use the reproducible Checklist for Critical Reading in the Appendix.

Across elementary school, middle school, and high school, checklists support students in increasingly complex self-assessment routines. These checklists are specific to reading in different content domains. In history, students' self-assessment strategies are enhanced with checklists that focus on the status of a text as a primary or secondary source, as well as on the trustworthiness and reliability of text. Each item on the checklist encourages students to reflect and self-assess. Combined, the items provide student self-assessment practice in going beyond a literal understanding of history. The history checklist is presented in Figure 10.3.

The next example reflects the district's use of checklists to help students

> **Paragraph and checklist on cues to determine source text status:**
> ☐ I determine when the text was written.
> ☐ I determine the purpose of the text.
> ☐ I determine the author of the text.
> ☐ I determine the type of text.
>
> **Cues to source type:**
> ☐ I check on the provenance of the text (where the text comes from).
> ☐ I determine the age of the text (the date of origination or publication).
> ☐ I check on the spelling and grammar of the text.

FIGURE 10.3. Sample checklist for reading history texts.

self-assess in relation to the CCSS. The complexity of the performance assessments that are used to determine students' attainment of standards raises the question of how students will independently and successfully navigate the path toward success. Checklist items related to the CCSS include the following:

☐ What reading must I do to help meet the standard?
☐ What are the related tasks that help me meet the standard?
☐ What resources should I consult to help meet the standard?
☐ What are good places to stop and check on my progress?

Nidus and Sadder (2016) suggest that checklists should be one of several components in any program that is designed to help students develop effective self-assessment routines. A concern is that some students will just "check" items on the checklist without engaging in the self-assessment routines that are required. The authors suggest that the use of checklists should be complemented by instruction that helps them to create attainable goals and carefully monitor their work and progress. Cicely is confident that her initial instruction and classroom discussions provide both good models of self-assessment and clear explanations of the value of self-assessment to help students move beyond the simple act of checking items.

In summary, checklists provide students with structured and sequenced opportunities to think about their work and to self-assess. Checklists serve initially as external prompts for student self-assessment, and these prompts can be internalized as students build their self-assessment repertoires. Given this potential, it is essential that we create checklists that guide students to important insights about their reading. As student reading develops, we should expect that checklists focus on increasingly complex and demanding aspects of reading self-assessment.

RUBRICS

Rubrics provide students with explicit goals and criteria for conducting assessment. When students use rubrics, they compare their own work against specific characterizations of performance and related grades. This process, giving a detailed accounting of one's own reading, represents a critical self-assessment behavior and is at the center of student readers' independence and success. When we use rubrics to help students learn to assess, we should follow the practices outlined above, related to teachers' questions and checklists. That is, start simple.

The act of comparing one's own work with the criteria included in a scoring rubric can be complex and overwhelming for some students, regardless of the complexity of the rubric. Starting simple means that the rubrics with which students learn to assess their work should focus on relatively simple reading processes and products. Consider the rubric in Table 10.1, which is used in fourth grade to help students learn to self-assess their performance at identifying a claim made in text and supporting evidence.

Students using the rubric in Table 10.1 are learning how to determine the differences between fact and opinion, to understand how authors make claims in relation to their purposes for writing, and to seek evidence for claims that are included in texts. This rubric provides information about what a student's work must include to earn the label "Proficient," and the associated grade that a student receives, based on their performance. Read left to right, the rubric reflects the developmental progression that students might experience in learning about claims and evidence in texts. Thus, the rubric provides a consistent message about expected outcomes of the claim/evidence unit, and it focuses students on the "must have" aspects of their reading performance. Both help students learn to self-assess their reading performance—the teacher does not have to be present for students to self-assess using the criteria listed in the rubric. Learning to evaluate and critique what we read is a developmental phenomenon, as is the ability to use increasingly complex rubrics in self-assessment. Introducing rubrics early in students' careers and familiarizing students with their use in self-assessment is a key to success.

TABLE 10.1. **Rubric for Identifying Claims in Text**

Category	Levels of student performance		
	Not apparent (1)	Developing (2)	Proficient (3)
Identifying a claim and supporting evidence in a text.	There is no indication that student identifies either claim or supporting evidence.	Student accurately identifies claim or supporting evidence.	Student accurately identifies claim and supporting evidence.

Self-awareness involves mindsets and strategies. Across the ages (and considerably earlier than the advent of attention to metacognition), readers managed to become self-aware, to monitor their construction of meaning, and to independently progress through acts of reading. That readers can develop self-assessment routines on their own is a tribute to the resourcefulness of some readers. However, we want self-assessment to develop as efficiently as possible. Helping students learn self-assessment involves helping them develop a self-assessment mindset and a set of self-assessment strategies.

AN IMPORTANT NEXT STEP: BEYOND TEACHER QUESTIONS, CHECKLISTS, AND RUBRICS

Students' self-assessment in reading is encouraged when we use particular teaching and assessment materials. As described in this chapter, teacher questions can help focus students on metacognitive aspects of reading. These questions can be followed or accompanied by checklists. The checklists serve as reminders of the types of questions to ask, and they model the content and focus of important questions. Rubrics help students focus on both broad and complex aspects of their reading and reading-related performances. Despite the individual and cumulative value of the above approaches, it is probable that students' mindfulness, reflection, self-awareness, and engagement will not flourish without supportive classroom talk.

How do students develop such mindsets and strategies? How can teachers help students perform increasingly complex reading tasks and help students reach ever greater reading achievement levels while providing them with the means to assess their own reading? The premise is that as we "do" reading assessment in the classroom, we can also teach reading assessment. Classroom talk features here. We can conduct reading assessment in relation to the goal of collecting valuable information about students and in relation to the goal of teaching reading assessment. Just as we can model, explain, and demonstrate reading comprehension strategies for our students, we can model, explain, and demonstrate assessment strategies. For example, we can provide think-alouds for students as we set goals for reading, develop a plan to meet the goals, and describe the necessary assessment routines and checkpoints that are built into the plan. Classroom talk can encourage the reflection and mindfulness that are essential to students' successful self-assessment, and we should advocate for related initiatives. Self-assessment develops over time, just as reading strategies and skills do. Yet, there are too few examples of schools that focus on self-assessment and metacognition across the school years.

SUMMARY

Helping students develop effective self-assessment mindsets and routines is often a neglected aspect of reading and reading assessment programs. This is unfortunate, as self-assessment is essential to student independence and success. Self-assessment is commonly linked with metacognition, and so focuses on the cognitive aspects of reading. Self-assessment also helps readers connect and appreciate their effort and reading outcomes. Self-assessment relates to building self-awareness and mindfulness and helping students make connections between their effort and outcomes. The benefits of becoming adept at self-assessment are local, as when students self-assess continually as they read. The benefits are also global, as students learn to better understand their strengths and needs and become more mindful individuals. Consider a third grader who, across an entire school year, learns how to set specific and broad reading goals, how to check on progress toward goals, and how to determine that goals are met. This student will also be managing local assessment—checking on understandings of individual words, sentences, and paragraphs. When successful, these self-assessment routines foster motivation and engagement and increased self-efficacy. The student who manages and monitors an act of reading can experience success and independence—key ingredients in building one's self-concept as a reader and in fostering enthusiasm and confidence related to reading.

Successful student readers set goals, plan their reading, read strategically, monitor their progress, and achieve their goals, all independently. The ability of students to self-assess is at the center of reading achievement. Thus, fostering students' self-assessment should be a focus of our instruction. This means we must teach, as well as do, assessment. Successful students commence, work through, and complete increasingly complex reading tasks as they read increasingly complex texts. No student is a truly independent reader without the mindset and strategies to continually self-assess.

Enhancing Your Understanding

1. As you plan a reading lesson, focus on the assessment that you will use. Determine what aspects of the assessments lend themselves to being the focus of teaching students self-assessment.

2. Self-assessment strategies are closely related to reading comprehension strategies. Choose one self-assessment strategy (e.g., asking self-assessment questions

or using a rubric from a performance assessment) and develop a teaching script that helps you model, explain, and think aloud in relation to the self-assessment strategy.

3. Prior to teaching a reading lesson, develop a checklist that helps students prepare for, work through, and complete the lesson. The contents of the checklist should reflect learning goals and important student tasks.

Reading Assessment Snapshot
ASSESSMENT SYSTEMS

Creating and managing a reading assessment system—for a classroom, a school, or a school district—can be a daunting task. While useful reading assessment systems demand considerable resources, we can appreciate the benefits of these systems by focusing on the "3 Cs" of *coverage, consistency,* and *communication.*

First, consider the comprehensive coverage provided by a robust reading assessment system. Are students' strategies and skills developing on schedule? Are students comprehending texts to grade-level expectation? Is motivation contributing to more—or less—student reading? What is the nature of students' metacognitive strategies and skill development? When an assessment system supplies data to answer these questions, our instruction is best guided to enhance student learning. There is comprehensive coverage of the influences on students' reading development, as well as documentation of their learning outcomes.

Next, consider the consistency afforded by a reading assessment system. Consistency helps familiarize students and teachers with assessment materials and procedures, and this familiarity contributes to assessment fluency: knowing what a particular assessment can provide and how it operates. In contrast, using disparate assessments across grades places a learning burden on both teachers and students. In addition, students moving from grade to grade within a consistent system can learn to be metacognitive as assessment materials and procedures are maintained across the years, providing a familiarity that promotes students assuming self-assessment (metacognitive) responsibilities.

Finally, a thoughtful reading assessment system promotes effective communication. When teachers have detailed information from formative assessments, they can communicate this to students to influence ongoing reading development. Furthermore, communication is enhanced between teachers as profiles of students' strengths and needs are shared from school year to school year. An effective reading assessment system also focuses on language that is comprehensible for all interested audiences. Parent–teacher meetings are enhanced by language that clearly communicates a student's current reading status and possible home and community supports for that student. In summary, a well-designed reading assessment system provides many benefits to teachers, students, and the broader school community. Initial work in creating a robust assessment system is demanding, but the rewards are considerable.

CHAPTER 11

Assessing Digital and Critical Reading

The advent of digital literacy reminds us of the importance of students' critical reading abilities. Students are enmeshed in social media and surrounded by explicit and subliminal messages to join, to mimic, to not be left out, and most of all to buy. They are inundated with information that may or may not be accurate or truthful. In this chapter, I focus on students' critical reading and digital reading development because the two require, at the core, specific strategies, skills, and mindsets. Fostering our students' development in these two key areas should be a priority, and here we explore approaches to related assessments across the grades.

DIGITAL READING

Consider the amount of information that our students encounter in digital form. *Forbes Magazine* (Wong, 2023) reports that in 2023 almost 5 billion people used social media; it estimates that there will be 5.85 billion worldwide users by 2027. Related, the average time spent with social media is approximately 145 minutes per day, with short videos the most popular medium and mobile phones the most frequently used device.

A recent study (Anderson et al., 2023) examined teenagers' social media habits, and nearly half (48%) reported that they use the internet "almost constantly." More than 15 years ago, Gulli and Signorini (2005) and Lawless and Schrader (2008) reported that the amount of information available on the internet to the average consumer has increased more than 60,000% in the last 20 years alone. No doubt these exponential increases in internet information continue. Research also indicates that the time students spend with daily use of digital devices is negatively related to reading comprehension test scores. Salmerón et al. (2022) report that "even small daily amounts (30 min.) of use of digital devices in . . . classrooms are negatively related to scores on a reading comprehension test, and that this relation is almost double in 4th compared with 8th grade" (p. 190). In addition, recent meta-analyses conclude that students' reading comprehension is better with traditional (print) reading when compared with digital reading (Furenes et al., 2021; List & Alexander, 2017).

Given the prevalence of digital reading, it is critical that its characteristics are well defined, as this helps us create and establish construct validity for related assessments. According to the American Library Association, digital literacy "requires skills in locating and using information and in critical thinking. Beyond that, however, digital literacy involves knowing digital tools and using them in communicative, collaborative ways through social engagement." The association also proposes that digital literacy involves "the ability to use information and communication technologies to find, evaluate, create, and communicate information, requiring both cognitive and technical skills" (American Library Association, 2024).

Not all that is required to be digitally literate is unique. In fact, digital literacy shares much in common with traditional literacy—the literacy associated with reading print materials (Afflerbach & Cho, 2009). Prior to the digital age, it was not uncommon to ask student readers to employ what are now labeled "21st-century reading skills and strategies." These strategies and skills include using multiple sources when constructing meaning, vetting the texts (and the sources of these texts) for trustworthiness and reliability, and using multimodal text resources to construct meaning to use in school- and life-related tasks and endeavors. These should remain as important goals for our teaching, and existing reading assessments—as they "fit" with digital reading texts and tasks—may be used effectively.

However, there are key differences between traditional print reading and digital reading; the latter is noted for the ease of access to information, the amount of information, and the sometimes questionable sources and qualities of texts found on the internet. Digital reading on the internet is also notable for the number of "distracters" embedded in texts that may take readers off task. Related, Coiro (2020) defines digital reading as "a range of multifaceted meaning-making experiences whereby readers engage with multiple texts for particular purposes that are situated in diverse contexts" (p. 12). Coiro also proposes four general strategies that are essential for successful digital reading: navigation, integration, monitoring, and evaluation. Navigation includes searching for and locating reading material on the internet, as well as the essential keyboarding skills that allow for navigation. Integration involves the syntheses of the different types of information that may be encountered in digital reading, including text, charts, tables, and embedded video and audio (Ahn, 2023). Monitoring involves the metacognitive mindsets and strategies that help readers plan, work through, and successfully complete digital reading tasks. Evaluation relates to readers' ability to critically appraise the content they encounter on the internet and to judge this content against standards including accuracy, truthfulness, and completeness. Thus, an important goal for assessment programs is maintaining a focus on critical reading strategies and skills while adding complementary foci on navigation, integration, monitoring, and evaluation.

In summary, digital reading is omnipresent. Digital reading requires that student readers must develop strategies and skills that are both similar to and in addition to traditional print reading strategies and skills. Student readers are born into the digital world and constantly use the internet, which provides a wealth of information from diverse sources at rapid speed. However, this content may be of unknown origin and murky intent. Assessment is needed to help us best chart the development of students' digital reading strategies and mindsets and to assist us in creating related instruction.

CRITICAL READING

In 2018, the Pew Research Center examined the ability of American adults to read critically, including the ability to accurately identify factual statements and opinion statements. It found that when given 10 statements, "about a quarter of Americans overall could accurately classify all five factual statements (26%) and about a third could classify all five opinion statements (35%)" (Gottfried & Grieco, 2018). Given that this research focused on adult readers, the need for fostering critical reading in school is apparent. There is considerable research focused on critical reading, how it develops, and how it contributes to individual student growth. Molden (2007) describes strategies that help students move beyond literal and inferential comprehension to critical understanding of text, and Karabay (2015) reports that instruction in critical reading enhanced students' media literacy. ten Dam and Volman (2004) describe the centrality of critical reading to "citizenship competence," reflecting the role of such reading in individuals' contributions to society. Koray and Çetinkılıç (2020) found that critical reading instruction in seventh-grade science courses had a significant, positive influence on students' academic achievement, science performance level, and problem-solving skills. Wells et al. (2020) describe the use of picture books to foster younger students' critical reading and literacy, focusing on authors' voices and perspectives, conducting visual analysis of illustrations, and investigating representation of people, ideas, and places. Related, Brown (1997) proposes that critical reading serves as a catalyst for changing schools into "communities of thinking," in which students engage with serious societal issues.

Critical reading involves students' orientations and strategic approaches to analyzing text, determining the accuracy and relevance of information, examining author intention and perspective, and investigating the trustworthiness and bias of a text or author (Braasch et al., 2022; Cervetti et al., 2001). Critical reading helps students investigate authors and purposes, posing questions such as "Why did the author write this?," "What devices and strategies does the author use to communicate the message?," "Is the author trying to manipulate me?," and "Is the information in this text accurate and truthful?" Reading critically requires that students not only construct meaning from text, but also evaluate and question that meaning. Critical reading requires that students first understand texts and then make judgments about what they read.

Accordingly, assessment should gauge growth as students construct meaning and learn to distinguish fact and opinion, examine claim–evidence structures in texts, determine if there is sufficient evidence to support a claim, discern an author's purpose, identify subtexts that dwell beneath actual words, and critically appraise how components of an argument work—or don't. When students do deep reading, they are in a position to critically examine authors' use of source material, determine text credibility and bias, and identify propaganda. Yet, instruction focused on critical reading may be insufficient and not prioritized, at least as is reflected in popular reading curricula. This is unfortunate. Ellis and Eberly (2015) argue that critical literacy should not be considered an "add-on to the existing curriculum" (p. 9). Rather, it should be a central focus of instruction that helps students understand how and why texts are written and how to develop both inquiring mindsets and healthy skepticism toward particular authors and texts.

Related conceptualizations of critical reading and critical literacy focus on social change and social justice. For example, Lewison et al. (2002) describe four dimensions of critical literacy: disrupting the commonplace, interrogating multiple viewpoints, focusing on sociopolitical issues, and taking ongoing action to promote social justice. These dimensions follow from Freire and Macedo's (1987) assertion that literacy involves an individual's relationship with the world in general, and Freebody and Luke's (1990) Four Resources Model, which situates critical reading in relation to (and in addition to) traditional foci of classroom reading instruction. These authors argue that reading instruction should help students not only learn the mechanics of decoding text, but also participate in the creation of meaning from text, analyze and evaluate texts, and use texts as needed in life.

In many classrooms, assessment focuses on decoding, reading fluently, gaining vocabulary, and constructing meaning. How students critically analyze and evaluate texts, or how they use what is learned to try to change their lives, is not as common. Suffice to say, assessments that describe how our students read critically, how they use reading and writing to enhance their (and others') lives, and how

Critical and Digital Reading Assessment

Given the importance of critical and digital reading, what should be our assessments? In the following section, I describe a series of assessments across elementary, middle, and high school that are intended to (1) reflect the developmental nature of students' critical and digital reading, (2) align with classroom curriculum and instruction that support this reading, and (3) provide both formative and summative information regarding the nature of students' reading.

Our examination of assessment is centered in Algonquin School District, which uses a curriculum that emphasizes digital and critical literacy. Accordingly, a first focus in elementary school is the assessment of students' keyboarding and internet navigation skills. In later elementary grades, students learn to determine fact and opinion and to identify and evaluate claim–evidence arguments. They further their understanding of persuasive language and propaganda. They conduct deep reading of advertisements and editorials. They develop strategies and mindsets for analyzing and critically evaluating texts. They participate in group projects that have the potential to contribute to social good. These individual aspects of critical and digital reading are assessed across students' school careers.

Keyboarding and Familiarity with Digital Devices and the Internet

Elementary students' keyboarding skills and familiarity with the internet are fundamental to success in school. Developing keyboarding skills is essential when students are engaged in tasks that demand access to—and navigation through—the internet and websites. Across the district, elementary teachers use a variation of the keyboarding assessment developed by Khoury-Shaheen and Weintraub (2022), who remind us that "poor keyboarding performance may affect [students'] efficiency of computer use and academic achievement" (p. 7). While we expect that many students are well versed in accessing and using the internet, their competency with keyboarding should be checked, especially with young children and in relation to the specific digital devices used in school. Such assessment evaluates the speed and accuracy of elementary students' keyboarding, as well as their ability to block, copy, paste, edit, and share texts. A reproducible form you can use to assess elementary students' digital and critical reading—the Checklist for Keyboarding and Internet Navigation Knowledge and Skills—is presented in the Appendix.

Using this checklist, teachers can determine if all students possess the knowledge needed to begin to realize and manage the resources of the internet. As they

literacy figures in promoting social justice are needed (Forzani et al., 2020). At this point in time, however, these assessments are more aspirational and less realized.

matriculate through elementary school, students should learn about the special language of the internet, a skill that may help them avoid the downsides and dark corners of being online, including inappropriate content, scams, and misleading information. Concurrently, they must develop internet search and navigation skills (Litt, 2013). Form 11.1 represents an assessment that focuses on a key foundation of critical digital reading: students' ability to identify the origin, author, purpose, and nature of the information in texts found on the internet. The items in Form 11.1 also anticipate the growth in critical and digital reading that is expected of elementary school students in the district. The assessment in Form 11.1 is used as developmentally appropriate. For example, younger elementary students learn how to identify websites using URL cues, while later in elementary school (and throughout middle school and high school), the focus includes critical appraisal of author and text purposes.

As with reading inventory assessment and performance assessment, students' ability to use cues, strategies, and skills related to digital and critical reading may provide the most useful information when it emanates from holistic internet reading performances. I note that many of the above assessment items focus on single aspects of becoming digitally literate and that a true test of a student's digital literacy is best reflected in an intact reading and related performance.

Related, the Integrative Multimodal Literacy Assessment (IMLA; Ly & Forzani, 2023) presents the opportunity to investigate both student motivations when using different modes of literacy and students' multimodal literacy performances. The IMLA consists of two parts. The first is a set of Likert-scale ratings with which students indicate the nature of their motivations (including interest, value, and self-efficacy) as related to linguistic, visual, aural, gestural, and spatial modes of literacy. The second part examines students' learning from multimodal texts, with text types and modes selected by the student, followed by a student response. The chosen response mode—focused on communicating what was learned from the multimodal texts—is drawing, writing, or creating an oral or video recording. The IMLA has the advantage of helping us evaluate both student motivation and student performance related to multimodal literacy.

In the following sections, we examine students engaged with assessment tasks that assume the ability to read and that focus on key aspects of digital and critical reading ability.

Identifying Facts and Opinions

As students learn to interact with the internet, a watershed moment in their critical reading development is when facts can be reliably distinguished from opinions. In school, this ability is directly tied to reading and related consequential decision making, including whether to trust a text or author (or both), vetting texts for

FORM 11.1 **Assessment of Student Website Evaluations**

Student name: _____

Student identifies URL clues as to origin of website:

☐ .edu Educational

☐ .org Nonprofit

☐ .com Commercial

☐ .gov Government

Student can determine who wrote the text and material on website:

☐ Who is the author?

☐ What are qualifications of the author?

☐ If there is no author, where does the text come from?

☐ If it is impossible to determine where the text comes from, why might that be?

Student identifies purpose of website:

☐ To sell things/advertise

☐ To entertain

☐ To provide information/teach

☐ To persuade

Student can determine nature of information found on website:

☐ Factual

☐ Opinion

☐ Nonsense

☐ Mixture

From *Understanding and Using Reading Assessment, K–12, Fourth Edition,* by Peter Afflerbach. Copyright © 2025 The Guilford Press. Permission to photocopy this material, or to download and print enlarged versions (*www.guilford.com/afflerbach2-forms*), is granted to purchasers of this book for personal use or use with students; see copyright page for details.

truth and accuracy, and building content-area knowledge based on factual information. Later in our students' lives, distinguishing fact from opinion helps citizens decide whom to vote for, whether to make a major purchase (e.g., home, car, education), and whether to believe—or not—the considerable number of written and spoken texts encountered daily. In effect, the ability to distinguish fact from opinion is a bedrock skill that helps individuals identify texts that may be truthful or dishonest, straightforward or misleading, and helpful or manipulative. We live in a digital era in which particular people and websites propose "alternative facts," where some public figures regularly lie, and where artificial intelligence is used to create alternate realities that are difficult to distinguish from truth. Clearly, the stakes could not be higher for students becoming educated consumers with digital and critical reading.

Accordingly, one focus of elementary reading instruction and assessment is fostering student learning of one foundation of critical reading: the ability to identify facts and opinions. Developing this ability helps students critically evaluate texts and authors. Students learn that facts are statements that can be verified, while opinions include an individual's feelings and beliefs.

In fourth grade, the assessment of critical reading focuses on students' ability to define, identify, and distinguish fact and opinion in text and describe how that determination is made. A unique feature of this assessment is that it is tailored to students and their prior knowledge. Accordingly, this requires that teachers familiarize themselves with student interests and the knowledge students already possess. The assessment example in Form 11.2 focuses on a group of students determining fact and opinion with a text and topic that the teacher has determined to be highly familiar. The assessment includes two generic questions that can be used with any topic (i.e., "Is this a fact or opinion? How can you prove it to be so?"), yet the assessment is customized by the teacher so that students can work in an area for which they have prior knowledge—in this case, ice hockey. (I note that other groups of students will, of course, have different areas of prior knowledge—such as cosplay, soccer, pets—and that assessment will need related adjustments in terms of text and topic.)

Note the advantages of conducting our assessments of fact and opinion in an area for which students have prior knowledge—and often opinions related to that knowledge. If students are reading in an area for which they have little or no prior knowledge, they may be dependent on outside (and often unknown) sources for information, especially the internet, to support their determination of fact or opinion. Making determinations of fact or opinion when the information used to make the decision is delivered by the internet—and may be inaccurate or incomplete—reduces the value of the exercise and the validity of the assessment.

Following students' response to the first question—the determination of fact or opinion—their written responses to the second question, "How can you prove it

FORM 11.2 **Assessment for Determining Fact and Opinion Statements**

Student name: _____

The Rangers' **won–lost–tied record is 12–4–4.**

Is this a fact or an opinion? How can you prove it to be so?

Student response: This is a fact. The NHL official website lists the Rangers' current won–lost–tied record as 12–4–4. The Rangers website also lists the won–lost–tied record as 12–4–4. Also, the *New York Daily News* lists the won–lost–tied record as 12–4–4.

The Rangers are the best team in the National Hockey League.

Is this a fact or an opinion? How can you prove it to be so?

Student response: This is a fact. The best team has the best record, and the Rangers have the most wins, the fewest losses, and the highest winning percentage.

The Rangers deserve to win the Stanley Cup.

Is this a fact or an opinion? How can you prove it to be so?

Student response: This is an opinion. Fans of other hockey teams believe that their team deserves to win the Stanley Cup. "Deserve" is a word that is difficult to support with facts for every team.

It's impossible to find a team that matches the Rangers for heart and determination.

Is this a fact or an opinion? How can you prove it to be so?

Student response: This is an opinion. The author of this statement did not do a detailed accounting of the heart and determination possessed by other teams in the NHL. The author did not describe how "heart" and "determination" are measured. Many sports fans believe that their team has the most heart and determination.

From *Understanding and Using Reading Assessment, K–12, Fourth Edition*, by Peter Afflerbach. Copyright © 2025 The Guilford Press. Permission to photocopy this material, or to download and print enlarged versions (*www.guilford.com/afflerbach2-forms*), is granted to purchasers of this book for personal use or use with students; see copyright page for details.

to be so?," are a window onto their critical reading and thinking processes. These responses provide teachers with further information on the students' strategy use.

The above assessment example illustrates the interface of digital literacy and critical literacy. Having students determine fact from opinion is a traditional strategy and skill set. Today, students' reasoning processes when determining fact and opinion are frequently informed by data they gather from the internet. When students are asked to determine if the statement "Around the globe, glaciers are melting at an alarming rate" is fact or opinion, many access internet resources. For example, students may use Google to navigate to Wikipedia, which then serves as a primary source of information. Subsequently, students may click through to a website sponsored by the petroleum industry, the Environmental Protection Agency, or both. The internet is infamous for rapidly accessible information that may or may not be truthful or accurate. Students must learn that opinions stated multiple times and opinions posed as facts do not, in fact, make them facts. The example in Form 11.3 presents an assessment of fact and opinion as part of critical reading on the internet that can contribute to student engagement. Consider the possible benefits—including motivation and engagement and deep reading—that are gained as students critically read and evaluate information obtained through the internet to determine fact and opinion for curriculum topics of high interest and importance.

In this example, answering the question "How can you prove it to be so?" not only provides the opportunity to examine the reasoning behind determining fact or opinion but also serves as an assessment of what a student knows and has learned in the lesson or unit.

Determining Claims and Evidence

Following the examination of fact and opinion in fourth grade, the sixth-grade critical reading curriculum in Algonquin School District classrooms focuses on claim and evidence structures in texts in the content areas. The district incorporates students' learning to determine claim and evidence structures, identify claims and evidence, and examine the legitimacy of claim and evidence into a problem-based learning unit. For example, in science class, students are tasked with investigating the claim made in an online article about growing plants. The claim is "The optimal conditions for sprouting seeds include moisture, heat, and light." The related hands-on experiment is intended to engage students as they construct science knowledge with digital resources, while creating the evidence that will support or refute the claim. Students must record information gathered from the internet-informed experiment to investigate the accuracy and truthfulness of the claim. They are, in effect, engaged in problem-based learning that will provide the evidence for examining the veracity of the claim.

FORM 11.3 Assessment for Determining Fact and Opinion Statements on the Internet

Student name: _____

Climate change is real.

Is this a fact or an opinion? How can you prove it to be so?

Human beings contribute to climate change.

Is this a fact or an opinion? How can you prove it to be so?

We should do all we can to help prevent climate change.

Is this a fact or an opinion? How can you prove it to be so?

What we do about climate change should be in relation to what other countries do about climate change.

Is this a fact or an opinion? How can you prove it to be so?

Climate change is a constant and the Earth is always going through cycles of cooling or heating.

Is this a fact or an opinion? How can you prove it to be so?

Students encounter vast resources as they search the internet for information on seeds and germination. They use their understanding of efficient search strategies to gather and synthesize information, reflecting the integration process for digital reading proposed by Coiro (2020). Building on strategies developed in the early elementary grades (e.g., how to use URL cues to determine the nature of internet sources and origin of information), students vet what they read to determine what is fact and what is opinion. They note that the .gov websites typically represent state departments of agriculture and that the .com websites are selling things. The students' combined internet searches reveal that different types of seeds sprout under vastly different conditions.

Based on the claim that moisture, light, and heat are optimal for sprouting seeds, students develop the focus question "What is the best environment for the seeds to sprout?" In answering the question, students are gathering evidence. The students create three growing conditions:

- Moist with light
- Moist with heat
- Moist with light and heat

Over the course of two weeks, three student teams investigate growing conditions, one team for each condition. Each team has the responsibility to plant seeds, provide the environment consistent with their assigned sprouting conditions, take daily notes and digital photographs, record their observations, and share their findings. Teams observe the number of seeds sprouted, the date and time of the seed sprouting, and the height of each sprout. In doing so, students are amassing data about what growing conditions are optimal for the seeds, while creating evidence that may (or may not) support the author's original claim. The assessment (Figure 11.1) is intertwined with the science curriculum.

The students examine and compare the evidence they created to determine if they support the text's original claim that "optimal conditions for sprouting seeds include moisture, heat, and light." At the conclusion of the unit, students have learned about seeds and how growing conditions influence germination. Moreover, they have gathered experimental data and used it to support what was once the author's unsubstantiated claim that light, moisture, and heat provide the healthiest environment for seed germination. Any assessment of critical reading should be accompanied by a check on students' actual comprehension of text. For example, evidence of each group's comprehension of the material downloaded from the internet is important as this construction of meaning provides the pathway to the examination of claim and evidence. I note that the preceding example of assessing students' claim–evidence arguments is complex and time-consuming. All of our assessments must pass the "doable" test: They must be created and used

> Is there evidence to support the claim "The optimal conditions for sprouting seeds include moisture, heat, and light"?
>
> Group members: _____
>
> 1. Conditions for growing seeds
>
>   *Moist with light*
>   Number sprouted: _____ Date of sprouting: _____ Average height of sprouts: _____
>
>   *Moist with heat*
>   Number sprouted: _____ Date of sprouting: _____ Average height of sprouts: _____
>
>   *Moist with light and heat*
>   Number sprouted: _____ Date of sprouting: _____ Average height of sprouts: _____
>
> 2. Based on your group's findings, describe the evidence you found on the internet and the sources of that evidence. Next, explain whether there is sufficient evidence to support the author's original claim: "The optimal conditions for sprouting seeds include moisture, heat, and light."

FIGURE 11.1. Sample assessment of evidence to support an author's claim.

within the parameters of school and district resources. While the above assessment demands resources, it is embedded in the existing science curriculum, it focuses on problem-based learning, and it requires (and assesses) students' fluency with the internet and digital literacy.

Another approach—one that is less resource-consuming and more traditional—to assessing students' strategies for determining claim and evidence begins with locating and identifying a claim in text. This can be done by students as evaluation focuses on highlighting the found claim. Subsequently, students are asked to locate and highlight the evidence provided in support of the claim. Building on this assessment, we can next evaluate their ability to judge the claim–evidence structure. These assessments should reflect both the students' reading achievement levels and their fluency in determining claim–evidence structures. Representative assessment questions are included in Form 11.4.

In summary, claim and evidence is a common structure in many written and spoken texts and students must become familiar with it to grow as critical readers and consumers of information. Students encounter a wealth of claims and evidence in digital reading—some logical, some questionable, some honest, and some misleading—that must be analyzed and evaluated, and assessments that help us understand students' development as educated consumers of claim and evidence are essential.

FORM 11.4 **Assessment of Students' Ability to Determine Claim–Evidence Structures**

Student name: _____

What claim is made in the text?

Is there evidence to support the claim?

Is the evidence relevant or appropriate for the claim?

Does the evidence provide support for all aspects of the claim?

Is the evidence real and valid?

Is this the best evidence that can support the claim?

From *Understanding and Using Reading Assessment, K–12, Fourth Edition,* by Peter Afflerbach. Copyright © 2025 The Guilford Press. Permission to photocopy this material, or to download and print enlarged versions (*www.guilford.com/afflerbach2-forms*), is granted to purchasers of this book for personal use or use with students; see copyright page for details.

Identifying and Analyzing Advertisements and Propaganda

By ninth grade, the students in Algonquin schools are well versed in critical and digital reading. They have worked through the curriculum that includes basic keyboarding and internet source identification, as well as understanding fact and opinion, and claim and evidence. Students are assumed to be able to construct literal understanding of text, on which the critical evaluation of text is based. Accordingly, the ninth-grade curriculum requires students to read and evaluate real-world texts that include advertisements and propaganda. The curriculum includes student discussions of why advertisements and propaganda exist, the means by which they may appeal to readers, and how to deconstruct them to determine how they are intended to manipulate the reader. Combined, these features reflect students' ability to navigate, integrate, evaluate, and monitor their reading (Coiro, 2020). As part of the assessment, students are asked questions to demonstrate comprehension and critical appraisal of advertising and propaganda texts.

Here, critical reading and digital reading curriculum and assessment are informed by the CRAAP Test, which emphasizes students' ability to examine and evaluate the *currency, relevance, authority, accuracy,* and *purpose* of texts. The CRAAP Test was developed by librarians at California State University, Chico as a tool for students to investigate and critically evaluate texts they locate on the internet. The assessment maps onto questions that guide critical reading instruction. Figure 11.2 presents assessment questions related to each of the five areas of the CRAAP Test (currency, relevance, authority, accuracy, and purpose).

As is evident, the CRAAP Test provides questions that help assess students' critical reading as well as inform related instruction. Answering the CRAAP questions accurately requires that students both construct meaning and critically evaluate that meaning. This is a further reminder that as our assessments focus on students' growing ability to read critically, it is imperative that we assess (and not assume) students' literal understanding of texts.

There is a veritable cornucopia of advertising and propaganda that provides texts suitable for learning and practicing aspects of critical reading. We do not have to search far for reading materials that can be vetted with the CRAAP Test. Students begin their critical reading unit focused on deconstructing and critiquing advertisements. Consider the advertisement in Figure 11.3 for the product Brain-Gro, similar to those found on the internet.

This advertisement is representative of many that are readily available on the internet; from this perspective, the internet can be seen as an infinite resource. Such advertisements can be chosen in relation to students' interests, which can add the filter of prior knowledge to the critical digital reading experience. In addition to the CRAAP questions described earlier, assessment is conducted with the rubric

> **Currency:** The timeliness of the information.
> - When was the information published or posted?
> - Has the information been revised or updated?
> - Is this the most up-to-date information available?
>
> **Relevance:** The importance of the information for your needs.
> - How well does the information relate to your topic or answer your question?
> - Have you looked at a variety of sources before determining you will use this source?
>
> **Authority:** The source of the information.
> - Who is the author/publisher/source/sponsor?
> - Is the author qualified to write on the topic?
> - Is there contact information, such as a publisher or email address?
> - Does the URL reveal anything about the author or source? (examples: .com, .edu, .gov, .org, .net)
>
> **Accuracy:** The reliability, truthfulness, and correctness of the content.
> - Where does the information come from?
> - Is the information supported by evidence?
> - Can you trust the source?
> - Is this fact or opinion?
> - Has the information been reviewed or refereed?
>
> **Purpose:** The reason the information exists.
> - What is the purpose of the information? Is it to inform, teach, sell, entertain, fool, or persuade?
> - Do the authors/sponsors make their intentions or purpose clear?
> - Is the information fact, opinion, or propaganda?

FIGURE 11.2. Sample assessment questions based on the CRAAP framework (California State University, Chico, 2010). CRAAP = currency, relevance, authority, accuracy, and purpose.

in Table 11.1, which focuses on students' ability to examine claims and evidence as they occur in advertisements.

Asking Critical Questions

In addition to the above performance task and assessment rubric, each advertisement contains information—statements and claims—that can be interrogated through student-generated critical questions. In ninth grade, critical questions are a key aspect of assessing students' ability to identify and then query aspects of advertisements and propaganda. For example, students reading the BrainGro advertisement demonstrate their comprehension of text, as well as their critical reading ability, by asking critical questions. Here are representative critical questions:

- Does BrainGro really grow your brain?
- The advertisement states, "Our leading doctor has been doing research for 43 years." Who is this doctor, what research has been conducted, and how is the research related to the product BrainGro?
- Does the fact that doctors received "monetary compensation" from the company making this product influence their recommendations to use the product?
- The advertisement claims that "All BrainGro products contain thoroughly studied and endorsed ingredients." What are these ingredients, who endorses them, and what are the qualifications of the endorsers?
- How can this company make claims about the beneficial, helpful effects of BrainGro when the following is included at the conclusion of the advertisement: "*Note: The above statements and claims have not been evaluated by*

Build and maintain your best, most powerful brain!

Take BrainGro health supplement every day!

As people age, brain function can deteriorate. As people lose brain function, their thinking slows down and is not reliable. Without brain function, life gets difficult. Simple tasks and thoughts are challenging. Everyday chores are a burden. Complex problem solving is impossible. Friends and family become distant.

No worries! You can take care of your brain and its health. Take BrainGro every day and take care of your brain! BrainGro is widely recommended by health professionals and doctors. It was developed in relation with several famous research universities. Here are results from a recent survey:*

- 100% of doctors would recommend BrainGro to create the highest level of brain function.
- 85% of doctors would recommend BrainGro to establish optimal cognitive processing.
- 91% of doctors would recommend BrainGro to create your best memory.
- 96% of doctors would recommend BrainGro for people who forget things.
- 94% of doctors would recommend BrainGro to keep the brain healthy.

All BrainGro products contain thoroughly studied and endorsed ingredients. Our leading doctor has been doing research for 43 years. BrainGro is used by many clinicians and patients around the world.

---

*These figures are the result of a survey of 30 doctors. Each doctor has a medical degree (MD) and was given monetary compensation to complete the survey.

Note: The above statements and claims have not been evaluated by the Food and Drug Administration. This product is not intended to diagnose, treat, cure, or prevent any disease.

FIGURE 11.3. Advertisement for BrainGro.

TABLE 11.1. **Rubric for Determining Claim, Evidence, and Warrant in Advertisements**

Grading level of performance	Demonstrated learning
1—Exemplary	Student identifies and describes the component parts of the argument presented in the advertisement. These components can include facts and opinions, and claims and evidence. Student notes that claims are supported or not supported. Student determines the quality of the claims. Student differentiates facts and opinions. Student describes the relationships of components of the argument and identifies the text structure of the argument.
2—Satisfactory	Student identifies and states advertisement's claims and evidence, or facts and opinions. Student does not identify all evidence; student does not distinguish fact and opinion. Student does not comment on quality of claims.
3—Unsatisfactory	Student fails to identify advertisement's claims and evidence, and fact and opinion.

the Food and Drug Administration. This product is not intended to diagnose, treat, cure, or prevent any disease"?

Examination of students' critical questions provides further assessment information related to their critical and digital reading development. First, students' critical questions allow the teacher to evaluate whether students understand both the text and subtext of what they read. Next, the critical questions originate from student mindsets informed by their learning about advertisements and propaganda. Follow-up discussions focused on critical questions can help us further understand students' reasoning and critical reading. Together, the questions derived from the CRAAP Test, the performance assessment rubric, and students' critical questions provide detailed information as to students' progress and attainment in the advertising and propaganda unit.

Scenario-Based Assessments

A capstone unit and assessment for 12th graders involves scenario-based assessments (SBAs; McCarthy et al., 2023; Sabatini, 2022; Sabatini et al., 2020). SBA focuses on digital and critical reading development, as well as situating assessment in contexts that are meaningful to students. SBAs directly address the integration of reading with digital texts on the internet. Sabatini et al. (2020) note that readers must choose, read, and critique vast amounts of information on the internet, some of dubious origin and opaque intent. To read such texts, students must use critical reading strategies. In relation, SBAs provide information on how students use what they understand from digital reading as they apply new understandings to locate and solve problems. McCarthy et al. (2023) note:

> Scenario-based assessment (SBA) is a technique to deliver tasks and items that can help measure how students read in the 21st century. In a typical SBA, students are provided with a context and purpose for reading a collection of thematically related sources in a simulated digital environment. Test takers collaborate with simulated peers and a teacher to understand an issue, to solve problems, make decisions or transfer what they know to a new situation. (p. 3)

Furthermore, Sabatini (2022) notes that SBAs typically emulate real reading situations regarding purpose and social interaction. The purpose and characteristics of SBAs align well with both the assessment program in Algonquin district schools and the district's commitment to literacy learning and social action. In particular, the district values students who use reading and literacy to inform efforts for positive social change.

The capstone project and related SBA are connected to the unit "Protecting Our Environment," which requires that students demonstrate learning from internet resources and then apply this knowledge to the problem of shrinking the school district's ecological footprint—how the consumption of natural resources might be reduced across the school year. This student work relates to four dimensions of critical literacy noted by Lewison et al. (2002): disrupting the commonplace, interrogating multiple viewpoints, focusing on sociopolitical issues, and taking ongoing action to promote social justice. In addition, the SBA on "Protecting Our Environment" reflects the observation that literacy involves students' relationship with the world in school and out of school (Freire & Macedo, 1987).

Within the unit, students are assigned to different small groups: Vehicles, Buildings, and Materials. A first task in the SBA is for students to conduct internet-aided research related to their assigned group. Students in the Vehicles group inventory the make, model, and year of each district-owned or -leased vehicle, including school buses, cars, mowers, and snowblowers, and determine the energy consumption of each. Buildings group members examine the energy consumption of schools, district offices, and playing fields, as well as related energy costs. Materials group members inventory school materials and their sustainability, including computer software and hardware, printers, paper, cleaning products, and the plates and utensils used in the cafeteria. All three groups also conduct research on the different options for maintaining or changing current school practice.

This SBA requires that students describe the paths they take through—how they navigate—the internet. This aspect of assessment invites students' metacognition related to strategy use, planning, and goal evaluation. Students are prompted to focus on their strategies and decision making as they assess their progress and accomplishments. In the process, students use the knowledge gained in their elementary, middle, and high school years. They use URLs as general cues about the nature of sources, they distinguish fact from opinion, and they locate and examine claims and evidence. They pose critical questions of the texts, videos, graphs, and charts that they encounter, and they apply the different criteria of the CRAAP Test as they vet internet content. The SBA requires that students provide an account of their plan to use internet resources, the resources they used, and questions raised by their critical reading. The SBA sheet is presented in Form 11.5.

Note that the above assessment example is focused on both students' interactions with the internet and the information they gather related to the environment and saving energy. SBA requires critical reading of texts found on the internet, which is at the heart of digital literacy. I describe aspects of SBA not because it is widely used, but because it can be viewed as a promise—a promise that future assessments might better reflect the purposeful, critical digital reading we want for our students. Curricula that foster digital literacy and critical reading can only make inroads when there are consequential assessments that describe both their importance and students' progress.

Throughout this chapter, the examination of assessments used in Algonquin School District reminds us of the value of fostering students' growth in digital and critical literacy. Nevertheless, the district is beholden to statewide standardized reading tests, and this places the district in a difficult place. The literacy curriculum used in Algonquin schools focuses on developing students' ability to navigate the internet and to critically evaluate the reading materials found there. It focuses on students using what they read to solve problems and increase their critical awareness. It encourages students to use their critical reading to try to effect positive change. However, the high-stakes tests used to measure student, teacher, and school success at reading do not share this focus. Thus, the current high-stakes test results underrepresent and may undermine students' and teachers' achievements. District administrators and teachers share the concern that this lack of assessment attention to essential learning could undo or severely limit the digital and critical literacy curriculum.

SUMMARY

Digital and critical reading are essential in the internet age. Reading on the internet creates opportunities and demands for student readers. Across the school years and across students' school experiences, it is important to use a program of related assessments that help us determine how students are learning the basics

FORM 11.5 **Scenario-Based Assessment:**
Planning, Working Through, and Completing

Group members: _____

UNIT: PROTECTING THE ENVIRONMENT

Keep a log of each website you accessed for this project.

Describe why and how you chose the websites that you accessed.

Describe what internet resources you used and how they contributed to your final project.

What internet resources were helpful?

How did you determine that these resources were helpful?

What internet sources were not helpful?

How did you determine that these resources were unhelpful?

From *Understanding and Using Reading Assessment, K–12, Fourth Edition,* by Peter Afflerbach. Copyright © 2025 The Guilford Press. Permission to photocopy this material, or to download and print enlarged versions (*www.guilford.com/afflerbach2-forms*), is granted to purchasers of this book for personal use or use with students; see copyright page for details.

of keyboarding and digital literacy, accessing information, using (and not being used by) the wealth of information available on the internet, determining fact and opinion, investigating claim and evidence, and critically appraising information. Assessing how students use the knowledge they gain from critical and digital reading should also be a priority. Assessment programs should continually reference our latest understanding of the benefits and challenges of critical reading and digital reading, along with the shared characteristics of critical reading in traditional (i.e., print) texts.

The assessment of critical and digital literacy has significant consequences for teachers and students. Such assessment informs us how students develop the ability to evaluate texts and how they navigate, integrate, and monitor their reading in internet environments. Assessment helps chart student growth, identify areas of need, and certify attainment of related standards. Also, assessment is immediately useful for teachers who are seeking information about students' progress at strategies and skills that are central to success—in school and out—in the digital age. Critical reading and digital reading assessment provides evidence that students *do not* transition from learning to read to reading to learn in elementary school. Rather, students continue to learn to read as they progress through middle school and high school, should the curriculum and our instruction challenge them to do so. The elementary students who are distinguishing fact and opinion, the middle schoolers who deconstruct an author's argument by identifying and critiquing the claim–evidence structure, and the high schoolers who regularly examine advertisements and propaganda for truth and accuracy are practicing reading strategies and skills that are essential for reading success. Assessment that describes this development is essential.

Enhancing Your Understanding

1. With your colleagues, create a list of the differences between traditional (print) reading and digital reading. Next, create a list of assessment priorities based on the differences you've determined.

2. Create a presentation for open school night in which you highlight the importance of students' critical reading and the assessments that can be used to describe students' growth in this area.

3. Explain why problem-based learning may be an ideal task for assessing both digital reading and critical reading.

4. Create an assessment that helps you to understand students' development in relation to identifying fact and opinion or claim and evidence.

Reading Assessment Snapshot
ASSESSMENT AND SCIENCE—OR SCIENCES?—OF READING

What are the important influences on our students' reading development? What contributes to their reading achievement? These questions should anticipate our reading assessments. As we identify the factors that influence reading development and achievement, we are describing the complex construct of reading and reading development. These constructs must be supported by research results—results that describe the foundations of reading, the benefits of particular approaches to reading instruction, and important outcomes of that instruction. Of course, research is a foundation of the science of reading.

What research? Throughout this book, I have argued that we do well to maintain a broad perspective on the science of reading. In fact, I suggest that a *sciences* of reading view is beneficial because we can learn much from the sciences affiliated with reading and human development. The vast majority of assessments used in schools reflect the cognitive perspective on reading: Strategies and skills and prior knowledge are used by students to construct meaning. It follows that we have attendant assessments of skill and strategy, many with impressive reliability and validity.

However, if our conceptualization of reading development is narrow—if the science of reading that we reference is not comprehensive—we risk missing factors that contribute to reading success. How does motivation impact students' reading development? How does metacognition pair with cognitive strategies and skills to encourage reading independence? How does student self-efficacy promote or impede reading? Coming to know these powerful influences and assessing their impact is important. Furthermore, if we assess reading development in a piecemeal fashion—a skill here, a strategy there—we miss opportunities to examine how our students use strategy, skill, and prior knowledge in concert to construct meaning.

In summary, the sciences of reading inform our understanding of reading development and achievement, and assessment should mirror the broad perspective provided by the sciences of reading. This helps us provide instruction that best supports student development. Assessment tied to the sciences of reading also helps us best represent our students' reading development and achievement and our own teaching successes.

Appendix

CONTENTS

Reading Assessment Inventory: Audiences and Purposes	227
Reading Assessment Inventory: What Is Assessed?	228
Using the CURRV Framework to Evaluate Reading Assessment	229
Conducting a Task Analysis to Enhance Reading Assessment	230
Critical Questions to Ask of Reading Inventory Information	231
Checklist for Constructing Effective Questions	232
Developing an Arc of Questions: From Relatively Simple to Increasingly Complex	233
Guidelines for Developing and Using Performance Assessments	234
Creating Consistent Approaches to Reading Assessment across Grade Levels and Content Areas	235
Checklist for Linguistic Modification of Reading Assessment	236
Assessing "the Other": Questions for Teachers and Administrators	237
Checklist for Planning Effective Formative Assessment	238
Formative Assessment Coverage That Contributes to Students' Achievement on High-Stakes Summative Assessments	239
Checklist for Self-Assessment	240
Checklist for Critical Reading	241
Checklist for Keyboarding and Internet Navigation Knowledge and Skills	242

The forms and checklists included here are intended to help teachers and administrators optimize their reading assessment efforts. They can be used for such tasks as conducting inventories of existing reading assessment, determining the specific audiences and purposes for reading assessment, performing linguistic modification of assessment materials for English learners, creating effective teacher questioning routines, developing formative reading assessments, and promoting students' self-assessment.

You may download and print the forms and checklists at this book's companion website. See the box at the end of the table of contents for details.

Reading Assessment Inventory: Audiences and Purposes

Note: See Table 1.1 ("Representative Audiences and Purposes for Reading Assessment") for examples.

1. Prepare a list of the audiences that are interested in reading assessment information for your classroom, school, or district (e.g., students, teachers, school administrators, parents).

2. List the purposes and uses of reading assessment information in relation to the above audiences.

3. Create a list of what assessments serve what audiences and what purposes (e.g., reading inventories provide teachers with information that is used to diagnose student reading development; high-stakes tests are used by administrators to gauge reading program effectiveness at the district level).

4. Determine if the needs of all important audiences and their purposes are fairly represented by the existing array of reading assessments used in your district or school.

Reading Assessment Inventory: What Is Assessed?

Assessment type	Cognitive reading strategies and skills	Motivation for reading	Social uses of reading	Independence in reading	Reading in collaborative learning environments	Choosing reading over attractive alternatives	Other (list)
Tests and quizzes							
Portfolios							
Performance assessments							
Teacher questions							
Reading inventories							
Teacher observations							
Other (list)							

From *Understanding and Using Reading Assessment, K–12, Fourth Edition*, by Peter Afflerbach. Copyright © 2025 The Guilford Press. Permission to photocopy this material, or to download and print enlarged versions (*www.guilford.com/afflerbach2-forms*), is granted to purchasers of this book for personal use or use with students; see copyright page for details.

Using the CURRV Framework to Evaluate Reading Assessment

Type of assessment: _____

What are the **C**onsequences of this assessment?

    Positive:

    Negative:

What is the **U**sefulness of this assessment?

    For these purposes:

    For these audiences:

What are the **R**oles and responsibilities related to this assessment?

    Teachers

    Students

    Administrators

    Parents

What are the **R**eliability issues related to this assessment?

What are the **V**alidity issues related to this assessment?

From *Understanding and Using Reading Assessment, K–12, Fourth Edition,* by Peter Afflerbach. Copyright © 2025 The Guilford Press. Permission to photocopy this material, or to download and print enlarged versions (*www.guilford.com/afflerbach2-forms*), is granted to purchasers of this book for personal use or use with students; see copyright page for details.

Conducting a Task Analysis to Enhance Reading Assessment

The reading and reading-related tasks are: _____

It is important to imagine the assessment task through the eyes of your students. Note here your insights into the reading task.

What must a student do to successfully complete the task?

Does student success at this task have prerequisites? What are they?

What component strategies and skills are needed to succeed at the task?

What prior knowledge and experience are needed to succeed at the task?

What strategies, skills, and knowledge that are not specific to reading are necessary to succeed at the task?

Are these related strategies, skills, and knowledge assessed? How?

How will the chosen assessment(s) inform you as to successful student performance?

How will the chosen assessment(s) be sensitive to all the factors that contribute to successful student performance?

Critical Questions to Ask of Reading Inventory Information

- Do the word lists and their grade-level designations reflect the approximate achievement levels of my students?

- Are the graded word lists and graded reading passages well coordinated?

- Do the graded word lists help in the accurate placement of students to read their first passage orally?

- Are there opportunities to examine students' oral reading fluency?

- How do the estimates of students' reading ability that are provided by a reading inventory compare with other reading assessment information and students' regular text comprehension performance in class?

- Are there comprehension questions that do not appear to address important aspects of the text (e.g., questions focused on information not central to understanding the text)?

- Are there comprehension questions that are vaguely worded and unclear to students?

- Do the text passages contain content that is more familiar to some of my students?

- Are there comprehension questions that are answered correctly by students when other indicators suggest that students have not comprehended well?

- Are there comprehension questions that can be answered because students have much prior knowledge about the text content and not because they understand the text?

- Do the texts and accompanying comprehension questions afford the opportunity to check students' critical and evaluative comprehension?

From *Understanding and Using Reading Assessment, K–12, Fourth Edition*, by Peter Afflerbach. Copyright © 2025 The Guilford Press. Permission to photocopy this material, or to download and print enlarged versions (*www.guilford.com/afflerbach2-forms*), is granted to purchasers of this book for personal use or use with students; see copyright page for details.

Checklist for Constructing Effective Questions

My questions:

☐ Are designed to assess student understanding.

☐ Are clearly worded so that students understand them.

☐ Represent the complexity of the task asked of students and the texts they read.

☐ Are in line with the materials being covered.

☐ Ensure that students think at various intellectual levels.

☐ Are logically ordered and are guided by students' responses.

☐ Reflect the objectives of the lesson.

☐ For students who answer incompletely are processing questions.

☐ Can be extended and modified to encourage students to answer difficult questions.

☐ In no way prevent students from demonstrating what they have learned.

From *Understanding and Using Reading Assessment, K–12, Fourth Edition*, by Peter Afflerbach. Copyright © 2025 The Guilford Press. Permission to photocopy this material, or to download and print enlarged versions (*www.guilford.com/afflerbach2-forms*), is granted to purchasers of this book for personal use or use with students; see copyright page for details.

Developing an Arc of Questions:
From Relatively Simple to Increasingly Complex

Text(s): _____

Bloom's taxonomy category (what students must do)	Related question
Remember	
Understand	
Apply	
Analyze	
Synthesize	
Evaluate/create	

From *Understanding and Using Reading Assessment, K–12, Fourth Edition*, by Peter Afflerbach. Copyright © 2025 The Guilford Press. Permission to photocopy this material, or to download and print enlarged versions (*www.guilford.com/afflerbach2-forms*), is granted to purchasers of this book for personal use or use with students; see copyright page for details.

Guidelines for Developing and Using Performance Assessments

- Determine if and why the performance assessment is needed. Remember that many performance assessments demand considerable effort and time to be worthwhile.

- Specify the important reading knowledge and outcomes that will be assessed by the performance assessment.

- Propose a specific performance that is composed of the reading knowledge and outcomes and conduct a task analysis.

- Based on the task analysis and in relation to research findings, specify the performance that allows students to demonstrate their learning and achievement.

- Specify the aspects of performance that will receive assessment attention and enable the identification and determination of student success.

- Determine the degrees of students' performance that will be identified using rubrics.

- Set performance levels and different levels of proficiency in relation to instructional goals and standards.

- Use the performance assessment to evaluate student learning and work, perhaps using checklists geared to important (i.e., "must have") aspects of the task, using rating scales that represent the continuum of expected student performance. Note that piloting helps fine-tune scoring guides to best cover and represent what students might do.

From *Understanding and Using Reading Assessment, K–12, Fourth Edition*, by Peter Afflerbach. Copyright © 2025 The Guilford Press. Permission to photocopy this material, or to download and print enlarged versions (*www.guilford.com/afflerbach2-forms*), is granted to purchasers of this book for personal use or use with students; see copyright page for details.

Creating Consistent Approaches to Reading Assessment across Grade Levels and Content Areas

What are the opportunities for coordinating assessments across grades in your school or district?

What are the opportunities for coordinating assessments across content areas in a particular grade in your school or district?

What types of formative reading assessment are consistent across the school years / elementary school years / middle school years / high school years?

What types of summative reading assessment are consistent across the school years / elementary school years / middle school years / high school years?

What are the benefits of consistent forms of and approaches to reading assessment for students?

What are the benefits of consistent forms of and approaches to reading assessment for teachers?

What are the benefits of consistent forms of and approaches to reading assessment for administrators?

From *Understanding and Using Reading Assessment, K–12, Fourth Edition,* by Peter Afflerbach. Copyright © 2025 The Guilford Press. Permission to photocopy this material, or to download and print enlarged versions (*www.guilford.com/afflerbach2-forms*), is granted to purchasers of this book for personal use or use with students; see copyright page for details.

Checklist for Linguistic Modification of Reading Assessment

☐ There are a reasonable number of questions, no more than are needed to sufficiently assess learning outcomes.

☐ All questions are written clearly and concisely.

☐ All directions and instructions are written clearly and concisely.

☐ Students are encouraged to give feedback on the comprehensibility of assessment directions and questions.

☐ Students receive feedback that is as specific as possible.

☐ When assessment is discussed with students, general terms such as *good, poor,* and *not adequate* are avoided.

☐ The feedback provided students mirrors the steps taken in teaching a lesson, including establishing goals, direct instruction, guided practice, independent practice, and assessment.

☐ Expectations for the task are clearly explained.

☐ Assessment is planned to include regular interactions with students to check for understanding.

From *Understanding and Using Reading Assessment, K–12, Fourth Edition*, by Peter Afflerbach. Copyright © 2025 The Guilford Press. Permission to photocopy this material, or to download and print enlarged versions (*www.guilford.com/afflerbach2-forms*), is granted to purchasers of this book for personal use or use with students; see copyright page for details.

Assessing "the Other": Questions for Teachers and Administrators

What aspects of student readers' development *besides* cognitive strategies and skills do we value (e.g., motivation and engagement, persistence in the face of challenges, self-concept and self-efficacy, attitudes toward reading, interests, attributions for reading success or failure)?

What available assessments focus on these important aspects of student readers' development?

What is our plan for gaining expertise in using these assessments?

What are our responsibilities related to developing, administering, and using these assessments?

How can we fit these assessments into our already crowded assessment schedule?

How can we help our school community understand the value of these assessments?

Checklist for Planning Effective Formative Assessment

☐ Is formative assessment developed alongside curriculum and instruction?

☐ Is formative assessment focused on *how* students learn, in addition to *what* students learn?

☐ Is formative assessment situated in the midst of instruction, as part of the teaching–learning–assessment cycle?

☐ Is formative assessment a major focus for teachers' professional development?

☐ Does formative assessment focus on the broad set of student learning outcomes that we expect from a successful reading program?

☐ Does formative assessment promote student motivation and engagement with both learning and assessment itself?

☐ Will formative assessment promote students' understanding of learning goals and criteria for judging their work?

☐ Does the content of formative assessment provide students with information that helps them know how to improve?

☐ Does formative assessment serve as a model of how to "do assessment" so that students learn independence?

☐ Is formative assessment capable of adjusting to the grain size of student learning—does it have the capacity to capture major and minor learning accomplishments?

From *Understanding and Using Reading Assessment, K–12, Fourth Edition*, by Peter Afflerbach. Copyright © 2025 The Guilford Press. Permission to photocopy this material, or to download and print enlarged versions (*www.guilford.com/afflerbach2-forms*), is granted to purchasers of this book for personal use or use with students; see copyright page for details.

Formative Assessment Coverage That Contributes to Students' Achievement on High-Stakes Summative Assessments

What is the complex learning goal (including Common Core State Standards) to be met?

What strategies, skills, and knowledge do students need to meet the learning goal?

Develop a list of the formative assessments that provide information on the development of these strategies, skills, and knowledge.

Is the formative assessment coverage of students development on the path to meeting the standard complete? What remains to be assessed?

Develop assessment tasks that encourage students to bring together all of the strategies, skills, and knowledge needed to do well on the summative assessment that maps onto the complex learning goal.

From *Understanding and Using Reading Assessment, K–12, Fourth Edition*, by Peter Afflerbach. Copyright © 2025 The Guilford Press. Permission to photocopy this material, or to download and print enlarged versions (*www.guilford.com/afflerbach2-forms*), is granted to purchasers of this book for personal use or use with students; see copyright page for details.

Checklist for Self-Assessment

Orientation and planning at the onset of reading

☐ I understand the reading task.

☐ I have a clear goal for my reading.

☐ I have the needed resources to succeed at reading.

☐ I keep track of all my responsibilities as a reader.

☐ When and where will I check on my progress?

☐ How will I check on my progress?

☐ Am I flexible so that as I read I can revise my plan?

☐ Am I flexible so that as I read I can change my goal?

Monitoring and selecting methods for being metacognitive

☐ When, where, and how am I checking on my progress?

☐ Against what standard am I making self-assessment decisions?

☐ I check to see if what I read makes sense.

☐ I am on the lookout for problems while I read.

☐ If I find a problem, I try to figure out what it is.

☐ Once I find the problem, I try to fix it.

☐ When the problem is fixed, I continue my reading.

Evaluation after reading

☐ Did I reach my goal for reading?

☐ If so, what contributed to my success?

☐ If not, what were the challenges I encountered?

From *Understanding and Using Reading Assessment, K–12, Fourth Edition*, by Peter Afflerbach. Copyright © 2025 The Guilford Press. Permission to photocopy this material, or to download and print enlarged versions (*www.guilford.com/afflerbach2-forms*), is granted to purchasers of this book for personal use or use with students; see copyright page for details.

Checklist for Critical Reading

☐ I try to determine what is fact and what is opinion when I read.

☐ I check to determine if the author provides evidence to support claims.

☐ I compare the text information with what I already know about the topic.

☐ I try to determine the author's purpose when it is not stated explicitly.

☐ I work to identify the subtext of the text I am reading.

☐ I try to determine the source of the text I am reading.

☐ I work to determine if the text I am reading is trustworthy.

Checklist for Keyboarding and Internet Navigation Knowledge and Skills

Student name: _____

☐ Is familiar with school digital devices

☐ Efficiently uses school digital devices

☐ Can keyboard appropriately (spelling, punctuation, grammar)

☐ Can type in Search bar

☐ Understands Search function

☐ Can click on links

☐ Can use Delete key

☐ Can use Cut function

☐ Can use Paste function

☐ Can identify appropriate internet links in relation to reading purpose

☐ Uses hyperlinks to efficiently navigate internet

Observations and concerns about keyboard familiarity:

Observations and concerns about keyboard fluency:

Observations and concerns about internet navigation:

From *Understanding and Using Reading Assessment, K–12, Fourth Edition*, by Peter Afflerbach. Copyright © 2025 The Guilford Press. Permission to photocopy this material, or to download and print enlarged versions (*www.guilford.com/afflerbach2-forms*), is granted to purchasers of this book for personal use or use with students; see copyright page for details.

References

Abedi, J. (2012). Validity issues in designing accommodations. In G. Fulcher & F. Davidson (Eds.), *Handbook of language testing*. New York: Routledge.

Abedi, J., Lord, C., Hofstetter, C., & Baker, E. L. (2000). Impact of accommodation strategies on English language learners' test performance. *Educational Measurement: Issues and Practice, 19*(3), 16–26.

Abedi, J., Lord, C., & Plummer, J. R. (1997). *Final report of language background as a variable in NAEP mathematics performance* (CSE Technical Report No. 429). Los Angeles: Center for the Study of Evaluation, National Center for Research on Evaluation, Standards, and Student Testing, University of California, Los Angeles.

Adams, M. J. (1990). *Beginning to read: Thinking and learning about print*. Cambridge, MA: MIT Press.

Afflerbach, P. (2002a). Teaching reading self-assessment strategies. In C. C. Block & M. Pressley (Eds.), *Comprehension instruction: Research-based best practices* (pp. 96–111). New York: Guilford Press.

Afflerbach, P. (2002b). The road to folly and redemption: Perspectives on the legitimacy of high-stakes testing. *Reading Research Quarterly, 37*(3), 348–360.

Afflerbach, P. (2022). *Teaching readers (not reading): Moving beyond skills and strategies to reader-focused instruction*. New York: Guilford Press.

Afflerbach, P., & Cho, B. (2009). Identifying and describing constructively responsive comprehension strategies in new and traditional forms of reading. In S. E. Israel & G. G. Duffy (Eds.), *Handbook of research on reading comprehension* (pp. 69–90). New York: Routledge.

Afflerbach, P., Cho, B., & Kim, J. (2011). The assessment of higher order thinking in reading. In G. Schraw & D. H. Robinson (Eds.), *Assessment of higher order thinking skills* (pp. 185–218). Charlotte, NC: Information Age.

Afflerbach, P., & Meuwissen, K. (2005). Teaching and learning self-assessment strategies in middle school. In S. E. Israel, C. C. Block, K. L. Bauserman, & K. Kinnucan-Welsch (Eds.), *Metacognition in literacy learning: Theory, assessment, instruction, and professional development* (pp. 141–164). Mahwah, NJ: Erlbaum.

Afflerbach, P., Pearson, P., & Paris, S. (2008). Clarifying differences between reading skills and reading strategies. *The Reading Teacher, 61*(5), 364–373.

Afflerbach, P., & VanSledright, B. (2001). Hath? Doth? What! The challenges middle school students face when reading innovative history text. *Journal of Adolescent and Adult Literacy, 44*(8), 696–707.

Ahn, H. (2023). *Competent readers' online multimodal reading strategies use* [Unpublished doctoral dissertation]. University of Maryland. ProQuest Dissertations and Theses Global.

Alexander, P. A. (2005). The path to competence: A lifespan developmental perspective on reading. *Journal of Literacy Research, 37*(4), 413–436.

Alexander, P. A. (2010). Reading into the future: Competence for the 21st century. *Educational Psychologist, 47*(4), 259–280.

Allington, R. L. (1983). The reading instruction provided readers of differing reading abilities. *The Elementary School Journal, 83*(5), 548–559.

Allington, R., & Gabriel, R. (2016). Classroom influences on individual differences. In P. Afflerbach (Ed.), *Handbook of individual differences in reading: Text and context* (pp. 196–208). New York: Routledge.

American Educational Research Association, American Psychological Association, & National Council on Measurement in Education. (2014). *Standards for educational and psychological testing*. Washington, DC: Author.

American Institutes for Research. (2024). *Essential components of MTSS*. https://mtss-4success.org/essential-components

American Library Association. (2024). *Digital literacy*. https://literacy.ala.org/digital-literacy

Anderson, L., & Bourke, S. (2000). *Assessing affective characteristics in the schools* (2nd ed.). Mahwah, NJ: Erlbaum.

Anderson, M., Faverio, M., & Gottfried, J. (2023, December 11). *Teens, social media and technology 2023*. Pew Research Center. www.pewresearch.org/internet/2023/12/11/teens-social-media-and-technology-2023

Anderson, R., & Pearson, P. (1984). A schema-theoretic view of basic processes in reading comprehension. In P. Pearson, R. Barr, M. Kamil, & P. Mosenthal (Eds.), *Handbook of reading research* (pp. 255–291). White Plains, NY: Longman.

Andrade, H. G. (2000). Using rubrics to promote thinking and learning. *Educational Leadership, 57*(5), 13–18.

Athey, I. (1985). Reading research in the affective domain. In H. Singer & R. Ruddell (Eds.), *Theoretical models and processes of reading* (3rd ed., pp. 527–557). Newark, DE: International Reading Association.

Azevedo, R., Rosário, P., Núñez, J. C., Vallejo, G., Fuentes, S., & Magalhães, P. (2023). A school-based intervention on elementary students' school engagement. *Contemporary Educational Psychology, 73*, 102148.

Bae, C., DeBusk-Lane, M. L., & Lester, A. (2020). Engagement profiles of elementary students in urban schools. *Contemporary Educational Psychology, 62*, 101880.

Baker, L., & Brown, A. (1984). Metacognitive skills in reading. In P. Pearson, R. Barr,

References

Bandura, A. (1998). Personal and collective efficacy in human adaptation and change. In J. Adair, D. Belanger, & K. Dion (Eds.), *Advances in psychological science: Vol. 1. Personal, social and cultural aspects* (pp. 51–71). Hove, UK: Psychology Press.

Bandura, A. (2006). Guide for constructing self-efficacy scales. In F. Pajares & T. Urdan (Eds.), *Self-efficacy beliefs of adolescents* (pp. 307–337). Charlotte, NC: IAP.

Barber, A. T., & Klauda, S. L. (2020). How reading motivation and engagement enable reading achievement: Policy implications. *Policy Insights from the Behavioral and Brain Sciences, 7*(1), 27–34.

Barzilai, S., & Strømsø, H. (2018). Individual differences in multiple document comprehension. In J. Braasch, I. Bråten, & M. McCrudden (Eds.), *Handbook of multiple source use* (pp. 99–116). New York: Routledge.

Beck, I., McKeown, M., Hamilton, R., & Kucan, L. (1997). *Questioning the author: An approach for enhancing student engagement with text.* Newark, DE: International Reading Association.

Berkeley, S., Mastopieri, M. A., & Scruggs, T. E. (2011). Reading comprehension strategy instruction and attribution retraining for secondary students with learning and other mild disabilities. *Journal of Learning Disabilities, 44*(1), 18–32.

Berliner, D., & Biddle, B. (1995). *The manufactured crisis: Myths, fraud, and the attack on America's public schools.* Cambridge, MA: Perseus.

Betts, E. (1946). *Foundations of reading instruction, with emphasis on differentiated guidance.* New York: American Book.

Bhattacharya, E. (2016). The influence of poverty on individual differences in reading. In P. Afflerbach (Ed.), *Handbook of individual differences in reading: Text and context* (pp. 305–317). New York: Routledge.

Black, P., & Wiliam, D. (1998). Inside the black box: Raising standards through classroom assessment. *Phi Delta Kappan, 80,* 139–144.

Bloom, B. S. (Ed.). (1956). *Taxonomy of educational objectives: The classification of educational goals. Handbook 1: Cognitive domain.* New York: David McKay.

Boekaerts, M., Pintrich, P., & Zeidner, M. (2000). *Handbook of self-regulation.* San Diego, CA: Academic Press.

Borkowski, J., & Turner, L. (1990). Transituational characteristics of metacognition. In W. Schneider & F. Weinert (Eds.), *Interactions among aptitudes, strategies, and knowledge in cognitive performance* (pp. 159–176). New York: Springer-Verlag.

Braasch, J. L. G., Haverkamp, Y. E., Latini, N., Shaw, S., Arshad, M. S., & Bråten, I. (2022). Belief bias when adolescents read to comprehend multiple conflicting texts. *Reading and Writing, 35*(6), 1759–1785.

Bracey, G. (2001). The 11th Bracey report on the condition of public education. *Phi Delta Kappan, 83,* 157–168.

Bråten, I., Strømsø, H. I., & Britt, M. A. (2009). Trust matters: Examining the role of source evaluation in students' construction of meaning within and across multiple texts. *Reading Research Quarterly, 44*(1), 6–28.

Brown, A. L. (1997). Transforming schools into communities of thinking and learning about serious matters. *American Psychologist, 52,* 399–413.

Brown, J., & Sanford, A. (2011). *RTI for English language learners: Appropriately using screening and progress monitoring tools to improve instructional outcomes.* Washington, DC: National Center on Response to Intervention, Office of Special Education Programs, U.S. Department of Education.

Cain, K., & Oakhill, J. (2011). Matthew effects in young readers: Reading comprehension and reading experience aid vocabulary development. *Journal of Learning Disabilities, 44*(5), 431–443.

California Department of Education. (n.d.). *Definition of MTSS.* www.cde.ca.gov/ci/cr/ri/mtsscomprti2.asp

California Department of Education. (1998). *English-language arts content standards for California public schools: Kindergarten through grade twelve.* www.cde.ca.gov/be/st/ss/documents/elacontentstnds.pdf

California State University, Chico. (2010). *Evaluating information—Applying the CRAAP test.* https://library.csuchico.edu/sites/default/files/craap-test.pdf

Carroll, J. M., & Fox, A. (1997). Reading self-efficacy predicts word reading but not comprehension in both girls and boys. *Frontiers in Psychology, 7,* 20–56.

Cazden, C. (1986). Classroom discourse. In Wittrock, M. C. (Ed.), *Handbook of research on teaching* (3rd ed., pp. 432–462). New York: Macmillan.

Cervetti, G., Pardales, M. J., & Damico, J. (2001). A tale of differences: Comparing the traditions, perspectives, and educational goals of critical reading and critical literacy. *Reading Online, 4*(9).

Chapman, J. W., & Tunmer, W. E. (1995). Development of young children's reading self-concepts: An examination of emerging subcomponents and their relationship with reading achievement. *Journal of Educational Psychology, 87*(1), 154–167.

Cho, B.-Y. (2014). Competent adolescent readers' use of internet reading strategies: A think-aloud study. *Cognition and Instruction, 32*(3), 253–289.

Christensen, L., Shyyan, V., Schuster, T., Mahaley, P., & Saez, S. (2012). *Accommodations manual: How to select, administer, and evaluate use of accommodations for instruction and assessment of English language learners.* Minneapolis: University of Minnesota, National Center on Educational Outcomes.

Clark, I. (2012). Formative assessment: Assessment is for self-regulated learning. *Educational Psychology Review, 24*(2), 205–249.

Clay, M. M. (1979). *Reading: The patterning of complex behaviour* (2nd ed.). Portsmouth, NH: Heinemann.

Clay, M. M. (1989). Concepts about Print in English and other languages. *The Reading Teacher, 42*(4), 268–276.

Clay, M. M. (2016). *An observation survey of early literacy achievement* (2nd ed.). Portsmouth, NH: Heinemann.

Clayton, F. J., West, G., Sears, C., Hulme, C., & Lervåg, A. (2020). A longitudinal study of early reading development: Letter–sound knowledge, phoneme awareness and RAN, but not letter–sound integration, predict variations in reading development. *Scientific Studies of Reading, 24*(2), 91–107.

References

Cohen, D., Tracy, R., & Cohen, J. (2017). On the effectiveness of pop-up English language glossary accommodations for EL students in large-scale assessments. *Applied Measurement in Education, 30*(4), 259–272.

Coiro, J. (2020). Toward a multifaceted heuristic of digital reading to inform assessment, research, practice, and policy. *Reading Research Quarterly, 56*(1), 9–31.

Common Core State Standards. (2024a). *English Language Arts Standards » Reading: Informational Text » Grade 4.* https://corestandards.org/ELA-Literacy/RI/4

Common Core State Standards. (2024b). *English Language Arts Standards » Reading: Informational Text » Grade 3.* https://thecorestandards.org/ELA-Literacy/RI/3

Cook, L., Eignor, D., Steinberg, J., Sawaki, Y., & Cline, F. (2014). Using factor analysis to investigate the impact of accommodations on the scores of students with disabilities on a reading comprehension assessment. *Journal of Applied Testing Technology, 10*(2), 1–33.

Datchuk, S. M., & Hier, B. O. (2019). Fluency practice: Techniques for building automaticity in foundational knowledge and skills. *Exceptional Children, 51*(6), 424–435.

Davis, A. (1998). *The limits of educational assessment.* Oxford, UK: Blackwell.

Durkin, D. (1978). What classroom observations reveal about reading comprehension instruction. *Reading Research Quarterly, 14*(4), 481–533.

Dweck, C. (1999). *Self-theories: Their role in motivation, personality, and development.* Philadelphia: Psychology Press.

Ellis, A., & Eberly, T. L. (2015). Critical literacy: Going beyond the demands of Common Core. *Illinois Reading Council Journal, 43*(2), 9–15.

Fairbairn, S. (2007). Facilitating greater test success for English language learners. *Practical Assessment, Research and Evaluation, 12*(11).

Finn, B., Miele, D. B., & Wigfield, A. (2023). The impact of remembered success experiences on expectancies, values, and perceived costs. *Contemporary Educational Psychology, 72*, 1–17.

Fitri, D., Sofyan, D., & Jayanti, F. (2019). The correlation between reading self-efficacy and reading comprehension. *Journal of English Education and Teaching, 3*(1), 1–13.

Fletcher, J. M., Francis, D. J., Boudosquie, A., Copeland, K., Young, V., & Kalinowski, S. (2006). Effects of accommodations on high-stakes testing for students with reading disabilities. *Exceptional Children, 72*(2), 136–150.

Forzani, E., Corrigan, J. A., & Slomp, D. (2020). Reimagining literacy assessment through a New Literacies lens. *Journal of Adolescent and Adult Literacy, 64*(3), 351–355.

Francis, E. (2021). *Deconstructing depth of knowledge: A method and model for deeper teaching and learning.* Indianapolis, IN: Solution Tree.

Frederiksen, N. (1984). The real test bias: Influences of testing on teaching and learning. *American Psychologist, 39*(3), 193–202.

Freebody, P., & Luke, A. (1990). Literacies programs: Debates and demands in cultural context. *Prospect: An Australian Journal of TESOL, 5*(3), 7–16.

Freire, P., & Macedo, D. (1987). *Literacy: Reading the word and the world.* South Hadley, MA: Bergin & Garvey.

Frijters, J. C., Tsujimoto, K. C., Boada, R., Gottwald, S., Hill, D., Jacobson, L. A., & Gruen, J. R. (2018). Reading-related causal attributions for success and failure: Dynamic links with reading skill. *Reading Research Quarterly, 53*(1), 127–148.

Furenes, M. I., Kucirkova, N., & Bus, A. G. (2021). A comparison of children's reading on paper versus screen: A meta-analysis. *Review of Educational Research, 91*(4), 1–35.

Gabriel, R., & Allington, R. (2016). *Evaluating literacy instruction: Principles and promising practices.* New York: Routledge.

Gambrell, L., Codling, R., & Palmer, B. (1996). *Elementary students' motivation to read* (Reading Research Report No. 52). Athens, GA: National Reading Research Center.

Gamse, B., Jacob, R., Horst, M., Boulay, B., & Unlu, F. (2008). *Reading First Impact Study final report* (NCEE 2009-4038). Washington, DC: National Center for Education Evaluation and Regional Assistance, Institute of Education Sciences, U.S. Department of Education.

Gottfried, J., & Grieco, E. (2018, October 23). *Younger Americans are better than older Americans at telling factual news statements from opinions.* Pew Research Center. *www.pewresearch.org/short-reads/2018/10/23/younger-americans-are-better-than-older-americans-at-telling-factual-news-statements-from-opinions*

Gulli, A., & Signorini, A. (2005). The indexable Web is more than 11.5 billion pages. Retrieved March 22, 2023, from *www.semanticscholar.org/paper/The-indexable-web-is-more-than-11.5-billion-pages-Gulli-Signorini/6108476b315f6586afff39dd072a3f4 f7949bc10*

Guthrie, J. T. (2001). Contexts for engagement and motivation in reading. *Reading Online, 4*(8).

Guthrie, J. T., & Klauda, S. L. (2016). Engagement and motivational processes in reading. In P. Afflerbach (Ed.), *Handbook of individual differences in reading: Text and context* (pp. 41–53). New York: Routledge.

Guthrie, J. T., Wigfield, A., & You, W. (2013). Instructional contexts for engagement and achievement in reading. In S. L. Christensen, A. L. Reschly, & C. Wylie (Eds.), *Handbook of research on student engagement* (pp. 601–634). New York: Springer Science.

Hamilton, L., Stecher, B., & Klein, S. (Eds.). (2002). *Making sense of test-based accountability in education.* Santa Monica, CA: RAND.

Hart, R., Casserly, M., Uzzell, R., Palacios, M., Corcoran, A., & Spurgeon, L. (2015). *Student testing in America's great city schools: An inventory and preliminary analysis.* Washington, DC: Council of Great City Schools.

Heath, S. (1983). *Ways with words: Language, life, and work in communities and classrooms.* New York: Cambridge University Press.

Henk, W. A., & Melnick, S. A. (1995). The Reader Self-Perception Scale (RSPS): A new tool for measuring how children feel about themselves as readers. *The Reading Teacher, 48*(6), 470–482.

Hiebert, E. H., Winograd, P. N., & Danner, F. W. (1984). Children's attributions for failure and success in different aspects of reading. *Journal of Educational Psychology, 76*(6), 1139–1148.

Hildebrandt, D. (2001). "But there's nothing good to read" (in the library media center). *Media Spectrum: The Journal for Library Media Specialists in Michigan, 28,* 34–37.

Hoff, E. (2006). How social contexts support and shape language development. *Developmental Review, 26*(1), 55–88.

Hoover, W. A., & Tunmer, W. E. (2022). The primacy of science in communicating advances in the science of reading. *Reading Research Quarterly, 57*(2), 399–408.

Huey, E. B. (1908). *The psychology and pedagogy of reading, with a review of the history of reading and writing and of methods, texts, and hygiene in reading.* New York: Macmillan.

Institute for Educational Sciences. (2008). *Reading First Impact Study Final Report.* https://ies.ed.gov/ncee/pubs/20094038/summ_b.asp

International Reading Association. (1999). *High-stakes assessments in reading: A position statement of the International Reading Association.* Newark, DE: Author.

Ivey, G., & Johnston, P. (2023). *Teens choosing to read: Fostering social, emotional, and intellectual growth through books.* New York: Teachers College Press.

Jewett, A. (1940). Detecting and analyzing propaganda. *The English Journal, 29*(2), 105–115.

Johnston, P. (1987). Teachers as evaluation experts. *The Reading Teacher, 40*(8), 744–748.

Johnston, P. H., & Winograd, P. N. (1985). Passive failure in reading. *Journal of Reading, 17*(4), 279–301.

Karabay, A. (2015). Effect of critical reading education on metacognitive reading strategies and media literacy. *Journal of Theory and Practice in Education, 11,* 1167–1184.

Kendeou, P., McMaster, K. L., & Christ, T. J. (2016). Reading comprehension core components and processes. *Policy Insights from the Behavioral and Brain Sciences, 3*(1), 62–69.

Kerlinger, F. (1986). *Foundations of behavioral research* (3rd ed.). New York: Holt, Rinehart and Winston.

Khoury-Shaheen, R., & Weintraub, N. (2022). Keyboarding assessments for elementary school students: Can they be uniform? *Computers and Education Open, 3,* 100091.

Kim, J. S., Burkhauser, M. A., Mesite, L. M., Asher, C. A., Relya, J. E., Fitzgerald, J., & Elmore, J. (2021). Improving reading comprehension, science domain knowledge, and reading engagement through a first-grade content literacy intervention. *Journal of Educational Psychology, 113*(1), 3–26.

Kober, N., Chudowsky, N., & Chudowsky, V. (2008). *Has student achievement increased since 2002? State test score trends through 2006–07.* Washington, DC: Center on Education Policy.

Koenig, J., & Bachman, L. (Eds.). (2004). *Keeping score for all: The effects of inclusion and accommodation policies on large-scale educational assessments.* Washington, DC: National Academies Press.

Kohn, A. (2000). *The case against standardized testing: Raising the scores, ruining the schools.* Portsmouth, NH: Heinemann.

Kohn, A. (2015). *Schooling beyond measure . . . and other unorthodox essays about education.* New York: Heinemann.

Koray, Ö., & Çetinkılıç, S. (2020). The use of critical reading in understanding scientific texts on academic performance and problem-solving skills. *Science Education International, 31*(4), 400–409.

Krathwohl, D. R. (2002). A revision of Bloom's taxonomy: An overview. *Theory into Practice, 41*(4), 212–218.

Kuhn, D., Cheney, R., & Weinstock, M. (2000). The development of epistemological understanding. *Cognitive Development, 15*(3), 309–328.

Lave, J., & Wenger, E. (1991). *Situated learning: Legitimate peripheral participation.* New York: Cambridge University Press.

Lawless, K., & Schrader, P. (2008). Where do we go now? Understanding research on navigation in complex digital environments. In J. Coiro, M. Knobel, C. Lankshear, & D. Leu, D. (Eds.), *Handbook of research in new literacies* (pp. 267–296). New York: Routledge.

Lee, V., & Burkam, D. (2002). *Inequality at the starting gate: Social background differences in achievement as children begin school.* Washington, DC. Economic Policy Institute.

Leipzig, D. H., & Afflerbach, P. (2000). Determining the suitability of assessments: Using the CURRV framework. In L. Baker, M. Dreher, & J. Guthrie (Eds.), *Engaging young readers: Promoting achievement and motivation* (pp. 159–187). New York: Guilford Press.

Leslie, L., & Caldwell, J. (2021). *Qualitative reading inventory* (7th ed.). New York: Pearson.

Leu, D. J., Kiili, C., & Forzani, E. (2016). Individual differences in the new literacies of online research and comprehension. In P. Afflerbach (Ed.), *Handbook of individual differences in reading: Text and context* (pp. 259–272). New York: Routledge.

Lewison, M., Flint, A. S., & Van Sluys, K. (2002). Taking on critical literacy: The journey of newcomers and novices. *Language Arts, 79*(5), 382–392.

List, A., & Alexander, P. A. (2017). Analyzing and integrating models of multiple text comprehension. *Educational Psychologist, 52*(3), 143–147.

Litt, E. (2013). Measuring users' internet skills: A review of past assessments and a look toward the future. *New Media and Society, 15*(4), 612–630.

Lonigan, C. J., Burgess, S. R., & Anthony, J. L. (2000). Development of emergent literacy and early reading skills in preschool children: Evidence from a latent-variable longitudinal study. *Developmental Psychology, 36*(5), 596–613.

Ly, C., & Forzani, E. (2023). Let's learn from them: Using the Integrative Multimodal Literacy Assessment Tool to support instruction for young children. *The Reading Teacher, 77,* 10.1002/trtr.2243.

Mansell, W., James, M., & the Assessment Reform Group. (2009). *Assessment in schools: Fit for purpose? A commentary by the Teaching and Learning Research Programme.* London: Economic and Social Research Council, Teaching and Learning Research Programme.

Massachusetts State Department of Education. (2024). Tiered Instruction within the MTSS Model. *www.doe.mass.edu/massliteracy/leading-mtss/tiered-instruction.html*

Mathewson, G. (1994). Model of attitude influence upon reading and learning to read. In R. Ruddell, M. Ruddell, & H. Singer (Eds.), *Theoretical models and processes of reading* (4th ed., pp. 1131–1161). Newark, DE: International Reading Association.

McCarthy, K. S., Steinberg, J., Dreier, K., O'Reilly, T., Sabatini, J., Butterfuss, R., & McNamara, D. S. (2023). The effects of prior knowledge in a scenario-based comprehension assessment: A multidimensional approach. *Learning and Individual Differences, 103,* 1–10.

McCracken, R. (1966). *Standard reading inventory.* Klamath Falls, OR: Klamath Printing.

McKenna, M. C., & Kear, D. J. (1990). Measuring attitude toward reading: A new tool for teachers. *The Reading Teacher, 43*(9), 626–639.

McNamara, D. S., Jacovina, M., & Varner, L. (2016). Higher order thinking in reading. In P. Afflerbach (Ed.), *Handbook of individual differences in reading: Text and context* (pp. 164–176). New York: Routledge.

McNamara, D. S., & Magliano, J. P. (2009). Self-explanation and metacognition: The dynamics of reading. In D. J. Hacker, J. Dunlosky, & A. C. Graesser (Eds.), *Handbook of metacognition in education* (pp. 60–81). New York: Routledge.

Mehan, H. (1979). *Learning lessons: Social organization in the classroom.* Cambridge, MA: Harvard University Press.

Melesse, S., & Enyew, C. (2020). Effects of reading strategies on grade one children's phonemic awareness performance. *Journal of Education and Learning, 14*(3), 385–392.

Messick, S. (1989). Validity. In R. Linn (Ed.), *Educational measurement* (3rd ed., pp. 13–103). New York: Macmillan.

Metsala, J., & David, M. (2016). Individual differences in word recognition. In P. Afflerbach (Ed.), *Handbook of individual differences in reading: Text and context* (pp. 93–106). New York: Routledge.

Moje, E. B., Ciechanowski, K. M., Kramer, K., Ellis, L., Carrillo, R., & Collazo, T. (2004). Working toward third space in content area literacy: An examination of everyday funds of knowledge and discourse. *Reading Research Quarterly, 39*(1), 38–70.

Molden, K. (2007). Critical literacy, the right answer for the reading classroom: Strategies to move beyond comprehension for reading improvement. *Reading Improvement, 44*(1), 50–56.

Monte-Sano, C., Schleppegrell, M., Sun, S., Wu, J., & Kabat, J. (2022). Discussion in diverse middle school social studies classrooms: Promoting all students' participation in the disciplinary work of inquiry. *Teachers College Record, 123*(1), 142–184.

Moore, K., Redd, Z., Burkhauser, M., Mbwana, K., & Collins, A. (2009). *Children in poverty: Trends, consequences, and policy options.* Washington, DC: Child Trends.

Moskal, B. M. (2003). Recommendations for developing classroom performance assessments and scoring rubrics. *Practical Assessment, Research and Evaluation, 8*(14).

Muenks, K., Wigfield, A., & Eccles, J. S. (2018). I can do this! The development and calibration of children's expectations for success and competence beliefs. *Developmental Review, 48,* 24–39.

Mullis, I. V. S., & Martin, M. O. (Eds.). (2015). *PIRLS 2016 Assessment Framework* (2nd ed.). Chestnut Hill, MA: TIMSS & PIRLS International Study Center, Boston College.

Mullis, I. V. S., & Martin, M. O. (2021). *PIRLS 2021 reading assessment framework.* Chestnut Hill, MA: IEA TIMSS & PIRLS, Boston College. https://pirls2021.org/frameworks/home/reading-assessment-framework

Muspratt, S., Luke, A., & Freebody, P. (1997). *Constructing critical literacies: Teaching and learning textual practice.* Creskill, NJ: Hampton.

Nag, S., Banu Vagh, S., Dulay, K. M., & Snowling, M. J. (2019). Home language, school language and children's literacy attainments: A systematic review of evidence from low- and middle-income countries. *Review of Education, 7,* 91–151.

National Assessment Governing Board. (2023). *Reading framework for the 2025 National Assessment of Educational Progress*. Washington, DC: Author.

National Assessment of Educational Progress. (2023). *The Nation's Report Card: Highlights*. https://nationsreportcard.gov/highlights/ltt/2023

National Association for the Education of Young Children & National Association of Early Childhood Specialists in State Departments of Education. (2003). *Where we stand on curriculum, assessment, and program evaluation*. Washington, DC.

National Center for Education Statistics, Institute of Education Sciences, U.S. Department of Education. (2024a). *Students with disabilities*. https://nces.ed.gov/programs/coe/indicator/cgg

National Center for Education Statistics, Institute of Education Sciences, U.S. Department of Education. (2024b). *English learners in public schools*. https://nces.ed.gov/programs/coe/indicator/cgf

National Commission on Excellence in Education. (1983). *A nation at risk: The imperative for educational reform*. Washington, DC: U.S. Government Printing Office.

National Council for the Social Studies. (1994). *Expectations of excellence: Curriculum standards for social studies*. Washington, DC: Author.

National Council of Teachers of English. (2000). *Resolution on urging reconsideration of high stakes testing*. St. Louis: Author.

National Governors Association & Council of Chief State School Officers. (2010). *Common Core state standards for English language arts and literacy in history/social studies, science, and technical subjects*. Retrieved April 10, 2016, from *www.corestandards.org/assets/CCSSI_ELA%20Standards.pdf*

National Institute of Child Health and Human Development. (2000). *Report of the National Reading Panel: Teaching children to read: An evidence-based assessment of the scientific research literature on reading and its implications for reading instruction*. Washington, DC: U.S. Government Printing Office.

Nevo, E., & Vaknin-Nusbaum, V. (2020). Enhancing motivation to read and reading abilities in first grade. *Educational Psychology, 40*(1), 22–41.

Nidus, G., & Sadder, M. (2016). More than a checklist. *Educational Leadership, 73*(7), 62–66.

Ogle, D. M. (1986). K-W-L: A teaching model that develops active reading of expository text. *The Reading Teacher, 39*(6), 564–570.

Organisation for Economic Co-operation and Development. (2011). *Participating countries/economies*. Paris: Author.

Organisation for Economic Co-operation and Development. (2021). *21st-century readers: Developing literacy skills in a digital world*. Paris: Author.

Pajares, F., & Urdan, T. (Eds.). (2006). *Self-efficacy beliefs of adolescents*. Greenwich, CT: Information Age.

Paris, S. G. (2005). Reinterpreting the development of reading skills. *Reading Research Quarterly, 40*(2), 184–202.

Paris, S. G., & Carpenter, R. D. (2003). FAQs about IRIs. *The Reading Teacher, 56*(6), 578–580.

Paris, S. G., Lipson, M. Y., & Wixson, K. K. (1983). Becoming a strategic reader. *Contemporary Educational Psychology, 8*(3), 293–316.

Parr, A. J. (2018). *Highly consequential statewide testing: Some of the impacts of a narrowed curriculum resulting from high stakes tests.* Olympia: Washington State Board of Education.

Partnership for Assessment of Readiness for College and Careers. (2010). *The Partnership for Assessment of Readiness for College and Careers (PARCC) application for the Race to the Top Comprehensive Assessment Systems Competition.* Retrieved June 20, 2011, from www.fldoe.org/parcc/pdf/apprtcasc.pdf

Partnership for Assessment of Readiness for College and Careers. (2017). *Grade 4 English language arts/literacy test booklet: Practice test.* Retrieved May 2, 2018, from https://parcc.pearson.com/resources/practice-tests/english/grade-4/pba/PC194822-001_4ELATB_PT.pdf

Pearson, P. D., & Johnson, D. D. (1978). *Teaching reading comprehension.* New York: Holt, Rinehart and Winston.

Pearson, P. D., Palincsar, A. S., Biancarosa, G., & Berman, A. I. (Eds.). (2020). *Reaping the rewards of the Reading for Understanding Initiative.* Washington, DC: National Academy of Education.

Pečjaka, S., & Pircb, T. (2018). Developing summarizing skills in 4th grade students. *International Electronic Journal of Elementary Education, 10*(5), 571–581.

Pellegrino, J., Chudowsky, N., & Glaser, R. (Eds.). (2001). *Knowing what students know: The science and design of educational assessment.* Washington, DC: National Academies Press.

Pennock-Roman, M., & Rivera, C. (2011). Mean effects of test accommodations for ELLs and non-ELLs: A meta-analysis of experimental studies. *Educational Measurement: Issues and Practice, 30*(3), 10–28.

Peura, P., Aro, T., Räikkönen, E., Viholainen, H., Koponen, T., Usher, E. L., & Aro, M. (2021). Trajectories of change in reading self-efficacy: A longitudinal analysis of self-efficacy and its sources. *Contemporary Educational Psychology, 64*(4), Article 101942.

Peura, P., Aro, T., Viholainen, H., Raikkonen, E., Usher, E. L., Sorvo, R., & Aro, M. (2019). Reading self-efficacy and reading fluency development among primary school children: Does specificity of self-efficacy matter? *Learning and Individual Differences, 73*, 67–78.

Phillips, S. E. (1994). High-stakes testing accommodations: Validity versus disabled rights. *Applied Measurement in Education, 7*(2), 93–120.

Pikulski, J., & Shanahan, T. (1982). Informal reading inventories: A critical analysis. In J. Pikulski & T. Shanahan (Eds.), *Approaches to the informal evaluation of reading* (pp. 94–116). Newark, DE: International Reading Association.

Popham, W. J. (1991). Appropriateness of teachers' test-preparation practices. *Educational Measurement: Issues and Practice, 10*(4), 12–15.

Popham, W. J. (1997). What's wrong—and what's right—with rubrics. *Educational Leadership, 55*(2), 72–75.

Pressley, M., & Afflerbach, P. (1995). *Verbal protocols of reading: The nature of constructively responsive reading.* Hillsdale, NJ: Erlbaum.

Raphael, T. E., & Wonnacott, C. A. (1985). Heightening fourth-grade students' sensitivity to sources of information for answering comprehension questions. *Reading Research Quarterly, 20*(3), 282–296.

Rasinski, T., Rupley, W., Paige, D., & Young, C. (Eds.). (2021). *Reading fluency.* Zurich, Switzerland: mdpiAG.

Rogers, C., Thurlow, M., Lazarus, S., & Liu, K. (2019). *A summary of the research on effects of test accommodations: 2015–2016.* Minneapolis: University of Minnesota, National Center on Educational Outcomes.

Sabatini, J. (2022). Scenario-based assessment: Design, development, and research. *Design Recommendations for Intelligent Tutoring Systems, 41.*

Sabatini, J., O'Reilly, T., Weeks, J., & Wang, Z. (2020). Engineering a twenty-first century reading comprehension assessment system utilizing scenario-based assessment techniques. *International Journal of Testing, 20*(1), 1–23.

Salmerón, L., Vargas, C., Delgado, P., & Baron, N. (2022). Relation between digital tool practices in the language arts classroom and reading comprehension scores. *Reading and Writing, 36,* 175–194.

Scarborough, H. S. (2001). Connecting early language and literacy to later reading (dis)abilities: Evidence, theory, and practice. In S. Neuman & D. Dickinson (Eds.), *Handbook of early literacy research* (Vol. 1, pp. 97–110). New York: Guilford Press.

Schatschneider, C., Fletcher, J. M., Francis, D. J., Carlson, C. D., & Foorman, B. R. (2004). Kindergarten prediction of reading skills: A longitudinal comparative analysis. *Journal of Educational Psychology, 96*(2), 265–282.

Schiefele, U., Schaffner, E., Möller, J., & Wigfield, A. (2012). Dimensions of reading motivation and their relation to reading behavior and competence. *Reading Research Quarterly, 47*(4), 427–463.

Schmuckler, M. A. (2001). What is ecological validity? *Infancy, 2*(4), 419–436.

Schunk, D., & Bursuck, W. (2016). Self-efficacy, agency, and volition. In P. Afflerbach (Ed.), *Handbook of individual differences in reading: Text and context* (pp. 54–66). New York: Routledge.

Schunk, D. H., & DiBenedetto, M. K. (2020). Motivation and social cognitive theory. *Contemporary Educational Psychology, 60,* 101832.

Shell, D. F., Colvin, C., & Bruning, R. H. (1995). Self-efficacy, attributions, and outcome expectancy mechanisms in reading and writing achievement: Grade-level and achievement-level differences. *Journal of Educational Psychology, 87*(3), 386–398.

Shepard, L. A., & Bliem, C. L. (1995). Parents' thinking about standardized tests and performance assessments. *Educational Researcher, 24*(8), 25–32.

Shrider, E., & Creamer, J. (2023). *Poverty in the United States: 2022.* Washington, DC: U.S. Census Bureau.

Shyyan, V., Thurlow, M., Christensen, L., Lazarus, S., Paul, J., & Touchette, B. (2016). *CCSSO accessibility manual: How to select, administer, and evaluate use of accessibility supports for instruction and assessment of all students.* Washington, DC: Chief Council of State School Officers.

Sireci, S. (2004). *Validity issues in accommodating NAEP reading tests.* Amherst: University of Massachusetts Amherst.

Sleeman, M., Everatt, J., Arrow, A., & Denston, A. (2022). The identification and classification of struggling readers based on the simple view of reading. *Dyslexia: An International Journal of Research and Practice, 28*(3), 256–275.

Smarter Balanced Assessment Consortium. (2010). *Race to the Top assessment program application for new grants: Comprehensive assessment systems.* Retrieved June 20, 2011, from *www.scribd.com/doc/53320952/Sbac-Final-Narrative-20100620-4pm*

Smarter Balanced Assessment Consortium. (2014, May 16). *English/language arts practice test scoring guide: Grade 4 performance task.* Retrieved April 2, 2017, from *www.smarterbalanced.org/wp-content/uploads/2015/11/G4_Practice_Test_Scoring_Guide_ELA_PT.pdf*

Snow, C. (2002). *Reading for understanding: Toward an R&D program in reading comprehension.* Santa Monica, CA: RAND.

Snowling, M. J., & Hulme, C. (2012). Children's reading impairments: From theory to practice. *Japanese Psychological Research, 55,* 10.1111.

Solheim, O. J. (2011). The impact of self-efficacy and task value on reading comprehension scores in different item formats. *Reading Psychology, 32*(1), 1–27.

Soto, C., Gutierrez deBlume, A. P., Rebolledo, V., Rodriguez, F., Palma, D., & Gutierrez, F. (2023). Metacognitive monitoring skills of reading comprehension and writing between proficient and poor readers. *Metacognition and Learning, 18,* 113–134.

Stahl, K. A. D., & Bravo, M. A. (2010). Contemporary classroom vocabulary assessment for content areas. *The Reading Teacher, 63*(7), 566–578.

Stanovich, K. E. (1986). Matthew effects in reading: Some consequences of individual differences in the acquisition of literacy. *Reading Research Quarterly, 21*(4), 360–407.

State of California Office of Education. (2024). *California Common Core State Standards for ELA/Literacy.* https://scoe.net/castandards/Documents/parent_overview_ela_3-5.pdf

Stevens, R. (1912). *The question as a measure of efficiency in instruction: A critical study of classroom practice.* New York: Teachers College Press.

Stiggins, R. J., & Conklin, N. F. (2002). *In teachers' hands: Investigating the practices of classroom assessment.* Albany: State University of New York Press.

Stretch, L. S., & Osborne, J. W. (2005). Extended time test accommodation: Directions for future research and practice. *Practical Assessment, Research and Evaluation, 10*(8), 1–8.

Supovitz, J. (2009). Can high stakes testing leverage educational improvement? Prospects from the last decade of testing/accountability reform. *Journal of Educational Change, 10,* 211–227.

Sutter, C. C., & Campbell, L. O. (2022). The role of academic self-determined reading motivation, reading self-concept, home reading environment, and student reading behavior in reading achievement among American Indian and Hispanic students. *Contemporary Educational Psychology, 70,* 1–12.

ten Dam, G., & Volman, M. (2004). Critical thinking as a citizenship competence: Teaching strategies. *Learning and Instruction, 14*(4), 359–379.

Texas Education Agency. (2017). *Texas Essential Knowledge and Skills for English language arts and reading.* Texas Administrative Code, Title 19, Part 2, Ch. 110, Subch. A, Rule

§110.7.   https://texreg.sos.state.tx.us/public/readtac$ext.TacPage?sl=R&app=9&p_dir=&p_rloc=&p_tloc=&p_ploc=&pg=1&p_tac=&ti=19&pt=2&ch=110&rl=7

Thompson, S., Morse, A., Sharpe, M., & Hall, S. (2005). *Accommodations manual: How to select, administer, and evaluate use of accommodations for instruction and assessment of students with disabilities* (2nd ed.). Washington, DC: Council of Chief State School Officers.

Thorndike, E. L. (1917). Reading as reasoning: A study of mistakes in paragraph reading. *Journal of Educational Psychology, 8,* 323–332.

Thurlow, M., & Bolt, S. (2001). *Empirical support for accommodations most often allowed in state policy.* Minneapolis, MN: National Center on Educational Outcomes.

Tierney, R. J., & Pearson, P. D. (2024). *Fact-checking the science of reading: Opening up the conversation.* Literacy Research Commons.

Tullis, J. G., & Goldstone, R. L. (2020). Why does peer instruction benefit student learning? *Cognitive Research: Principles and Implications, 5,* Article 15. https://cognitiveresearchjournal.springeropen.com/articles/10.1186/s41235-020-00218-5

Unrau, N. J., Rueda, R., Son, E., Planin, J. R., Lundeen, R. J., & Muraszewski, A. K. (2018). Can reading self-efficacy be modified? A meta-analysis of the impact of interventions on reading self-efficacy. *Review of Educational Research, 88*(2), 167–204.

van den Broek, P., Mouw, J., & Kraal, A. (2016). Individual differences in reading comprehension. In P. Afflerbach (Ed.), *Handbook of individual differences in reading: Text and context* (pp. 138–150). New York: Routledge.

Van Keer, H., & Verhaeghe, J. P. (2005). Effects of explicit reading strategies instruction and peer tutoring on second and fifth graders' reading comprehension and self-efficacy perceptions. *Journal of Experimental Education, 73*(4), 291–329.

VanSledright, B. A. (2010). *The challenge of rethinking history education: On practices, theories, and policy.* New York: Routledge.

VanSledright, B. A. (2013). *Assessing historical thinking and understanding: Innovative designs for new standards.* New York: Routledge.

Veenman, M. (2016). Metacognition. In P. Afflerbach (Ed.), *Handbook of individual differences in reading: Text and context* (pp. 26–40). New York: Routledge.

Veenman, M., van Hout-Wolters, B., & Afflerbach, P. (2006). Metacognition and learning: Conceptual and methodological issues. *Metacognition and Learning, 1,* 3–14.

Verhoeven, L., & Snow, C. (Eds.). (2001). *Literacy and motivation: Reading engagement in individuals and groups.* Mahwah, NJ: Erlbaum.

Vidal Rodeiro, C., & Macinska, S. (2022). Equal opportunity or unfair advantage? The impact of test accommodations on performance in high-stakes assessments. *Assessment in Education: Principles, Policy and Practice, 29*(4), 462–481.

Vygotsky, L. S. (1978). *Mind in society: The development of higher psychological processes.* Cambridge, MA: Harvard University Press.

Walpole, S., & McKenna, M. C. (2006). The role of informal reading inventories in assessing word recognition. *The Reading Teacher, 59*(6), 592–594.

Wang, M. C., Haertel, G. D., & Walberg, H. J. (1990). What influences learning? A content analysis of review literature. *Journal of Educational Research, 84*(1), 30–43.

Wang, X., Jia, L., & Jin, Y. (2020). Reading amount and reading strategy as mediators of the effects of intrinsic and extrinsic reading motivation on reading achievement. *Frontiers in Psychology, 11,* 586346.

Watson, J. B. (1913). Psychology as the behaviorist views it. *Psychological Review, 20*(2), 158–177.

Webb, N. L. (2002). Depth of knowledge: Four content areas. Retrieved April 3, 2018, from *http://schools.nyc.gov/NR/rdonlyres/2711181C-2108-40C4-A7F8*

Weisleder, A., & Fernald, A. (2013). Talking to children matters: Early language experience strengthens processing and builds vocabulary. *Psychological Sciences, 24*(11), 2143–2152.

Wells, M. S., Morrison, J. D., & López-Robertson, J. (2020). Building critical reading and critical literacy with picturebook analysis. *The Reading Teacher, 76*(2), 191–200.

White, S., Sabatini, J., Park, B. J., Chen, J., Bernstein, J., & Li, M. (2021). *The 2018 NAEP oral reading fluency study.* Washington, DC: National Center for Education Statistics.

Wigfield, A., & Eccles, J. S. (2000). Expectancy–value theory of achievement motivation. *Contemporary Educational Psychology, 25*(1), 68–81.

Wiggins, G. (1998). *Educative assessment: Designing assessments to inform and improve student performance.* San Francisco: Jossey-Bass.

Wolf, D. (1987, Winter). The art of questioning. *Academic Connections,* 1–7. Retrieved October 28, 2003, from *www.exploratorium.edu/IFI/resources/workshops/artofquestioning.html*

Wong, B. (2023, May 18). *Top social media statistics and trends of 2024.* Forbes Advisor. *www.forbes.com/advisor/business/social-media-statistics*

Wright, T. S., Cervetti, G. N., Wise, C., & McClung, N. A. (2022). The impact of knowledge-building through conceptually-coherent read alouds on vocabulary and comprehension. *Reading Psychology, 43*(1), 70–84.

Xie, Y., Wang, J., Li, S., & Zheng, Y. (2023). Research on the influence path of metacognitive reading strategies on scientific literacy. *Journal of Intelligence, 11*(5), 1–16.

Zee, M., Rudasill, K. M., & Bosman, R. J. (2021). A cross-lagged study of students' motivation, academic achievement, and relationships with teachers from kindergarten to 6th grade. *Journal of Educational Psychology, 113*(6), 1208–1226.

Zhang, D., Wang, Q., Ding, Y., & Liu, J. J. (2014). Testing accommodation or modification? The effects of integrated object representation on enhancing geometry performance in children with and without geometry. *Journal of Learning Disabilities, 47*(6), 569–583.

Zimmerman, B. J., & Moylan, A. R. (2009). Self-regulation: Where metacognition and motivation intersect. In D. J. Hacker, J. Dunlosky, & A. C. Graesser (Eds.), *Handbook of metacognition in education* (pp. 299–315). New York: Routledge/Taylor & Francis.

Zuriff, G. E. (2000). Extra examination time for students with learning disabilities: An examination of the maximum potential thesis. *Applied Measurement in Education, 13*(1), 99–117.

B

Bias, 2, 35, 135
Blending, 45–46, 46f, 53f. *See also* Phonemic awareness
Bloom's taxonomy of learning, 78, 78t, 91–93, 92t
Brief constructed-response items, 123–125, 125t

C

Checklist: Concepts about Print and Reading (Form 2.3), 40, 41
Checklist for Constructing Effective Questions, 85, 232
Checklist for Critical Reading, 195, 241
Checklist for Keyboarding and Internet Navigation Knowledge and Skills, 205–206, 242
Checklist for Linguistic Modification of Reading Assessment, 149, 236
Checklist for Planning Effective Formative Assessment, 182, 238
Checklist for Self-Assessment, 195, 240
Checklist: Knowledge of Letter Sounds (Form 2.2), 37, 39
Checklist: Naming Upper- and Lowercase Letters (Form 2.1), 37
Checklist: Naming Upper- and Lowercase Letters (Form 2.1), 38
Checklists, self-assessment, 193–196, 194f, 196f, 198. *See also* Forms; Self-assessment; *individual checklists*
Claim and evidence structures. *See also* Critical reading
  critical and digital reading assessment and, 210, 212–214
  rubric for determining claim, evidence, and warrant in advertisements and, 215–216, 218t
Classroom practices. *See also* Classroom-based assessments; Elementary classrooms; High-stakes assessment
  assessment systems and, 200
  critical reading and, 204–205
  formative assessment and, 180–181
  Kindergarten classrooms, 2–3, 42–47, 46f
  middle school classrooms, 4, 105–114, 108f, 112f
  prekindergarten classrooms, 36
  self-assessment and, 192
Classroom talk, 193. *See also* Discussions
Classroom-based assessments. *See also* Classroom practices; Reading inventories
  accommodation in assessment and, 150–153
  authentic assessment and, 187
  formative assessment and, 2, 180–182
  ongoing classroom-based assessments, 42, 43t, 45–47, 46f, 48
  strategies and skills and, 52t, 74
  technology and, 75
Cognition, 24, 26, 223
Cognitive strategies, 18. *See also* Comprehension; Strategy use
Collaboration, 177

Common Core State Standards (CCSS). *See also* Standards
  formative and summative assessments and, 183–184, 185, 186
  high-stakes testing and, 79–80, 117–118, 122, 137
  noncognitive aspects of reading to assess, 160–161
  performance assessments and, 100
  reading inventories and, 56
  self-assessment and, 196
Communication, 200
Comparisons, 131–132
Competency tests, 118
Complexity, 187
Comprehension. *See also* Inferential comprehension; Literal comprehension
  accommodation in assessment and, 151–152
  advocacy for reading assessment and, 116
  confounds and, 157
  defining reading and, 21
  equity and, 35
  focus of assessment and, 18
  high-stakes testing and, 123–124
  listening comprehension, 58, 58t, 59f, 64–65, 65f
  model of reading assessment and, 24–25
  noncognitive aspects of reading to assess and, 161
  overview, 1, 7–9, 54
  performance assessments and, 110
  purposes for assessing reading and, 15–16
  reading inventories and, 55, 56–57, 58t, 59f, 61–64, 65f, 73
  self-assessment and, 191, 192, 195
  strategies and skills and, 50–51, 52t, 54, 54f, 55
  teacher questioning and, 76–78, 88–89, 92t, 96–97
Comprehension questions, 54f, 56, 57–58, 61, 62–64, 65f, 72–73
Comprehensive Test of Phonological Processing (CTOPP), 51f, 52t
Computer-adaptive testing, 125. *See also* Technology in reading assessment
Concepts about print and reading, 37, 40–42, 47
Concurrent validity, 135. *See also* Validity of assessments
Conducting a Task Analysis to Enhance Reading Assessment form, 49, 230
Confounds, 95, 113, 157
Consequences of assessment
  accommodation in assessment and, 153
  assessing "the other" and, 172, 174
  CURRV model and, 27–28, 27f, 31
  digital reading and, 216–218
  critical reading and, 212–218
  high-stakes testing and, 126–131, 128f, 138
  performance assessments and, 107–109, 108f
  reading inventories and, 68–69
  teacher questioning and, 92–93
Consistency, 139, 200
Consonants, 61–62, 119
Construct validity, 30–31, 96, 135, 136–137. *See also* Validity of assessments
Constructed response items, 123–125, 125t

Index

Construction of meaning. *See also* Meaning constructed from text
　digital literacy and, 202
　emergent literacy and early reading knowledge assessments and, 47
　overview, 51, 54
　self-assessment and, 190, 191
Content areas, 10, 109, 121, 139. *See also* Learning
Context clues, 53f
Convergent questions, 87–88
Cooperation, 177
Coordinating assessment, 10, 28, 200
Coverage, 200
CRAAP (currency, relevance, authority, accuracy, and purpose of texts) Test, 215–216, 216f, 217f, 218, 220
Creating Consistent Approaches to Reading Assessment across Grade Levels and Content Areas form, 139, 235
Critical analysis, 4–5, 8, 85, 93, 202. *See also* Critical reading
Critical comprehension, 96. *See also* Comprehension; Critical reading
Critical Questions to Ask of Reading Inventory Information form, 231
Critical reading
　asking critical questions, 216–218, 217f
　critical and digital reading assessment, 205
　determining claims and evidence and, 210, 212–214
　identifying and analyzing advertisements and propaganda, 215–216, 216f, 217f, 218t
　identifying facts and opinions and, 206, 208–210, 211
　overview, 12, 201, 203–220, 213f, 216f, 217f, 218t, 222
　rubric for determining claim, evidence, and warrant in advertisements and, 215–216, 218t
　scenario-based assessments (SBAs) and, 218–220, 221
　self-assessment and, 195
Critical/evaluative questions, 54f. *See also* Comprehension; Questions/questioning
Cueing responses
　accommodation in assessment and, 147
　performance assessments and, 103t, 104–105, 104f, 108–109, 108f
Curriculum
　formative assessment and, 180
　high-stakes testing and, 127–128, 136
　performance assessments and, 113–114
　summative assessment and, 178, 182
CURRV (consequences, usefulness, roles/responsibilities, reliability, and validity) model, 26–32, 27f
CURRV Model to Evaluate Reading Assessment form, 27

D

Decoding skills
　model of reading assessment and, 24
　performance assessments and, 110
　reading inventories and, 57, 58t, 61–62
　self-assessment and, 191
　strategies and skills and, 55
　teachers' reading inventories and, 65–66
Defining reading, 20–23
Deletion of initial or final sound, 46f
Demonstrations, 111, 193
Depth of knowledge, 78
Developing an Arc of Questions: From Relatively Simple to Increasingly Complex form, 92, 233
Development
　accommodation in assessment and, 145
　assessing "the other" and, 175
　defining reading and, 22–23
　emergent literacy and early reading knowledge assessments and, 47
　model of reading assessment and, 26
　multi-tiered systems of support and, 48
　overview, 9, 12, 32–33
　performance assessments and, 110
　sciences of reading and, 223
　self-assessment and, 188, 190–192, 195
　teacher questioning and, 81
　validity of assessments and, 30
Diagnostic assessments
　accommodation in assessment and, 145
　example illustrating, 44
　high-stakes testing and, 127–128
　multi-tiered systems of support and, 42, 43t, 47
　overview, 66–67, 67f, 72
Differential boost, 145, 154
Differential impact, 152
Digital portfolios, 4, 75. *See also* Portfolios; Technology in reading assessment
Digital reading. *See also* Technology in reading assessment
　asking critical questions, 216–218, 217f
　critical and digital reading assessment, 205
　determining claims and evidence and, 210, 212–214
　high-stakes testing and, 124
　identifying and analyzing advertisements and propaganda, 215–216, 216f, 217f, 218t
　identifying facts and opinions and, 206, 208–210, 211
　keyboarding skills and, 205–206
　overview, 8–9, 12, 201–203, 220, 222
　rubric for determining claim, evidence, and warrant in advertisements and, 215–216, 218t
　scenario-based assessments (SBAs) and, 218–220, 221
Disability. *See* Accommodation in assessment; Students with learning disabilities
Discussions
　assessing responses to questions in, 89–90
　performance assessments and, 111
　self-assessment and, 193, 196
　small-group discussions, 3
Districts
　assessment systems and, 200
　coordination of assessment across grades and content areas and, 10
　defining reading and, 20–21

Districts (*continued*)
   high-stakes testing and, 131–132
   purposes for assessing reading and, 15–17, 16*t*
Divergent questions, 87–88. *See also* Questions/questioning
Diversity, 71, 127, 184
   goals of reading instruction, 17, 130
   levels of understanding, 86, 93–96
   purpose for assessing, 16
   students, 4, 67, 156, 168, 172, 183
   theories informing reading instruction, 16
Dynamic Indicators of Basic Early Literacy Skills (DIBELS), 51*f*, 52*t*

E

Early reading, 12, 36, 37–49, 46*f*. *See also* Development; Emergent literacy
Easy CBM, 51*f*, 52*t*
Ecological validity. *See also* Validity of assessments
   CURRV model and, 30–31
   high-stakes testing and, 135–136
   reading inventories and, 73
   teacher questioning and, 96
Educational achievement. *See* Reading achievement
Educational equity. *See* Equity
Elementary classrooms. *See also* Classroom practices; Early reading
   assessing "the other" and, 163–175, 165*f*, 166*f*, 169*f*
   emergent literacy and early reading knowledge and, 36
   overview, 3–4, 9
   reading inventories and, 67–74
   self-assessment and, 192–196, 194*f*, 196*f*
   teacher questioning and, 90–96, 92*t*
Elementary Reading Attitude Survey, 168, 168*f*
Elkonin boxes, 45
Emergent literacy, 36, 37–49, 46*f*. *See also* Development; Early reading
Engagement
   assessment of, 159–160, 171, 172, 173
   emergent literacy and early reading knowledge and, 48
   formative and summative assessments and, 181, 185, 186
   goals of assessment and, 7
   high-stakes testing and, 121
   overview, 5, 9, 158, 162
   performance assessments and, 111
   purposes for assessing reading and, 17
English learners (ELs), 31–32, 35, 141, 143, 148–149, 156. *See also* Accommodation in assessment; Language diversity
Environmental factors, 36, 48. *See also* Classroom practices
Equity
   accommodation in assessment and, 153, 155
   assessment, 12, 35
   high-stakes testing and, 119, 134
   overview, 1–2, 12, 35
   performance assessments and, 107
   teacher questioning and, 95
Evaluation after reading, 190, 194*f*, 202, 203
Evidence. *See also* Critical reading
   critical and digital reading assessment and, 210, 212–214
   rubric for determining claim, evidence, and warrant in advertisements and, 215–216, 218*t*
Example papers, 110
Executive functioning, 189
Expertise of teachers, 11–12, 179, 180–181. *See also* Teachers
Expository text structure, 124
Extended constructed-response items, 125*t*

F

Facts, identifying, 206, 208–210, 211
Fairness, 153, 155. *See also* Equity; Reliability
Family. *See* Parents
Feedback, 3, 107, 151–152, 181, 184
   authentic assessment, 191
   formative, 107
   motivation, 28
   self-assessment, 112
Fix-it strategies, 58*t*, 190
Fluency
   emergent literacy and early reading knowledge assessments and, 47
   focus of assessment and, 18
   high-stakes testing and, 119, 121
   noncognitive aspects of reading to assess and, 161
   overview, 1, 54
   reading inventories and, 55, 57, 58*t*, 59*f*, 65*f*, 73
   self-assessment and, 191
   strategies and skills and, 50–51, 52*t*, 53*f*, 54, 55
   teachers' reading inventories and, 65–66
   technology and, 75
Focus of assessment, 17–19, 19*f*, 33
Formative assessment
   accommodation in assessment and, 150–153
   assessing "the other" and, 170–171
   characteristics of, 180–182
   coordination of assessment across grades and content areas and, 10
   CURRV model and, 29
   need for, 179–180
   overview, 2, 178–179, 182–186
   performance assessments and, 107
   purposes for assessing reading and, 14–17, 16*t*
   self-assessment and, 188
Formative Assessment Coverage That Contributes to Students' Achievement on High-Stakes Summative Assessments form, 185, 239
Forms
   Assessing "the Other": Questions for Teachers and Administrators form, 176, 237
   Assessment for Determining Fact and Opinion Statements (Form 11.2), 208, 209
   Assessment for Determining Fact and Opinion Statements on the Internet (Form 11.3), 210, 211
   Assessment of Student Website Evaluations (Form 11.1), 206, 207

Index

Assessment of Students' Ability to Determine Claim–Evidence Structures (Form 11.4), 213, 214
Checklist: Concepts about Print and Reading (Form 2.3), 40, 41
Checklist for Constructing Effective Questions, 85, 232
Checklist for Critical Reading, 195, 241
Checklist for Keyboarding and Internet Navigation Knowledge and Skills, 205–206, 242
Checklist for Linguistic Modification of Reading Assessment, 149, 236
Checklist for Planning Effective Formative Assessment, 182, 238
Checklist for Self-Assessment, 195, 240
Checklist: Knowledge of Letter Sounds (Form 2.2), 37, 39
Checklist: Naming Upper- and Lowercase Letters (Form 2.1), 37, 38
Conducting a Task Analysis to Enhance Reading Assessment form, 49, 230
Creating Consistent Approaches to Reading Assessment across Grade Levels and Content Areas form, 139, 235
Critical Questions to Ask of Reading Inventory Information form, 231
CURRV Model to Evaluate Reading Assessment form, 27
Developing an Arc of Questions: From Relatively Simple to Increasingly Complex form, 92, 233
Formative Assessment Coverage That Contributes to Students' Achievement on High-Stakes Summative Assessments form, 185, 239
Guidelines for Developing and Using Performance Assessments form, 111, 112*f*, 234
Healthy Readers Profile (Form 8.1), 172, 173
Reading Assessment Inventory: Audiences and Purposes form, 16, 227
Reading Assessment Inventory: What Is Assessed? form, 19, 228
Scenario-Based Assessment: Planning, Working through, and Completing (Form 11.5), 220, 221
Using the CURRV Framework to Evaluate Reading Assessment form, 229
Frustration reading level, 56–57, 59*f*, 60, 66–67, 67*f*, 70, 74. *See also* Reading levels
Funding decisions, 127, 130, 144

G

Gates–McGinitie Reading Tests, 51*f*, 52*t*
Glossaries, 148
Goals, 6–7, 17, 199. *See also* Focus of assessment; Instructional goals; Purposes for assessing reading
Grade levels, 59–60, 62, 65*f*, 139. *See also* Reading levels
Graded word lists. *See* Word lists
Gray Oral Reading Test (GORT), 51*f*

Group projects, 177
Guessing, 61, 88–89
Guidelines for Developing and Using Performance Assessments form, 111, 112*f*, 234

H

Healthy Readers Profile (Form 8.1), 172, 173
High school classrooms, 4–5, 149–155. *See also* Classroom practices
High-stakes assessment. *See also* Standardized testing; Summative assessment
  accommodations and, 140, 144, 145, 149–155
  all assessment is high stakes, 6
  characteristics of, 121–126, 125*t*
  classroom assessment, 6
  consequences of, 126–131, 128*f*, 138
  controversies with, 119–121
  formative assessment and, 179
  history of, 117–119
  overview, 6, 31, 117, 138, 178
  purposes for assessing reading and, 15
  reliability of, 134–135
  roles and responsibilities related to, 132–134
  teacher questioning and, 79–80, 94, 95
  usefulness of, 131–132
  validity of, 135–137
Home literacy experiences, 36. *See also* Emergent literacy; Parents

I

Identifying struggling and at-risk students. *See* Screening; Struggling readers; Students with learning disabilities
Illustrations
  assessing understanding of, 183, 185, 203
Independence, 3, 111, 134. *See also* Independent reading level; Reading independently
Independent reading level, 56–57, 60, 66, 67*f*, 70, 74. *See also* Reading independently; Reading levels
Individualized education plan (IEP), 141–142, 150, 152
Individuals with Disabilities Education Act, 141–142
Inequity, 1–2, 35, 107. *See also* Equity
Inferences, 25, 29–30, 72
Inferential comprehension. *See also* Comprehension; Inferential questions
  focus of assessment and, 18
  high-stakes testing and, 123–124
  initiate–respond–evaluate (IRE) discourse and, 78
  reading inventories and, 58*t*, 63
  teacher questioning and, 83–84, 92–93, 94, 96
Inferential questions. *See also* Comprehension; Inferential comprehension; Questions/questioning; Teacher questioning
  overview, 83–84
  reading inventories and, 56, 62, 63
  strategies and skills and, 54*f*
Informational text structure, 124

Initiate–respond–evaluate (IRE) discourse form, 77–78, 86–87
Instruction. *See also* Instructional goals; Learning
  accommodation in assessment and, 144, 150–153
  accountability and expertise and, 11–12
  assessing "the other" and, 172
  assessment systems and, 200
  authentic assessment and, 187
  consistent assessment and, 139
  critical reading and, 203
  CURRV model and, 28
  educational decision making and, 127
  emergent literacy and early reading knowledge assessments and, 46–47
  focus of assessment and, 17–18
  formative assessment and, 179–182
  high-stakes testing and, 119, 127–128, 129, 130–131, 132–134, 136
  how, where, and when to administer assessments and, 19–20
  model of reading assessment and, 24–25
  multi-tiered systems of support and, 48
  ongoing classroom-based assessments and, 46–47
  performance assessments and, 102–103, 107–108, 109, 111, 114
  process and product assessment and, 98
  reading inventories and, 68–69, 70–71
  self-assessment and, 188, 196
  strategies and skills and, 51
  teacher questioning and, 82–84
Instructional goals. *See also* Instruction
  defining reading and, 20–21
  focus of assessment and, 17–19, 19f
  formative assessment and, 2, 10, 155, 181, 238
  high-stakes testing and, 129
  overview, 5
  performance assessments and, 111
  purposes for assessing reading and, 15
  summative assessment and, 178, 182
Instructional reading level, 56–57, 60, 66–67, 67f, 70, 74. *See also* Reading levels
Integration of information, 202–203
Integrative Multimodal Literacy Assessment (IMLA), 206
Interests
  assessing "the other" and, 171–172
  assessment of, 168–169, 169f, 171
  interest inventories, 121
  overview, 158, 163
Internet. *See* Critical reading; Digital reading
Interpretation, 24, 25, 26
Isolation sounds, 46f

K

Kauffman Assessment Battery for Children (KABC), 51f
Keyboarded responses, 147–148
Keyboarding skills, 205–206
Kindergarten classrooms, 2–3, 42–47, 46f. *See also* Classroom practices; Early reading; Elementary classrooms; Emergent literacy
Knowledge, 85–86, 92t, 94, 152. *See also* Learning; Prior knowledge
KWL (know, want, learn) strategy, 82–83, 98. *See also* Teacher questioning

L

Language diversity, 71, 95. *See also* Accommodation in assessment; English learners (ELs)
Learning. *See also* Instruction
  assessment systems and, 200
  authentic assessment and, 187
  focus of assessment and, 18
  formative assessment and, 180–182
  performance assessments and, 107, 109, 112f, 113–114
  process and product assessment and, 98
  role of assessment in, 10–11, 179–181
  self-assessment and, 191
  teacher questioning and, 84–86, 87, 94
Learning disabilities. *See* Students with learning disabilities
Learning environments, 36, 48. *See also* Classroom practices
Letter knowledge, 37, 38, 47, 119
Letter sounds, 37, 39, 46f, 47, 119
Lexiles, 62. *See also* Grade levels
Limited English proficiency (LEP). *See* English learners (ELs)
Linguistic modifications, 148–149, 150–151
Listening comprehension, 58, 58t, 59f, 64–65, 65f. *See also* Comprehension
Listening to students, 89–90, 184. *See also* Students
Literal comprehension. *See also* Comprehension; Literal questions
  focus of assessment and, 18
  high-stakes testing and, 123–124
  initiate–respond–evaluate (IRE) discourse and, 78
  reading inventories and, 58t, 63
  teacher questioning and, 83–84, 93, 94, 96
Literal questions, 54f, 56, 63, 83–84. *See also* Comprehension; Literal comprehension; Questions/questioning; Teacher questioning
Look-backs, 63–64

M

Matching, 46f, 53f. *See also* Phonemic awareness
Matthew effect, 163
Meaning constructed from text. *See also* Comprehension; Construction of meaning
  digital literacy and, 202
  emergent literacy and early reading knowledge assessments and, 47
  formative and summative assessments and, 180, 184
  model of reading assessment and, 24
  overview, 8
  reading inventories and, 61–62
  self-assessment and, 190, 191

Index

Memorization, 77, 85
Memory, 63–64
Metacognition
   assessment of, 160
   assessment systems and, 200
   critical and digital reading assessment and, 219–220
   defining reading and, 23
   formative and summative assessments and, 185, 186
   goals of assessment and, 7
   high-stakes testing and, 121
   independence in reading and, 189
   overview, 1, 5, 9
   reading inventories and, 57, 58*t*, 61–62
   sciences of reading and, 223
   self-assessment and, 192, 193, 194*f*, 198, 199
   teacher questioning and, 85
   teachers' reading inventories and, 65–66
Metacomprehension, 93
Middle school classrooms, 4, 105–114, 108*f*, 112*f*. *See also* Classroom practices
Mindfulness, 189, 190–191
Mindsets, 190–191, 193, 199
Miscue analysis, 60–61, 61*f*, 65–66
Model of reading assessment, 23–32, 27*f*, 33–34
Modeling, 111, 193
Monitoring strategies
   digital literacy and, 202, 203
   formative and summative assessments and, 185, 186
   reading inventories and, 58*t*
   self-assessment and, 190, 193, 194*f*, 195, 199
Morphological analysis, 53*f*
Motivation
   assessment of, 159–160, 164–165, 165*f*, 171, 172, 173
   assessment systems and, 200
   CURRV model and, 28
   defining reading and, 22–23
   emergent literacy and early reading knowledge and, 48
   formative and summative assessments and, 181, 185, 186
   goals of assessment and, 7
   high-stakes testing and, 121, 125, 128
   model of reading assessment and, 25
   overview, 1, 4, 5, 9, 158, 162
   performance assessments and, 111
   purposes for assessing reading and, 17
   sciences of reading and, 223
   self-assessment and, 190
Motivation to Read Profile (MRP), 163, 165, 165*f*, 171
Multiple-choice questions, 88–89, 116, 122, 123–125, 125*t*
Multi-tiered systems of support (MTSS)
   emergent literacy and early reading knowledge assessments and, 36, 42, 43*t*, 46–47
   example illustrating types of assessments, 42–47, 46*f*
   overview, 12
   reading inventories and, 70
   teacher questioning and, 96

N

Narrative report cards, 158, 159*f*, 161, 171
Narrative text structure, 124
National Assessment of Educational Progress (NAEP), 21–22, 35, 118, 127, 132
National School Lunch Program, 127, 128*f*
No Child Left Behind Act (NCLB)
   accommodation in assessment and, 144
   assessing "the other" and, 174
   formative and summative assessments and, 184
   high-stakes testing and, 117–118, 120
   noncognitive aspects of reading to assess and, 160
   reading inventories and, 55, 73
Noncognitive aspects of reading. *See also* Attitudes; Motivation; Self-efficacy
   assessing collaboration and cooperation, 177
   assessing in struggling readers, 170–175
   assessing "the other" and, 163–175, 165*f*, 166*f*, 169*f*
   assessment of motivation, 4–5, 17–19, 21–22, 26, 164–165, 165*f*, 171–174, 181–185, 206
   assessment of self-efficacy, 4, 9, 22–23, 48, 160–167, 171–174
   formative and summative assessments and, 186
   history of, 159–161
   overview, 158, 159*f*, 161–163, 175–176
Nonsense words, 53*f*, 119
Norm-referenced testing
   high-stakes testing and, 122–123
   overview, 19–20
   performance assessments and, 110
   scoring and reporting of, 126
   validity of assessments and, 31

O

Objectives, 111. *See also* Instructional goals; Purposes for assessing reading
Observation
   assessing responses to questions in retellings and discussions, 89–90
   assessing "the other" and, 175
   concepts about print and reading and, 40
   formative and summative assessments and, 184
   model of reading assessment and, 24, 25, 26
On my own category of QAR, 83
Ongoing classroom-based assessments, 42, 43*t*, 45–47, 46*f*, 48. *See also* Classroom-based assessments
Opinions, identifying, 206, 208–210, 211
Oral reading
   reading inventories and, 56–57, 58*t*, 59*f*, 60–63, 61*f*, 65*f*, 70–71, 72
   retelling and comprehension questions and, 62–63
   teachers' reading inventories and, 65–66
Orientation and planning phase of reading, 189, 193, 194*f*
Other factors to assess. *See also* Attitudes; Engagement; Interests; Motivation; Noncognitive aspects of reading; Self-efficacy
   assessing in a struggling reader, 170–175
   attitudes toward reading, 167–168, 168*f*

Other factors to assess (*continued*)
  collaboration and cooperation, 177
  consequences and usefulness of assessing "the other" and, 172, 174
  engagement and, 173
  formative and summative assessments and, 186
  motivation and, 164–165, 165f, 173
  overview, 158, 159f, 161–164, 170–172, 173, 175–176
  reliability and, 174–175
  roles and responsibilities related to, 174
  self-concept and self-efficacy and, 165–167, 166f
  students' attributions for success and failure, 169–170
  students' reading interests, 168–169, 169f
  validity and, 175
Outcomes, 17, 18, 145, 199

P

Parents
  advocacy for reading assessment and, 116
  defining reading and, 20–21
  high-stakes testing and, 133, 134
  home literacy experiences, 36
  performance assessments and, 109
Partnership for Assessment of Readiness for College and Careers (PARCC), 79–80, 100, 179, 185
Passage independence, 88–89, 134. *See also* Reading passages
Peabody Picture Vocabulary Test (PPVT), 52t
Peer evaluation, 86–87
Performance assessments
  advocacy for reading assessment and, 116
  characteristics of, 100–105, 103t, 104f
  consequences and usefulness of, 107–109, 108f
  CURRV model and, 28
  history of, 99–100
  overview, 5, 31, 99, 105–107, 114–115
  reliability of, 113
  roles and responsibilities related to, 109–112, 112f
  validity of, 113–114
Perseverance, 4, 22–23, 130
Phonemic awareness
  emergent literacy and early reading knowledge assessments and, 42–47, 46f
  focus of assessment and, 18
  high-stakes testing and, 119
  noncognitive aspects of reading to assess and, 161
  overview, 1, 54
  reading inventories and, 55, 73
  strategies and skills and, 50–51, 52t, 53f, 55
  teacher questioning and, 96
  technology and, 75
  types of assessments and, 42–47, 46f
Phonics
  emergent literacy and early reading knowledge assessments and, 47
  focus of assessment and, 18
  high-stakes testing and, 119
  noncognitive aspects of reading to assess and, 161
  overview, 1, 2–3, 54
  reading inventories and, 55, 58t, 73
  strategies and skills and, 50–51, 52t, 53f, 55
  teacher questioning and, 96
  technology and, 75
Phonological Awareness Literacy Screening (PALS), 51f, 52t
Pilot testing, 122–123
Planned questions, 87–88. *See also* Questions/questioning
Planning, 180, 199, 220
Politicians, 16t, 120–121, 129
Portfolios, 4, 31, 75, 116
Poverty, 120–121, 127, 128f
Preferential seating, 146. *See also* Accommodation in assessment
Prekindergarten education, 36. *See also* Classroom practices; Early reading; Emergent literacy
Primary source documents, 4, 105–114, 108f, 112f. *See also* Source texts
Principals. *See* Administrators
Print concepts, 37, 40–42, 47
Prior knowledge
  confounds and, 157
  equity and, 35
  high-stakes testing and, 134–135, 137
  overview, 4
  reading inventories and, 55, 65f, 73
  teacher questioning and, 81, 88–89
Process-oriented assessments, 7, 57, 98
Product assessments, 7, 98
Programme for International Student Assessment (PISA), 118, 132
Progress in International Reading Literacy Study (PIRLS), 21–22, 132
Progress monitoring assessments
  accommodation in assessment and, 145
  multi-tiered systems of support and, 42, 43t, 47, 48
  self-assessment and, 199
  technology and, 75
  types of assessments and, 44
Prompts, 147, 148–149
Pronunciation, 70–71
Propaganda
  asking critical questions and, 216–218, 217f
  identifying and analyzing, 215–216, 216f, 217f, 218t
  rubric for determining claim, evidence, and warrant in advertisements and, 215–216, 218t
Purposes for assessing reading, 14–17, 16t, 33, 71

Q

Qualitative Reading Inventory-7, 59–60, 67–68, 70, 71
Question–answer relationships (QAR), 82, 83. *See also* Teacher questioning
Questioning the author strategy, 83

Index

Questions/questioning. *See also* Inferential questions; Student questions; Teacher questioning
  comprehension questions, 54f, 56, 57–58, 61, 62–64, 65f, 72–73
  critical/evaluative questions, 54f
  divergent questions, 87–88
  literal questions, 54f, 56, 63, 83–84
  overview, 84–89
  planned questions, 87–88
  scriptally implicit questions, 80–81
  textually explicit and textually implicit questions, 80–81

R

Rate of reading, 57, 58t, 61
Reader interests. *See* Interests
Reader Self-Perception Scale, 163
Reading, defining, 20–23
Reading achievement
  CURRV model and, 28, 29
  defining reading and, 21–22
  formative assessment and, 191–192
  high-stakes testing and, 128, 129–130, 131
  overview, 9
  sciences of reading and, 223
  self-assessment and, 190
  summative assessment and, 178
  teachers' reading inventories and, 65–66
Reading Assessment Inventory: Audiences and Purposes form, 16, 228
Reading Assessment Inventory: What Is Assessed? form, 19
Reading attitudes, 158, 163, 167–168, 168f, 171
Reading comprehension. *See* Comprehension
Reading concepts. *See* Concepts about print and reading
Reading development. *See* Development
Reading First, 184
Reading independently, 188–189, 192. *See also* Independence; Independent reading level
Reading interest survey, 164, 171
Reading inventories
  accommodations and, 140
  advocacy for reading assessment and, 116
  characteristics of, 57–65, 58t, 59f, 61f, 65f
  consequences and usefulness of, 68–69
  critical and digital reading assessment and, 206
  CURRV model and, 28
  focus of assessment and, 18
  overview, 31, 55–57, 67–68, 74
  purposes for assessing reading and, 15
  reading passages and, 60–62, 61f
  reliability of, 72–73
  retelling and comprehension questions and, 62–64
  roles and responsibilities related to, 70–71
  silent reading and listening comprehension and, 64–65, 65f
  strategies and skills and, 54
  teachers' inventories, 65–66, 73–74
  using information from, 66–67, 67f
  validity of, 73–74
  word lists and, 59–60

Reading levels, 56–57, 59f, 60, 62, 65f, 66–67, 67f, 70, 72, 74. *See also* Frustration reading level; Grade levels; Independent reading level; Instructional reading level; Zones of proximal development
Reading passages
  high-stakes testing and, 123–124, 134, 137
  reading inventories and, 57–59, 58t, 59f, 60–62, 61f, 65f, 71, 72–73
Reading program effectiveness, 16–17, 20, 182
Reading rate. *See* Rate of reading
Reading Self-Concept Scale (RSCS-30), 163, 166–167, 166f
Reading Self-Efficacy Questionnaire, 163
Reading strategies and skills. *See* Skills; Strategy use
Reliability
  accommodation in assessment and, 154–155
  aspects of, 29–30
  assessing "the other" and, 174–175
  CURRV model and, 26–27, 27f, 29–30, 31
  high-stakes testing and, 134–135
  performance assessments and, 113
  reading inventories and, 72–73
  teacher questioning and, 95
  universal screening instruments and, 43
Rereading, 56–57
Response formats, 147–148
Response to Intervention (RTI), 145
Responsibilities related to assessment. *See* Roles and responsibilities related to assessment
Retellings. *See also* Comprehension; Summarizing strategies
  assessing responses to questions in, 89–90
  formative and summative assessments and, 184
  model of reading assessment and, 25
  reading inventories and, 58t, 62–64, 73
  strategies and skills and, 54f
Right there category of QAR, 83
Roles and responsibilities related to assessment
  assessing "the other" and, 174
  consequences and usefulness of, 153–154
  CURRV model and, 27, 27f, 29, 31
  high-stakes testing and, 132–134
  performance assessments and, 109–112, 112f
  reading inventories and, 70–71
Rubrics
  benefits of, 102–103
  CURRV model and, 29
  for determining claim, evidence, and warrant in advertisements and, 215–216, 218t
  overview, 5, 10, 11, 114–115
  performance assessments and, 101, 102–103, 103t, 107–108, 110, 112f, 114–115
  roles and responsibilities related to, 109
  self-assessment and, 193, 197–198, 197f
Running records, 69, 73–74. *See also* Classroom-based assessments; Reading inventories

S

Scaffolding instruction, 102–103
Scenario-Based Assessment: Planning, Working through, and Completing (Form 11.5), 220, 221

Scenario-based assessments (SBAs), 218–220, 221
School administrators. *See* Administrators
Schools
    accommodation in assessment and, 144
    accountability and, 11–12
    assessment systems and, 200
    consistent assessment and, 139
    coordination of assessment across grades and content areas and, 10
    defining reading and, 20–21
    focus of assessment and, 18
    high-stakes testing and, 120–121, 127, 130, 131–132
    overview, 1
    performance assessments and, 109
    purposes for assessing reading and, 15–17, 16*t*
Sciences of reading, 12–13, 20, 120, 223
Scoring guides, 102, 107–108, 109, 110
Screening
    accommodation in assessment and, 145
    high-stakes testing and, 119
    multi-tiered systems of support and, 42, 43*t*
    overview, 2–3
    universal screening instruments and, 42, 43, 43*t*, 47
Scriptally implicit questions, 80–81. *See also* Questions/questioning; Teacher questioning
Secondary source documents, 4, 105–114, 108*f*, 112*f*. *See also* Source texts
Segmenting, 46*f*, 53*f*. *See also* Phonemic awareness
Self-assessment. *See also* Metacognition; Self-corrections
    checklists and, 193–196, 194*f*, 196*f*, 198
    development of, 190–192
    formative assessment and, 181
    overview, 3, 10–11, 188–190, 192–193, 198, 199
    performance assessments and, 108–109, 108*f*, 110–111
    rubrics and, 197–198, 197*f*
    teacher and student questioning, 193
    teacher questioning and, 193, 198
Self-awareness, 189, 191, 198
Self-concept, 165–167, 166*f*
Self-corrections, 57, 58*t*, 61, 61*f*, 65–66
Self-efficacy
    assessment of, 159–160, 165–167, 166*f*, 171
    defining reading and, 22–23
    emergent literacy and early reading knowledge and, 48
    formative and summative assessments and, 181, 186
    goals of assessment and, 7
    model of reading assessment and, 25
    overview, 4, 5, 9, 158, 162, 163
    sciences of reading and, 223
    self-assessment and, 190–191
    validity of assessments and, 30
Self-esteem, 28
Self-evaluation, 86–87
Self-monitoring, 15
Self-perception, 121
Short constructed responses, 123–125, 125*t*
Sight word vocabulary, 18, 58*t*, 65–66. *See also* Vocabulary

Silent reading, 58*t*, 59*f*, 63, 64–65, 65*f*
Skills. *See also* Reading inventories; Strategy use
    accommodation in assessment and, 144
    digital literacy and, 202
    focus of assessment and, 18
    high-stakes testing and, 130
    model of reading assessment and, 24
    noncognitive aspects of reading to assess and, 160–161
    overview, 3, 8, 50–55, 51*f*, 52*t*, 53*f*–54*f*, 61–62, 74
    reading development and reading achievement and, 9
    reading inventories and, 67–74
    self-assessment and, 191
    teachers' reading inventories and, 65–66
    validity of reading inventories and, 73
Smarter Balanced Assessment Consortium (SBAC), 79–80, 100, 179, 185
Social change, 204
Socratic method, 76. *See also* Teacher questioning
Sound boxes, 45
Source texts. *See also* Primary source documents; Secondary source documents
    digital literacy and, 202
    formative and summative assessments and, 185
    performance assessments and, 102, 103*t*, 104–114, 104*f*, 108*f*, 112*f*
    rubrics and, 102, 103*t*
Special-needs students, 144. *See also* Accommodation in assessment; Students with learning disabilities
Speech, 70–71
Speed in reading, 57, 58*t*, 61
Spelling patterns, 53*f*
Spoken responses, 75, 147–148, 151, 185
Spontaneous questions, 87–88
Stakeholders. *See also* Administrators; Parents; Students; Teachers
    advocacy for reading assessment and, 116
    defining reading and, 20–21
    high-stakes testing and, 120–121, 128–129, 131
    overview, 32
    purposes for assessing reading and, 16–17, 16*t*
Standardized testing. *See also* High-stakes assessment
    accommodation in assessment and, 145, 147, 149–155
    controversies with, 119
    focus of assessment and, 18
    overview, 19–20, 122–123
    reliability of, 134–135
    validity of assessments and, 31
Standards
    accommodation in assessment and, 154
    assessing "the other" and, 174
    authentic assessment and, 187
    formative and summative assessments and, 183–184, 185, 186
    high-stakes testing and, 79–80, 117–118, 122, 136, 137
    noncognitive aspects of reading to assess and, 160–161
    overview, 5
    performance assessments and, 100, 113–114

Index

reading inventories and, 56, 73
self-assessment and, 196
summative assessment and, 178, 182
Stanford Diagnostic Reading Test (SDRT), 51*f*, 52*t*
Strategy use. *See also* Reading inventories; Skills
  critical and digital reading assessment and, 220
  critical reading and, 204
  digital literacy and, 202
  focus of assessment and, 18
  high-stakes testing and, 130
  KWL (know, want, learn) strategy, 82–83
  model of reading assessment and, 24
  noncognitive aspects of reading to assess and, 160–161
  overview, 4, 8, 50–55, 51*f*, 52*t*, 53*f*–54*f*, 61–62, 74
  performance assessments and, 110
  process and product assessment and, 98
  purposes for assessing reading and, 17
  reading development and reading achievement and, 9
  reading inventories and, 67–74
  self-assessment and, 188–189, 190–191, 193, 199
  teachers' reading inventories and, 65–66
  validity of reading inventories and, 73
Struggling readers, 43, 170–175. *See also* Accommodation in assessment; English learners (ELs); Students with learning disabilities
Student questions. *See also* Questions/questioning; Students
  asking critical questions, 216–218, 217*f*
  self-assessment and, 191, 193
  teacher questioning and, 86–87
Student responsibilities, 111–112. *See also* Self-assessment
Student-focus, 6–7
Students. *See also* Self-assessment; Student questions; Students with learning disabilities
  accommodation in assessment and, 152
  consistent assessment and, 139
  coordination of assessment across grades and content areas and, 10
  defining reading and, 20–21
  equitable education and, 35
  high-stakes testing and, 120–121, 127, 128*f*, 131, 133
  listening to, 89–90, 184
  purposes for assessing reading and, 15–17, 16*t*
Students with learning disabilities, 31–32, 141–143, 144, 146–148, 156. *See also* Accommodation in assessment; Students
Substitution, 46*f*, 61*f*
Summarizing strategies, 24–25
Summative assessment. *See also* High-stakes assessment
  accommodation in assessment and, 149–155
  assessing "the other" and, 170–171
  characteristics of, 182
  coordination of assessment across grades and content areas and, 10
  CURRV model and, 29
  formative assessment and, 179

multi-tiered systems of support and, 42, 43*t*, 47, 48
overview, 178–179, 182–186
performance assessments and, 107
purposes for assessing reading and, 14–17, 16*t*
self-assessment and, 188
types of assessments and, 44–45

T

Tape-recording assessments, 69, 71, 72
Task analysis
  assessing collaboration and cooperation and, 177
  emergent literacy and early reading knowledge and, 49
  formative and summative assessments and, 183–184
  performance assessments and, 101–102, 107–108, 109, 112*f*
  teacher questioning and, 95
Taxonomies, 78, 78*t*, 92*t*, 96
Taxpayers, 16*t*, 129, 131
Teacher questioning. *See also* Inferential questions; Literal questions; Questions/questioning; Teachers
  assessing responses to questions in retellings and discussions, 89–90
  categorizing and classifying questions, 78, 78*t*, 80–81
  consequences and usefulness of, 92–93
  CURRV model and, 28
  effective questions, 84–89
  formative assessment and, 179
  history of, 76–78
  influence of testing on, 79–80
  instructional perspectives on, 82–84
  overview, 31, 76, 90–92, 92*t*, 96–97
  reliability of, 95
  roles and responsibilities related to, 94–95
  self-assessment and, 193, 198
  validity of, 96
Teachers. *See also* Teacher questioning
  accommodation in assessment and, 143
  accountability and, 11–12
  advocacy for reading assessment and, 116
  assessment systems and, 200
  bias and, 35
  consistent assessment and, 139
  coordination of assessment across grades and content areas and, 10
  defining reading and, 20–21
  equity and, 35
  expertise and, 11–12
  focus of assessment and, 18
  formative and summative assessments and, 179, 180–181
  high-stakes testing and, 120–121, 127, 130–131, 132–134, 138
  motivation and, 162
  purposes for assessing reading and, 15–17, 16*t*
  summative assessment and, 182
  teachers' reading inventories and, 65–66, 73–74
  technology and, 75
  usefulness of assessment and, 28–29

Technology in reading assessment, 75, 124, 125, 126, 147–148. *See also* Digital reading
Test anxiety, 134, 135
Test of Reading Comprehension (TORC), 51*f*, 52*t*
Test of Word Reading Efficiency (TOWRE), 51*f*, 52*t*
Test preparation, 28, 31, 119, 130, 131, 133–134, 135, 149. *See also* High-stakes assessment
Text comprehension. *See* Comprehension
Texts, source. *See* Primary source documents; Secondary source documents; Source texts
Textually explicit and textually implicit questions, 80–81. *See also* Questions/questioning; Teacher questioning
Theories of learning, 78, 78*t*
Think and search category of QAR, 83
Think-alouds, 193, 198
Timed tests, 145, 148
TOWRE Sight Word and Phonemic Decoding, 52*t*

U

Universal screening assessments, 42, 43, 43*t*, 47. *See also* Screening
Untimed tests, 145, 148
Usefulness of assessment
  accommodation in assessment and, 153
  assessing "the other" and, 172
  CURRV model and, 27, 27*f*, 28–29, 31
  high-stakes testing and, 131–132
  performance assessments and, 107–109, 108*f*
  reading inventories and, 68–69
  teacher questioning and, 92–93
Using the CURRV Framework to Evaluate Reading Assessment form, 229

V

Validity of assessments
  accommodation in assessment and, 144, 152, 154, 155
  assessing "the other" and, 175
  critical and digital reading assessment and, 208
  CURRV model and, 26–27, 27*f*, 30–31
  high-stakes testing and, 135–137
  performance assessments and, 102, 113–114
  reading inventories and, 73–74
  rubrics and, 102
  teacher questioning and, 96
  universal screening instruments and, 43
Venn diagrams, 185
Verbal responses, 75, 147–148, 151, 185

Vocabulary
  accommodation in assessment and, 148
  emergent literacy and early reading knowledge assessments and, 40, 47
  focus of assessment and, 18
  formative assessment and, 178
  high-stakes testing and, 123
  noncognitive aspects of reading to assess and, 161
  overview, 1, 3, 4, 8–9, 54
  performance assessments and, 110
  purposes for assessing reading and, 15–16
  reading inventories and, 55, 58*t*, 70, 73
  strategies and skills and, 50–51, 52*t*, 53*f*, 54, 55
  teacher questioning and, 87, 88
  teachers' reading inventories and, 65–66
Vowels, 119

W

Wait time, 88–89
When assessment should occur, 19–20, 71
Where assessment should occur, 19–20
Woodcock–Johnson Test of Achievement, 51*f*, 52*t*
Word identification, 61–62
Word lists, 57–60, 58*t*, 59*f*, 62, 65*f*, 72
Word meanings, 51, 53*f*, 54. *See also* Vocabulary
Word recognition
  model of reading assessment and, 24
  performance assessments and, 110
  reading inventories and, 58*t*, 59*f*
  strategies and skills and, 51, 54
Words correct per minute (WCPM), 52*t*, 53*f*
Written responses
  accommodation in assessment and, 147–148, 151
  critical and digital reading assessment and, 208, 210
  formative and summative assessments and, 185
  high-stakes testing and, 137
  technology and, 75

Z

Zones of proximal development. *See also* Reading levels
  accountability and expertise and, 11
  formative and summative assessments and, 179–180, 181, 186
  performance assessments and, 102–103
  reading inventories and, 61, 66–67, 67*f*
  self-assessment and, 188, 191

CASES in HEALTHCARE FINANCE

AUPHA/HAP Editorial Board for Graduate Studies

Timothy D. McBride, PhD, Chair
Washington University in St. Louis

John Baker, PhD
University of Arkansas for Medical Sciences

Simone Cummings, PhD
Washington University

Connie J. Evashwick, ScD, FACHE
St. Louis University

Sherril B. Gelmon, DrPH, FACHE
Portland State University

Thomas E. Getzen, PhD
Temple University

Diane M. Howard, PhD, FACHE
Rush University

Christy H. Lemak, PhD
University of Michigan

John M. Lowe III, PhD
Simmons College

Dawn Oetjen, PhD
University of Central Florida

Mark Pauly, PhD
University of Pennsylvania

Bernardo Ramirez, MD
University of Central Florida

Lydia Reed
AUPHA

Andrew T. Sumner, ScD
Georgia State University

Andrea W. White, PhD
Medical University of South Carolina

Lesly Wilson, PhD
University of South Carolina